JOHN DEWEY'S
LATER
LOGICAL THEORY

SUNY series in American Philosophy and Cultural Thought
―――――――――
Randall E. Auxier and John R. Shook, editors

JOHN DEWEY'S LATER LOGICAL THEORY

JAMES SCOTT JOHNSTON

Cover photo of John Dewey (date unknown) is from Wikimedia Commons.

Published by State University of New York Press, Albany

© 2020 State University of New York

All rights reserved

No part of this book may be used or reproduced in any manner whatsoever without written permission. No part of this book may be stored in a retrieval system or transmitted in any form or by any means including electronic, electrostatic, magnetic tape, mechanical, photocopying, recording, or otherwise without the prior permission in writing of the publisher.

For information, contact State University of New York Press, Albany, NY
www.sunypress.edu

Library of Congress Cataloging-in-Publication Data

Name: Johnston, James Scott, author
Title: John Dewey's Later Logical Theory / James Scott Johnston, author.
Description: Albany : State University of New York Press, [2020] | Includes bibliographical references and index.
Identifiers: ISBN 9781438479415 (hardcover : alk. paper) | ISBN 9781438479422 (pbk. : alk. paper) | ISBN 9781438479439 (ebook)
Further information is available at the Library of Congress.

10 9 8 7 6 5 4 3 2 1

Contents

LIST OF TABLES	vii
ACKNOWLEDGMENTS	ix
INTRODUCTION	1
CHAPTER 1 Dewey's Logical Education, 1915–1937: From Lectures on the Types of Logical Theory to *Logic: The Theory of Inquiry*	9
CHAPTER 2 Dewey's Logical Development 1916–1924	35
CHAPTER 3 Dewey's Logical Development 1925–1932	75
CHAPTER 4 Dewey's Logical Development 1933–1937	131
APPENDIX 1	175
NOTES	179
REFERENCES	223
INDEX	233

Tables

1 Dewey's Logical Development 1915   33

2 Dewey's Logical Development 1916–1924   73

3 Dewey's Logical Development 1925–1932   129

4 Dewey's Logical Development 1933–1937   173

Acknowledgments

This book began as an extension of the themes of *John Dewey's Earlier Logical Theory* into the period 1916-1937. As such, it had its germination back in 2008, when I first broached the idea of a chronological accounting and discussion of Dewey's 40 year's journey to *Logic: The Theory of Inquiry*. The research for this book began in earnest in 2013, with a visit to the Center for Dewey Studies and two weeks of intensive reading of Dewey's papers and familiarization with the then newly published Lectures.

I wish to acknowledge the following individuals for their assistance in the coming-to-be of this book:

To Jim Garrison and Larry Hickman for reading and commenting on earlier drafts.

To Larry Hickman and James Downhour at (now shuttered) Center for Dewey Studies at S.I.U. in Carbondale, Il for their hospitality in hosting me during my session with the Special Collections at the Morris Library.

To Arthur Sullivan for conversations regarding Bertrand Russell.

To graduate students Michelle Mahoney and Emma Pearce for help with Dewey's voluminous correspondence.

To graduate student Bryan Heystee for helping me to compile the index.

To graduate student Liu Jia for help with collecting the vast secondary literature related to Dewey's Logic.

Finally, I wish to thank *Education Sciences* for the use of material on pp. 41–44 and 46–48 from "The Logic of Democracy and Education," *Education Sciences*, 7, 2, 2017, 1–8.

Introduction

Dewey began his logical odyssey in 1890, with a paper written for *Open Court* titled "Is Logic a Dualistic Science?"[1] Dewey's conclusion was sadly affirmative, and he attempted over the next forty years to combat the distinction made between logical form and matter. Dewey would continue to write on logical topics through the 1890s, though he did not produce a logical treatise until 1903 with the publication of *Studies in Logical Theory*, which was a combined effort with colleagues at the University of Chicago.[2] This treatise caught the attention of a number of prominent intellectuals, including William James, who applauded the effort, and C. S. Peirce, who did not.[3] The centerpiece of *Studies*—the critique of Kantian-inspired formal logic best represented by Rudolph Hermann Lotze—would remain a fixture for Dewey in subsequent papers on logical theory, psychology, and theory of knowledge into the second and third decades of the twentieth century.

If there was a single issue that dominated Dewey's early forays into logical theory, it was this false division set up by formal logicians—ancient and modern—between form and matter. This topic more than any other occupied Dewey's first major publication on logical theory in 1890, and formed the centerpiece of the first chapter of *Studies*. It continued to concern Dewey's overall pattern of thinking as articulated in *How We Think* (1910), and was a key subject in the introduction to *Essays in Experimental Logic* in 1916.[4] The form-matter distinction was important on a number of intersecting levels. To begin with, Dewey thought the distinction false to fact. It was not the case, Dewey claimed, that there were rival ontological domains of existence; one ideal, the other material. This was a holdover from ancient Greek metaphysics imbued in modern philosophy. On another level, this view continued to frustrate the adoption of science as a natural attitude in contemporary scholarship. Furthermore, empiricist logics—those that eschewed ontological domains in favor of complex inductive accounts of rules and principles—very often failed to extirpate the form-matter dualism from their accounts. This in turn made it difficult for aspiring naturalistic accounts to find legitimate precedents in logical theory. Finally, and perhaps most ominously, if the public was unable to count on existing scholarship for aid in its development of science as a natural attitude—if science itself remained fractured on the question of its ontological commitment to a number of dualisms and their corollaries arising from the form-matter distinction (mind-body dualism, property dualism, phenomenalism, epiphenomenalism)—what could it offer in the way of sage advice to the public, to whom the decision of how to apply the results of science was left?

For Dewey, then, there was much at stake in these early forays into logical theory. Dewey took his logical cues from a number of past thinkers and present colleagues, including Aristotle, J. S. Mill, C. S. Peirce, William James, G. H. Mead, Charles Darwin, and, later, F. H. Woodbridge, Franz Boas, and mathematicians and physicists including Isaac Newton, Albert Einstein, Arthur Eddington, Percy Bridgman, Neils Bohr, Max Planck, and Werner Heisenberg. But the earliest and most profound influence, from the standpoint of his earlier logical theory, was G. W. F. Hegel.[5] It was Hegel who first helped Dewey articulate the philosophical impetus behind the criticism of the form-matter distinction. And it was Hegel who gave Dewey an understanding of the interpenetration of form and matter through overcoming various obstacles to analysis and synthesis and induction and deduction in the performance of operations of inquiry. Dewey would throw off his Hegelian "garb" in the last decade of the nineteenth century, but the "Hegelian bacillus" would remain.[6]

That the "bacillus" proved to be resistant to the increasingly functionalist and instrumentalist direction Dewey would take in the years after his period of Hegelianism meant that overcoming the form-matter distinction would continue to partially drive his attempts at reconstructing logical theory. Dewey would make several attempts at overcoming this distinction in the years 1900–1916. To begin with, he would argue an account of logical theory that was genetic-historical, rather than formalist and a priori; he would approach topics and issues in logical theory from a developmental standpoint. Problems and issues, rather than formal rules and principles, would be given center stage in this argument. In such an account, operations drive inferences, and the context or problem to which inquiry is beholden drives operations. There is a good deal of ink spent on the movements within inquiry; beginnings-to-endings and analysis-to-synthesis, which culminate in a "double movement"; a back-and-forth from whole-to-part-to-whole, as the original problem advancing inquiry and its operations is resolved.[7]

Approaching topics and issues from a developmental standpoint insists on a theory of experience that accompanies the account of inquiry's pattern. Inquiries have beginnings and endings—both of which are experiential. Dewey had to account for how what is experienced in an immediate experience becomes refined (to use a term Dewey would later adopt). This requires an account of immediate experience and an account of the ways in which the products or results of immediate experience are logically ordered and settled. Dewey would only grope toward full accounts of these, as he gradually put together an account of experience that satisfied questions of immediacy and refinement. Dewey was assailed by critics of both idealist and realist camps along the way. (I discuss the realist camps in chapter 1.) By 1915—the year prior to Dewey's next major venture in logical theory—Dewey had amassed a burgeoning though still incomplete theory of logical forms together with the context in which these forms operate. This context was increasingly spelled out in the period 1903–1915 as experience. Almost the entire introduction to his *Essays in Experimental Logic* (1916)—Dewey's second treatise on logical theory—was devoted to the role of experience in inquiry. In the introduction to *Essays*, Dewey thought he had what would satisfy critics; an account of experience in which traits of existence of things immediately felt and had, existed (MW 10, 323). This, it was hoped, would ward off the critics' insatiable appetite for "really real" objects existing in the universe. These traits of existence were felt; they were qualitative, not measurable by instruments. They were found in all beginnings and endings, and their presence (and absence) constituted in part the satisfaction to the felt difficulty that initiated all inquiry. This account of experience was to be conjoined with an account of operations and inferences to produce a total accounting of inquiry that was self-sufficient in that it relied on no ontological dualism between form and matter, ideals and materials, to function.

By 1910, Dewey had the basic "double movement" of inquiry articulated: "a movement from the given partial and confused data to a suggested comprehensive (or inclusive) entire situation; and back from this suggested whole . . . to the particular facts, so as to connect these with one another and with additional facts to which the suggestion has directed attention" (MW 6, 242). This "double movement" would characterize the pattern of inquiry from 1910 on. *There was in all inquiry a double continuity operative; the second continuity operates between parts and whole—confused data and facts—that in turn emerges from a first continuity—an existential to-and-fro—in the immediacy of having and undergoing and experience.* Establishing an account of the conjoining of the first and second *continuity* is a project to which Dewey would increasingly turn as he moved toward his consummate statement on logical theory; the 1938 *Logic*.[8] But experience in 1916 was still underdeveloped in comparison to the robust and complex account Dewey provided in *Experience and Nature* (1925) and other, later works.[9] Dewey had traits of existence that were qualities of things, but no account as of yet how these qualities are continuous with inquiry, or reflection. Much work had to be done to fill in the context in which inquiry operates. Beyond this, Dewey had made little progress in his theory of logical forms, which consisted chiefly of accounts of deduction and induction against the backdrop of the operations of analysis and synthesis. This was detailed in texts such as *How We Think* (1910), but not beyond this. Until 1915, with the article "The Logic of Judgments of Practice," the *hypothetical* nature of all judgments was mostly implicit in Dewey's work.[10] With this article, and this particular account of judging and judgments, Dewey would dive into *Essays in Experimental Logic* with the premise of the basic hypothetical nature of all claims and assertions at the forefront of his arsenal. And with this in hand, Dewey was able to turn his account of propositions and their role in judgments in a way that avoided the ontological dualism set up between form and matter by generations of previous logicians, while maintaining a functional distinction between universals and generic propositions (kinds) that would ensure the domain of each was not reduced to the other. The problem of integrating formal logical methods, which were regnant at the time of the 1938 *Logic*, with a genetic-historical accounting of inquiry in various contexts and of various subject matters, was foremost on Dewey's mind in the period of 1916–1937. This required nothing less than a reformulation of logical theory. What his reformulation consisted of would occupy Dewey for the next twenty-two years.

After *Essays*, Dewey did not produce another logical treatise until 1938, with the publication of *Logic: The Theory of Inquiry*. Other than the now-published lectures, Types of Logical Theory of 1915–1916 and

1927–1928, there is no single text to which we can turn to examine Dewey's logical theory in this period. Indeed, specifically logical works in this period are less than plentiful in comparison to the earlier period (1890–1916), in which two treatises and several articles dealing directly with logical theory, as well as numerous associated texts on psychology, theory of knowledge, thought, and method, were produced. Instead, there are approximately a dozen scattered articles dealing exclusively with logical theory, and three of these were published in 1936. Various issues regarding Dewey's logical theory are discussed in books and articles devoted to other topics, including education, experience, psychology, philosophy, knowledge, art, and politics. Important information also emerges from Dewey's correspondence with key figures. The task of bringing together this mass of scattered material differentiates this work from the examination and analysis of his earlier period, where texts and articles are ready to hand for investigation.

Complicating the issue of the paucity of specifically logical works by Dewey in this period is the lack of scholarship on Dewey's progress toward the 1938 *Logic*. Indeed, what material there is concentrates either on Dewey's metaphysics or theory of knowledge (exemplified *in Experience and Nature* and *The Quest for Certainty*), or the very late *Journal of Philosophy* articles (1936) that formed the nucleus of Dewey's account of universal, existential, and generic propositions. This lack of scholarship suggests that Dewey spent little time or energy on logical topics—a suggestion falsified by the existence of correspondence and class lectures; correspondence and lectures that show Dewey was hard at work on a logical treatise from approximately 1925 to 1938. Unfortunately, other than pointing to the existence of these materials, together with what does exist in Dewey's publication record during the years 1916–1937, little attempt has been made to sort through this mass and develop from it a cogent and coherent account of Dewey's logical development in this period. This I do in what follows.

The publication of Dewey's correspondence and class lectures have made the articulation of Dewey's logical development in these years a much easier task than otherwise. Dewey wrote no treatise on logic between 1917 and 1938. He wrote fewer articles on logic in this period than he did in the period of 1890–1916. And there are fewer articles detailing logical theory in philosophic, epistemological, and psychological topics compared to his earlier period. Nevertheless, there are important articles and texts that bear on Dewey's logical theory; and this is particularly the case with respect to the contexts in which logical theory operates. These include experience, education, habit, language, culture, art, applied science, and politics. Indeed, these contexts are far more richly developed than in the previous period. In the case of experience, two of Dewey's texts—*Experience and Nature* (1925/1929) and *Art as Experience* (1934)—hold the solution to the question of continuity's role in inquiry; a question that Dewey made front and center to his 1938 *Logic*.[11]

Continuity turns out to be the key to logical theory by 1938, and experience, the key to continuity. Dewey makes this claim in earnest in 1916 and gives us a fuller articulation in 1925 and 1934. The relationship between continuity as a logical trait of inquiry and continuity as a generic trait of existence—what I am calling *double continuity*—forms much of the backdrop to Dewey's logical development in this period. To see that this is the case, however, we must venture beyond the few articles Dewey wrote on logic in these twenty-two years and look at many of his other publications, his class lectures, and his correspondence. And we must broaden the search beyond his specifically logical works to examine his works on experience, habit, education, language, culture, art, applied science, and politics. In *John Dewey's Earlier Logical Theory*, I used a set of themes to articulate what remained for Dewey to accomplish in the years between the 1916 publication of *Essays* and the 1938 *Logic*.[12] These themes are "Traits, Meanings, and the Indeterminacy of Situations," "the Existential Matrices of Inquiry (biological and social)," "Scientific and Social Inquiry," and "Propositions and Inferences in Inquiry." I follow these themes in chapters 2, 3, and 4. I break the content covered into three roughly equivalent periods for ease of presentation: 1916–1924, 1925–1932, and 1933–1937.

Chapter 1 begins our discussion with the logical education Dewey received from predecessors and colleagues during the period 1916–1937 by way of specific reference to logical theory. It opens with a brief history of Dewey's gains in logical theory up to and including 1915: the year immediately prior to the publication of *Essays*. It follows with a detailed exposition of various thinkers important to Dewey in framing his logical theory in this period, as well as colleagues who had important roles to play in this regard. Also discussed are various topics and issues Dewey grappled with in moving toward the 1938 *Logic*. Chapters 2, 3, and 4 discuss these thinkers, colleagues, topics, and issues in more detail. This constitutes the content of the periods I assign for the purpose of presentation: 1916–1924, 1925–1932, and 1933–1937, together with the themes mentioned above. Despite the strongly descriptive and historical gloss much of this material receives (a gloss, I might add, that has not been prevalent, at least not in philosophical scholarship), I do have a primary thesis, which I defend: *that continuity as both a logical trait and a generic trait of existence is the key to understanding Dewey's logical theory and that continuity—which Dewey made central to the articulation of the 1938 Logic—is a metaphysical as well as logical concern.* The existential trait of continuity is bound up with the logical trait of continuity in an inquiry. This is the account of *double continuity* Dewey attempts to articulate in his experiential works and the 1938 *Logic*.

A secondary thesis—one that I am prepared to defend but admit requires stronger textual evidence than I provide—is the importance for Dewey's logical theory of Peirce's methods of pragmatism/pragmaticism generally, and his accounts of causality and causal relations specifically. *If Hegel emerges as the key figure in moving Dewey to account for the failure of the form/matter distinction, and is the key figure in moving him toward a reconstructive accounting of his own in the years 1890–1915, then in the years 1916–1938, Peirce emerges as the key figure in gradually moving Dewey from an account in which the enmeshment of experience and inquiry remains undertheorized to one in which each is understood as fully enmeshed with the other.* Dewey's account of how these come to be is developed in the period between 1916–1937 is put to work in the 1938 *Logic*. What this account looks like and how it works is a central aim of this book.

Chapter 1

Dewey's Logical Education, 1915–1937

From Lectures on Types of Logical Theory to *Logic: The Theory of Inquiry*

In this chapter, I discuss the logical education of Dewey in the period 1915–1937 and the settings and individuals in and from which Dewey's ongoing development in logical theory took place. Much of Dewey's development in this period consisted of further refinement of the logical theory first articulated in *Studies in Logical Theory* (1903) and other early essays and lectures; the whole of which I have called Dewey's *earlier* logical theory.[1] But novel interventions also occurred in this later period. It is these novel interventions that this chapter highlights. However, before I discuss these novel interventions and those thinkers that Dewey drew upon, it will do to discuss the accomplishments of Dewey's earlier logical theory. These accomplishments form the material for part 1 of this chapter: Dewey's logical theory circa 1915. The year 1915 is a milestone in Dewey's logical education, for it is the year prior to the publication of Dewey's *Essays in Experimental Logic*. This was a busy year in which Dewey was gathering his sources for the upcoming book; publishing his lengthy retort against Bertrand Russell, "The Logic of Judgments of Practice"; penning the lengthy introduction to accompany *Essays*; and delivering the first of two years' worth of the history of logic in spring courses at Columbia University.[2]

Part 2 discusses the continuity of these influences and looks at the development of Dewey's logical theory in the period 1916–1924. In this period, there is evidence of renewed thinking regarding Aristotle and J. S.

Mill (especially to be found in the lectures on logical theory of 1915–1916), and a surge of interest in C. S. Peirce. Aristotle, Mill, and particularly Peirce would continue to influence Dewey in the periods beyond. Dewey gave his second course of Types of Logical Theory in 1916, in which detailed discussions of historical logical theories, most importantly (again) Aristotle, Mill, and Russell, were prevalent. The ongoing estimation of Peirce for Dewey's own logical theory began in earnest in 1916 with the publication of "The Pragmatism of Peirce." Finally, Dewey's interlocutors in correspondence, particularly Scudder Klyce, helped him work toward a more thoroughgoing role for experience in logical theory.

Part 3 continues with an examination of Dewey's logical theory through these themes and pays attention to the ongoing influence of Aristotle, Mill, Russell, and Peirce, together with anthropologist Franz Boas, and the philosophical insights of leading international physicists that Dewey was following in the years 1925–1932. These physicists, including Einstein, Neils Bohr, Arthur Eddington, Max Planck, and Werner Heisenberg, were important in the debate over the new, or quantum physics and its relevance for philosophical accounts of causality in particular. The arguments they generated proved important for Dewey's own accounting of material, space, time, and causality. Also important for Dewey's ongoing logical development are a series of lectures titled Types of Logical Theory that he provided to graduate students at Columbia University in 1927–1928. In these, Dewey again discusses the logics of Aristotle, Mill, as well as formal logicians of significance, such as Russell. With these lectures, novel arguments regarding logical operations, propositions, causality, temporality, and the pattern of inquiry were put forward, arguments that would find their way into Dewey's 1938 *Logic*. Most notable during these years is a beginning concentration on the distinctions between universal and generic-existential judgments, a concentration that would continue through to 1938. Beyond this was Dewey's remarkable account of experience, developed at length in 1925 with *Experience and Nature* and followed by important articles, particularly "Qualitative Thought" (1930). These key texts on experience would serve Dewey's ongoing account of *double continuity*—a continuity of the existential to-and-fro inherent in doing and undergoing conjoined with the logical continuity of serial ordering in and through the operations of inquiry.

Part 4 deals with the years 1933–1937. Having developed a sophisticated theory of experience, and having dealt at length with the role of science to society and to the public, in these years Dewey worked tirelessly to refine his theory of propositions and judgments. Work on *Logic: The Theory of Inquiry*, although begun as early as 1925, was earnestly undertaken more or less uninterrupted only in these last few years. Increasingly, Dewey's interlocutors of most benefit to his logical theory were his friends and students, especially including Joseph Ratner, Sidney Hook, and (after 1934) Arthur Bentley. The correspondence between these shows Dewey continuing to hone his arguments for propositions and judgments. By 1938, the year of the *Logic*'s publication, the functional differentiation of generic and universal propositions—the last significant move in Dewey's logical theory—was fully in place.

Part 1: Dewey's Logical Theory circa 1915

By 1915, the year before the publication of *Essays in Experimental Logic*, Dewey had given twenty-five years of consideration to the topic of logical theory and had devoted many articles, lectures, and a book to the enterprise. When approached by the University of Chicago Press to contribute a second volume on logical theory, Dewey decided to take the essays he wrote for the earlier, *Studies in Logical Theory* (1903), and conjoin them with various other essays written in the interim. Most of these only peripherally dealt with logical topics, though they included assessments of leading schools of thought (pragmatism as understood by William James, Bertrand Russell's Analytic Realism, Critical Realism, including the so-called Six Realists); branches of philosophy, including philosophy of psychology and the theory of knowledge; as well as his evolving theory of experience. Dewey also included in *Essays* his recent "The Logic of Judgments of Practice" (1915), which targeted Russell's claim there could be no objective judgments of value. To all of this he added a lengthy introduction. Dewey's themes of instrumentalism, a duly qualified non-naive realism, a theory of experience, together with an apparatus for countering claims of subjectivism and idealism, all factored into the introduction Dewey wrote for *Essays*. The introduction is particularly notable for the attention Dewey gives to experience and to the (temporal) continuity bound up in experiencing (e.g., MW 10, 320). Experience, in the introduction to *Essays*, is meant to refer, first, to the inexpressible beyond of our cognition, and second, to the here and now of (all) our existence (e.g., MW 10, 324).[3] While reflection is the *locus classicus* of inquiry, and logical theory thereby, insufficient attention had been given to role of experience in inquiry, and to the beginnings and endings of inquiry. A fuller and instrumental accounting of these beginnings and endings is championed in the pages of the introduction. A fully instrumental theory of experience, Dewey thought, would help logical theory battle a number of faulty characteristics that had dogged it, especially in the latter half of the nineteenth century.

Dewey noted a chief problem with logical theory in the latter half of the nineteenth century concerned its reliance on sense-psychology. This reliance was often cashed out in *phenomenalism*, the view that there were mental intermediaries operating between the world and mind such as sensations, sense-qualia, impressions, and the like, and that the chief job of logic was to give form to this matter (MW 8, 51–52). Dewey though this reliance was in evidence in early thinkers of the empiricist tradition such as Locke, and infected others such as Kant and leading thinkers of the British associationist school, including J. S. Mill and Walter Jevons. It also pervaded the accounts of idealist thinkers such as R. M. Lotze, who figured prominently in Dewey's *Studies*. Certain newer realists, most notably Bertrand Russell, were also thought to rely on a faulty sense-psychology, and Dewey took note of this in the introduction to *Essays* and in an earlier work (republished in *Essays*) titled "The Existence of the World as a Logical Problem."[4] Giving a proper accounting of experience, or so Dewey thought, would alleviate many of the problems generated by phenomenalism.

Beyond this, Dewey was also keen to oppose those who considered his work on psychology, the theory of knowledge, and philosophy generally, to be in the idealist camp. These charges were mounted by Russell, but also by the so-called Critical Realists. These latter were composed of American philosophers, led by Arthur Lovejoy and E. B. McGilvary, who criticized pragmatism generally and Dewey specifically for a subjectivist view of knowledge whereby the limits imposed by human experience close off the possibility of objective facts beyond the mind-world interface.[5] This episode came to a head in 1910 with the publication of "The Program and First Platform of the Six Realists," followed by a volume of essays titled *The New Realism*.[6] Dewey and E. B. Spaulding debated the platform in 1912, with Dewey concluding that any realism that attempts to draw deductive conclusions from concepts alone is "Platonic-medieval" (MW 6, 138).[7]

The post-1903 contributions to *Essays* contained a number of deliberate claims designed to foil critics, all the while maintaining key conclusions from *Studies*. Post-1903, the central feature of logical theory is not the concept; rather, it is inquiry. Inquiry is reflective, and arises from an unsettled or indeterminate situation. Inquiry is functional, and has a specific task that is set by a concrete and empirical situation (MW 10, 327). Reflection terminates when the situation is settled. The products or outcomes of reflection are turned to meanings. Meanings, in turn, imply relationships. These relationships are brought to bear on further unsettled situations as habit. Meanings serve both as functions and as signs. Reflection is the proper domain of inquiry, and occupies a mediate position between beginning (of an unsettled situation) and ending (the settling of an unsettled situation) (MW 10, 327–28). This is best demonstrated through a genetic-historical accounting of the development of science, which is discussed both in the introduction to *Essays* (e.g., MW 10, 330–32) and in *Studies* (e.g., MW 2, 308–9). It is to this that Dewey adds his developing account of experience.

Existences are matters of, and for, experience. Brute existences are the stuff of experience, not colors, sensations, sense-qualia, or impressions. The understanding of existences already shaped by mental processes and put forth as primitive has been the failure of British sense-psychology and associationism, and has infected twentieth-century programs of realism, such as Russell's. Brute existences are prior to inquiry, and it is in inquiry that existences are differentiated and discriminated; analyzed into separate "components" such as sensations. What we have in brute existences are qualities and "traits"; "specific existential traits uniquely belonging to it; the entities of simple data as such" (MW 10, 343). Things ("*res*") have traits that are very often paired, and operate in a double movement; a back-and-forth, a to-and-fro (MW 10, 323). Indeed, this is a thesis Dewey maintained since at least *Studies*. Individual articles, such as "The Postulate of Immediate Empiricism," buttressed this claim (MW 3, 116). Beyond this, Dewey challenged the Analytic Realism of Russell and the Critical Realism of the Six Realists, while maintaining his distinction from certain forms of idealism. It is not that Dewey castigates realism or idealism *tout court*; it is rather that a certain faulty feature, common to many realisms and idealisms, remains to limit their utility in solving logical problems: the neglect of "the temporally intermediate and instrumental place of reflection . . ." (MW 10, 332). Universal, absolutist, and rationalist systems of logic, whether realist or idealist in name, have a strong tendency to commit to the sidelining of inquiry, and this Dewey cannot abide. An idealist accounting of logical theory that makes room for the temporal, existential, intermediate, and instrumental would be justified insofar as it does: likewise, for a realist accounting. An accounting that does not, whether through fixed and final categories of reflection, or objects immune to experiential inquiry (such as sense-qualia, sensations, or impressions), cannot be justified.

Despite the gains Dewey made with *Essays*, much work remained in light of his 1938 *Logic*. I have categorized this work across four themes, first articulated in *John Dewey's Earlier Logical Theory*. These themes are "Traits, Meanings, and the Indeterminacy of Situations," "The Existential Matrices of Inquiry (biological and social)," "Scientific and Social Inquiry," and "Propositions and Inferences in Inquiry." By 1916, Dewey had a nascent theory of experience, consisting in traits of brute existences, which were qualitative; felt. Inquiry supplied the wherewithal to order and control these traits, with the "product" being logical objects, concepts of relations, and inferences articulated as tools of operation. What Dewey didn't yet have was a finely wrought distinction between experience as "gross and macroscopic" and as "refined" (LW 1, 15–17), together with all the qualifications that this portends. Though continuity was marked especially for its importance in *Studies* and *Essays*, without the fine-grained distinctions Dewey would develop, the account remained question-begging. This would have to wait until *Experience and Nature* (1925) and beyond (LW 1, 15–17). Indeed, it wouldn't be until *Art as Experience* (1934) that Dewey would be able to take full advantage of a *double continuity*—an account consisting of temporality specific to both immediate *and* reflective experiences linked together in a seamless continuity—a temporality necessary for his further claims regarding scientific causality in the 1938 *Logic*.

Developing an intricate account of experience necessitated filling in the context of biology and culture as they formed the framework against which inquiry operates. Dewey's famous second and third chapters in the 1938 *Logic* on the matrices of inquiry were products of much reflection in the years 1915–1916: the role of biology in human experiencing, the role of language in and upon biology, and the role of signs and symbols in language continued to occupy Dewey. Progress was made in numerous articles and books, perhaps most importantly in the account of habit formation in the context of adaptation, beginning with the introduction to *Essays* (1916) and *Democracy and Education* (1916), and continuing to *Human Nature and Conduct* (1922). Dewey's regard for science and the public also continued in this period. By the end of 1915, Dewey had yet to develop a sophisticated account of public inquiry and had only begun to examine the burgeoning criticism of positivism, some of which was beginning to be directed his way the following year.[8] The detailed argument for the distinction between physical and social science, so important for the 1938 *Logic*, began in earnest in the period immediately following *Essays*, notably with *Democracy and Education*.

The most important consideration for Dewey in 1933–1937, and the issue that perplexed him longest, was that of propositions and, specifically, the nature of generic and universal propositions. This was only hinted at in works leading up to *Essays* (e.g., MW 6, 16–17; 254). Propositions were practical or abstract; practical propositions were existential, in that they referred to some activity, whereas abstract propositions were purely symbolic/mathematical. The roles of induction and deduction were uncomfortably paired with practical and abstract propositions. But the rigorous identification of various propositions into functional kinds was wanting in 1916. And there was a great deal at stake for Dewey in getting some categorization of functional kinds into view: for Dewey's realist critics, especially Russell, were of the opinion that Dewey had surrendered deductive argumentation to fancy, leaving (as with Mill) only induction to do the heavy lifting of logic.[9] For Dewey had, in *Essays* and elsewhere, downplayed the suitability of purely formal methods of argumentation such as symbolic logic for solving existential matters (e.g., MW 10, 144). *Dewey would have to show that universal propositions were propositions in which no material existence was needed for proof in a judgment, yet must have some sort of connection to existential propositions in which material existence was predicated.* As we shall see, this problem would not be satisfactorily solved until 1936.

Part 2: Dewey's Logical Education, 1916–1924

By 1916, Dewey had held his appointments as professor of philosophy and pedagogy at Columbia and Teachers' College for twelve years.[10] Of course, 1916 was the year of a number of important publications, including *Democracy and Education* as well as *Essays*. For Dewey's philosophy of education, it was a year of culmination of ideas that had been germinating since at least *School and Society* (1899); for Dewey's logical theory, it was a restatement of his earlier commitments in *Studies* (1903), as well as a synopsis of his theory of knowledge during the years 1903–1915, together with his response to critics of *Studies* and beyond. Importantly for us, it was the harbinger of relationships new and renewed with central thinkers in the history of philosophy, as well as current thinkers on the forefront of importance. Chief among the former is Aristotle and John Stuart Mill. Of emerging importance for Dewey in this period is Charles Saunders Peirce. Of immediate contemporary importance is Bertrand Russell. The correspondence with Scudder Klyce also emerges as important for Dewey in this (and the next) period.

Aristotle

Most commentators agree that Dewey's interest in Aristotle began in the first several years of his tenure at Columbia under the influence of his colleague in the department of philosophy, F. H. Woodbridge.[11] As a result, it is said that Dewey's realism was sharpened and placed in the foreground when responding to critics that claimed he was a closet idealist.[12] Woodbridge also had a salutary effect on Dewey in the latter's "discovery" of Aristotle.[13] I have discussed Dewey's relationship to Aristotle in the years leading up to 1916 elsewhere;[14] here, I want to quickly discuss what Dewey made of Aristotle in 1915–1916 in regards to his lectures delivered at Columbia University on the types of logical theory.[15]

Altogether, approximately sixty pages of written text on Aristotle are found in the typed manuscript of the lectures. Aristotle is the first of the eight historical thinkers and types of logic Dewey dealt with.[16] Dewey's discussion of Aristotle leads him to two important conclusions bearing on logical theory. First, logic is social. Logic is social because definitions and the like are essential ingredients of argument, and argument is social (TLT, 1915, Aristotle).[17] This in turn leads Dewey to stress logic as a "tool"; a technology for "the practical relations of life" (TLT, 1915, Aristotle). Of course, Dewey had long argued that logic was social; at least as early as *Studies* this was a feature of inquiry. But this reading of Aristotle gave Dewey a historical voice that was otherwise unavailable to him in the earlier period. The second bears directly on Dewey's distinction between universal and existential propositions. It was Dewey's conclusion that Aristotle operated with existential propositions; propositions about "facts of the matter" (TLT, 1915, Aristotle). This gets fleshed out in Dewey's description of Aristotle's account of induction and deduction. It contributes to Dewey's conclusion that Aristotle was a philosopher of relations, for whom the concept was the relation of universal and particular. Altogether, Dewey found Aristotle an ally in matters of the sociality of logic and the practical application of logical propositions to facts, even as he rejects the latter's talk of divinity and a priori analytics.[18] Dewey would return to Aristotle in his 1927–1928 Types of Logical Theory and draw ever new consequences from this latest reading.

Mill

Mill occupies a very unique place in Dewey's logical theory, as he is often the point of departure in Dewey's own accounts of induction and deduction. Like James, Dewey is sympathetic to Mill's attempt at refusing formalism in logic. Like James, Dewey is skeptical that Mill accomplishes his task. And like James, Dewey finds Mill to have reinvented the wheel in proclaiming induction superior to deduction and invariably chides Mill in his accounts of these.[19] In the period prior to 1916, Mill's logical theory is treated in several places, most notably *Outline of a Critical Theory of Ethics* (EW 3, 274–76);[20] *Lectures on Ethics*, 1900–1901: Lectures on the Logic of Ethics 1900,[21] and *Studies* (1903) (MW 3, 368–75). The general criticism is that Mill's "hedonism" is indebted to a sense-psychology in which associations produce immediate satisfactions irrespective of the social milieu of which they form a part. Furthermore, in *Studies*, Dewey concluded that Mill was led astray by the classical empiricist view that reality was ultimately diffused into sensations (MW 3, 368).[22]

In the 1915–1916 Types of Logical Theory, Mill received his fullest treatment thus far. According to the typed manuscript, the lecture on Mill began on March 29, 1915, and carried forward until April 26, 1915. Altogether, the section on Mill constitutes approximately twenty pages.[23] In Dewey's description of Mill's account of induction on March 31, 1915, there is a strong critique of the hidden reliance Mill places in hypothesis formation and induction (TLT, March 31, 1915). Yet Mill's account of deduction is also shown to rely on a faulty sense-psychology in which "occurrences" are sensations linked together at face value rather than being products of inquiry (TLT, March 31, 1915). (A similar falsity is noted in Locke's theory of knowledge in his account of March 16 and March 26, 1916: sensory data are for Locke "primitive" rather than products of inquiry [TLT, March 16, 1916].)[24] In these passages, Locke and Mill are compared unfavorably with William James. Mill's account of deduction will serve to make Dewey's account against sense-psychology all that clearer in future discussions, notably the 1927–1928 Types of Logical Theory and especially in Chapter 8 of *Logic: The Theory of Inquiry* (LW 12, 147–48).

Russell

Russell is the most discussed of Dewey's contemporary interlocutors. Indeed, there is recent Dewey scholarship discussing their rival views on metaphilosophy, psychology, theory of knowledge, and logic.[25] The debate between the two began in earnest as early as 1914—the year Dewey responded to Russell's *The Problem of the External World as a Field for Scientific Method in Philosophy*.[26] Dewey would carry his basic criticisms of Russell forward to the 1938 *Logic* and beyond. For his part, Russell would take the opportunity to criticize Dewey's logical theory in the 1939 *Library of Living Philosophers* series on Dewey and again in his *History of Western Philosophy* (1945).[27] The differences between Dewey and Russell were manifold: first and foremost was Russell's commitment to an abstract and formalist logic in which judgments were seemingly reduced to numerical coefficients. This "mathematicization" of logic would constitute the chief impediment to Dewey's recognition of the "new logic" as an improvement over syllogistic methods. Beyond this, Dewey took issue with Russell's reliance on sense-psychology: a holdover from classical empiricism in which reality is first taken in through the senses and mental intermediaries such as sensations, sense-qualia, and the like are said to account for the interface of world and mind. Dewey makes this quite clear in a number of places in 1915–1916, including especially "The Logic of Judgments of Practice" (1915) (MW 8) and the introduction to *Essays* (1916) (MW 10). But it was also a chief concern for Dewey's 1915–1916 Types of Logical Theory. Russell is purportedly the chief figure in Dewey's section on "Recent Logistic"; however, the actual discussion of Russell does not appear in the extant typescript. Russell is variously invoked in Dewey's passages on Locke and Mill, however, and Dewey suggests that Russell succumbs to the same faulty sense-psychology that they do (TLT, March 16, 1916; March 26, 1916). Dewey's unpublished lecture to the Philosophical Club at Columbia University in 1916, republished as "Logical Objects" (MW 10) in the *Middle Works*, carries over chief concerns regarding Russell's formalism and sense-psychology from "The Logic of Judgments of Practice" (MW 8, 1915) and the introduction to

Essays (MW 10, 1916): Russell is again criticized for making the atomic ingredients of "molecular propositions" foundational instead of products of inquiry (MW 10, 94–95). In 1918–1924, with the exception of Russell's investigations of Western influences on China, Dewey was more or less silent on Russell (MW 13, 215–18).[28]

Peirce

If Dewey's logical forays of the 1890s were most heavily influenced by Hegel, then beginning in the period 1916–1924, that influence shifts to Peirce. There has been some documentation of this in the Dewey literature.[29] While it is the case that Dewey's earliest encounters with Peirce were sub-satisfactory (he chafed at the logic course taken with Peirce while a graduate student at Johns Hopkins, and he had an awkward and difficult correspondence with Peirce over the publication of *Studies*),[30] by 1916 he had come to see the overall affinities between his own instrumentalism and Peirce's pragmatic-pragmaticistic method. Dewey wrote his first full-length article on Peirce for the *Journal of Philosophy, Psychology, and Scientific Methods* in 1916, titled "The Pragmatism of Peirce."[31] The article was notable for Dewey's account of Peirce's notion of truth-as-meaning, and for agreeing with Peirce that a *causal* theory of meaning and reality is demanded of right beliefs.[32] Peirce also helped Dewey to begin to see the role the nominalism-realism debate plays in his own logical theory and theory of knowledge. While Dewey (and Peirce) clearly rejects strong forms of conceptualism (think a priori philosophies of mind), the question of at least residual traces of nominalism in Dewey's empiricism remains.[33] The solution, as Dewey would develop beginning here and continuing to the 1938 *Logic*, was to reject the poles of the debate in favor of a melioristic position that avoids the abstractions common to both.

Klyce

Scudder Klyce was a figure who caused Dewey no small amount of trepidation. If Dewey's biographers are to be believed, Klyce was partly responsible for Dewey's self-examination of character.[34] Klyce was a tempestuous autodidact with a good deal of scientific knowledge, including the history of the sciences. He was also a confirmed Buddhist and idealist, and (as his letters to Dewey make clear) monist. Their correspondence began in 1913, with Klyce submitting to Dewey a copy of his self-published

The Universe. It ended rather abruptly in 1928 after Klyce's publication of the philosophical roman à clef *Dewey's Suppressed Psychology*. Klyce's stubborn refusal to countenance Dewey's realism and anti-nominalism was partly responsible for the demise of the correspondence.[35] Yet Klyce's early correspondence with Dewey proved invaluable for Dewey's ongoing account of continuity. Responding to the publication of Dewey's *Essays* in 1916, Klyce took the opportunity to chastise Dewey for neglecting scientists' understanding of temporality. For Klyce, Dewey hesitated to take the full step toward monism and declare time and space immediately real and not beholden to the past and future (e.g., Klyce to Dewey, July 24, 1916, 03554). Dewey would respond by modifying his account of continuity to take into consideration immediate temporality as well as the scientific-historical temporality discussed in *Essays*. Dewey's emergent account of the role of time in continuity would find its way into *Experience and Nature* (1925) and "Qualitative Thought" (1930), as well as other articles in the period 1925–1932.

Part 3: Dewey's Logical Education, 1925–1932

In 1920, Dewey published *Reconstruction in Philosophy*, and in 1922, *Human Nature and Conduct*.[36] The former was gathered from lectures Dewey gave in 1919 at the Imperial University of Tokyo; the latter from lectures given in 1918 at Leland Stanford University. Though Dewey broke no new logical ground in either, each was valuable for fleshing out the context in which inquiry operates. This context—both experiential and habitual—also played a significant role in Dewey's most important work of the period: *Experience and Nature* (1925). The roles of intelligent method and language in scientific (and philosophical) development were turned toward an account of the interaction of the human organism and its world in what would become Dewey's great treatise on metaphysics. *Experience and Nature* not only was of tremendous importance for Dewey's account of experience; it also supplied Dewey's fullest statement to date of the relationship between the two aspects of double continuity—the continuity of immediate experiencing together with the continuity built up in inquiry. The temporal-spatial dimensions of these continuities—unified in the activity of inquiry—were made manifest. Dewey would continue this stress on double continuity in "Qualitative Thought" (1930) and other articles in the period.

In terms of Dewey's interlocutors, Aristotle, Mill, and Peirce factored heavily. As well, Dewey became increasingly interested in the debates among physicists endorsing the "new physics": atomic physics, relativity, and the quantum-mechanical method. These included Einstein and Eddington, but also Neils Bohr, William Rutherford, Max Planck, and Werner Heisenberg. Dewey often claimed he could not follow the complicated mathematics involved in their debates, but he did follow the gist of the arguments and worked to incorporate the findings into his overall pattern of inquiry.[37] Some of their conclusions (especially Heisenberg's) were of interest for Dewey in regard to his account of spatio-temporality. Finally, Dewey's correspondence, particularly with Albert Barnes, Joseph Ratner, and Sidney Hook, furnished him with colleagues to discuss his ongoing program in logical theory. This would bear fruit, particularly in the years 1934–1937, when frequent exchanges between Ratner, Hook, and Dewey on the manuscript that would become *Logic: The Theory of Inquiry* were under way.

Aristotle

Dewey reencountered Aristotle in this time period. From the point of view of logical theory, the two great confrontations occurred in the years up to and including 1925, with *Experience and Nature*, and again, in 1927–1928, with Dewey's lectures on types of logic given as a graduate course at Columbia University.[38] In *Experience and Nature*, Aristotle is given pride of place as nearest to the path of a naturalistic metaphysics and a proponent of a pluralistic philosophy (LW 1, 47–48). In the 1927–1928 lectures, Dewey is more specific about the logical import of Aristotle's *Organon*. Aristotle's account of the syllogisms, while restricted to a logic of universal and particular, is the basis for an entire set of operations that is propositionalized.[39] The conclusion of a set of syllogisms operates as a leading hypothesis in a further judgment (e.g., TLT, October 10, 1927): instead of being a formal arrangement of fixed and stable claims, the syllogism becomes the basic operation in a nascent judgment. The syllogism returns to its former glory, not as the *fons et origo* of formal logic, but rather as a functional set of conditions that must be in place for any new scientific judgment. *That* we operate syllogistically in experimental conditions is a given for Dewey; *how* we operate with syllogisms is transformed. Rather than syllogisms having pride of place at the inception of any and all specific set of inferences, they take on an intermediary function as we move from the conclusion of one judgment to another in an ongoing inquiry: the syllogism place of prominence is to function as an intermediary in inquiry.

Mill

Dewey's reencounter with Mill also took place in the context of the 1927–1928 Types of Logical Theory. Indeed, Dewey discussed a number of empiricist-oriented logicians and logics in these lectures. All of them drew on a faulty sense-psychology that privileged sensations and associated givens as mental intermediaries between world and mind; all of them subsequently reduced knowledge to an affair of the phenomenalistic perception of basic qualities.[40] Consonant with the 1915–1916 lectures, Dewey chides Mill for his sense-psychology, as well as his inflation of induction to the detriment of deductive operations. He also chides Mill for formalizing the operation of induction; what should be an operation of testing phenomena for their stability in future inquiry is rendered into a formal procedure to which material must comply in order for there to be valid inference (TLT, December 12, 1927). However, Dewey does agree with Mill that induction is a sort of test; Dewey calls it a "material test" in which "phenomena" are tested as to their stability to make further inferences—what Dewey calls "fact" (TLT, December 12, 1927). The upshot is that *both* induction *and* deduction are tests; the former material, the latter formal.

Russell

The ongoing debate with Russell was reinvigorated by Dewey's 1927–1928 Types of Logical Theory. Like Aristotle and Mill, Russell appears and reappears throughout the manuscript. Dewey's earlier criticisms of Russell in *Essays* and the 1915–1916 Types of Logical Theory also reappear. The context, aside from sense-psychology, is propositions, specifically abstract and mathematical propositions. Of course, Russell's "molecular propositions," and the "atomic facts" that underlay them, come in for especial criticism. But Russell is no mere foil for Dewey's operational account of judgments. Dewey acknowledges the *positive* accomplishment of formal logical methods in these lectures. Formal logic helps us see the "barrenness" of the syllogistic form (TLT, December 7, 1927). The formal logic of syllogisms has nothing to say about material or existences. The syllogism is of purely abstract import. However, this implies that propositions about existences cannot (straightforwardly) be formal. Claims such as "This is of X" can refer only to singular instances of existence; other propositions must therefore deal with kinds and classes (All of X are of this kind) and universals (All X's have feature or characteristic Y). This licensing of inference would be extremely important in the following period (1933–1937) in helping Dewey get clearer on the relationship between existential, generic, and universal propositions and their functional nature.

Doubtless in light of Russell's formalism, Dewey began to canvass various functional roles of judging. He enumerated these in the 1927–1928 Types of Logical Theory. What was unique about these, which Dewey stressed throughout, was their *role-given* nature. Depending on how we wish to use them, judgments could be universal, particular, abstract. But they could also be refined as directive judgments, judgments of command and request, judgments of desire, judgments of inquiry or inquiring-into, judgments of advice and council, and commands (imperatives) (TLT, January 9, 1928). What matters with regard to judgments is their *class*: and this in turn on the *function* they serve. If what we want to do is direct a certain course of events, then judgments of the class "directive" come into play: likewise, for examining the relationships between ideas or concepts; we will want abstract judgments for this examination.

Peirce

Dewey discussed Peirce in a number of places in this period, including "The Development of American Pragmatism"[41] and the 1927–1928 Types of Logical Theory. He also reviewed the first volume of the *Collected Works of Charles Saunders Peirce* (1931). Indeed, Dewey began his lectures on logic proper with an exposition of Peirce's "The Fixation of Belief" (TLT, October 5, 1927). The stress in Dewey's lecture was on formal and material logics, the falsity of "the sharp separation between knowledge and belief," and the importance of continuity and discontinuity (TLT, October 5, 1927). It is the business of logical theory to overcome "gaps, discrepancies, and discontinuities in subject matter" (TLT, October 10, 1927). Additionally, Dewey repeats his early claim from "The Pragmatism of Peirce" (1916) in "The Development of American Pragmatism"; Peirce gives us a theory of meaning. The ability of the concept to grasp its cases in extension—to have applicability to human conduct—is the meaning of the proposition. This requires us to set up the conditions to be met in terms of hypotheses; conjectures that do, or do not, bear out the anticipated consequences. Furthermore, Peirce gives us an account of *immediate* meanings: meanings that consist in habits with qualitative dimensions. This would serve Dewey's own theory of meaning in *Experience and Nature* and elsewhere.

Physics and the Physicists

It is during this period, and especially with respect to *Experience and Nature* (1925), that Dewey began to discuss in earnest the ontological relationship between situations and events and the inquiry that refines these, chiefly through temporalization. This went hand in hand with Dewey's examination of developments, particularly in celestial and quantum physics, that revolutionized science in the early half of the twentieth century. As with most philosophers of the time, Dewey was fascinated by the claims of these (mostly) European physicists. Though Dewey often demurred in his correspondence with interlocutors regarding his mathematical education, we may surmise that Dewey read these thinkers with some sophistication, for he did have a background in mathematics and was for two years a high-school mathematics teacher before returning to graduate school. Dewey was very likely familiar with Einstein before 1920 (for he is mentioned in *Reconstruction*) and gradually became familiar with Eddington, Bohr, Planck, and Heisenberg in the 1920s.[42] By 1927, Dewey was clearly familiar with all of these, as his correspondence and class lectures display.[43] The overarching questions with respect to Dewey's engagement with these physicists have to do with their contribution to Dewey's overall accounting of a philosophy of science for logical theory.

Dewey scholars have made more of the importance of the conclusions of the relativity and indeterminacy of phenomena for Dewey's attacks on epistemology and less for his logical theory. It is certainly the case that Dewey used the conclusions, particularly of Einstein and Heisenberg, as experimental vindication for his critique of British sense-psychology and the tradition of epistemology to which it was beholden.[44] But there is more going on here. Dewey is also looking for validation of the claim that there is something irreducibly outside of and beyond our capture as temporal phenomena, and that time, the construction of a series of inquired-into events, is a constraint of inquiry. This anti-nominalistic realism of Dewey's complements and, indeed, helps to buttress his nascent philosophy of science, for it corroborates his thesis, put forward as early as 1905, that there are "thats" whose impingement upon us cannot be fully predicted and that lie beyond time.⁴⁵ It will do to discuss this in more detail in order to prepare for the analysis of Dewey's correspondence and claims in Dewey's 1927–1928 Types of Logical Theory, *The Quest for Certainty*, and his correspondence with Ratner and Hook.

In claiming that space and time were absolute, Newton also claimed that matter (mass) was invariant. Given a bounded space, one could calculate the exact position of a body *and* its velocity. The "invariance" hypothesis maintained its currency through to the latter half of the nineteenth century, until it was upended by the experiments of Albert Michelson and Edward Morley, who were attempting to prove the existence of aether. The results of the Michelson-Morley experiments are well-known. By shining a beam of light upon a mirror that was partly coated in silver, they hypothesized that if aether existed, there would be a difference in the speed with which light recombined when reflected back by the mirror. Of course, it turned out there was no difference. This was the beginning of the end of the invariance hypothesis, whose conclusion was only fully borne out in Einstein's theory of special relativity. The key to Einstein's calculations lay in part in the earlier work done by H. A. Lorentz, whose own calculations on transforms served to bridge James Clerk Maxwell's laws of electromagnetism with existing mechanics. The fourth transform of Lorentz's in particular is of benefit to solving problems of wavelength among two observers. This proved beneficial to Einstein in his demonstration that mass is not constant, but rather modified in the conservation of momentum.⁴⁶

One reading of Heisenberg's influence on Dewey is read off his conclusion that one cannot simultaneously locate the location and the velocity of an object. In studies of the wave-particle dualism of light (which Heisenberg helped to establish), the observation changes what is observed.⁴⁷ But what was at stake for Heisenberg was less this relativistic conclusion (though it was important) than the measure of the limits of the temporal relationship between a particle, described as a wave-function, and its momentum, or the product of the particle's mass and velocity. What was at stake, in other words, was the utility of Erwin Schrödinger's formula for precisely predicting the location of a particle in a defined field. The solution to Schrödinger's formula is probabilistic, meaning that the likely location will be limited to a certain specified region, and within a certain range.⁴⁸ Schrödinger relies on a discrete sum as a constant: the so-called Planck's Constant, which is a (statistical) summation of fixed values of energy from a continuous series of energies, first ascertained in Max Planck's studies on blackbody radiation as early as 1900. The indeterminacy in Heisenberg's principle of indeterminacy refers specifically to the position of the particle as a wave-function to that of its momentum. We can, with the formula for the principle, assign a numerical value to this uncertainty, given two operators.[49] What we cannot do is predict with absolute certainty where the particle will be at any given time. Indeed, the modified Planck's Constant that the principle insists we must work with is much reduced compared with the original Constant.[50] There is an element of chance in every prediction of phenomena; an element that cannot be fully eliminated. Heisenberg's thesis leads to two notable conclusions: first, our predictions are not infallible. Second, there is chance built into every attempt at ascertaining phenomena in time-determinations, here represented as mathematical operators. But there is a third conclusion, which Heisenberg himself notes, though it is not addressed in prevailing Dewey scholarship: there is an element of chance in the universe such that we cannot predict with complete accuracy temporal-spatial events.[51] For Heisenberg, the "chance" of this chance can be calculated probabilistically, with respect to mathematical operators as representations of physical variables. But this chance cannot be calculated with absolute accuracy. This conclusion *does* bring him in line with Einstein, though it was a conclusion Einstein largely refused to admit.[52] Most importantly, and as we shall see, it serves to aid Dewey in his long-held claim that *his is a realist theory of logical forms* that does not admit brute facts lie in a temporal-spatial dimension that is constructed through a historical series of events set in inquiry. Rather, brute facts (as events or situations) evince their own temporality, which is qualitatively distinct from the temporality of ordering:[53] what is refined in inquiry and settled in a temporal series is limited by undergoing an experience of an event or situation, the qualities of which cannot be (fully) predicted. The discussion of temporality as regards the conclusions of the new physics chiefly occurs in Dewey's ongoing correspondence with Joseph Ratner and Sidney Hook at and beyond the presentation of the 1927–1928 Types of Logical Theory, as well as in *Quest for Certainty* (1929).

Franz Boas

Boas, a colleague of Dewey's at Columbia, had an enormous impact on Dewey.[54] We see this particularly in *Reconstruction in Philosophy* and *Human Nature and Conduct*, where Dewey's accounts of early religion, mythology, customs, and speech groups owe a great debt to the work of Boas and his pupils. But we also see this debt in *Experience and Nature*, particularly in the accounts of experience, communication, meanings, and language, as well as the methods of ethnology. Important for *Experience and Nature* is the characterization of the contexts in which early man becomes aware of its powers of refinement in the move from primary to secondary experience. This account then becomes important in distinguishing primary experience from secondary or refined experience, while preserving the continuity that is built up in both. Dewey captures this sentiment in his transition from chapter 1 (of the 1929 edition) to chapter 2 in *Experience and Nature*.

Dewey's Correspondence

The correspondence in this period served as the main vehicle for Dewey's communication of his findings on physical science and temporality. It also served to bring notice to Dewey's commitment to write a treatise on logic. This involved three interlocutors in particular: Albert Barnes, Scudder Klyce, and Sidney Hook. Dewey of course, communicated with many more people, but these serve as the figures most responsible for his logical education in this period. Dewey's correspondence with Albert Barnes in this period is chiefly notable for the first pronouncement that a treatise on logic would be forthcoming. On December 4, 1925, Dewey sent to Barnes a letter in which he indicated he was working on a "new treatise," which would be "an introduction to logical theory" (Dewey to Barnes, December 4, 1925, 04215). At the time, Dewey was putting together the course on logic he would deliver in 1927–1928, and this is the context in which the letter was written. Dewey's correspondence with Klyce at this time was, by contrast, at its nadir. Klyce had become less and less tolerable toward what he saw as Dewey's equivocation in matters of idealism and the theory of knowledge. For Klyce, a confirmed idealist, Dewey's relativism toward matters such as truth was tantamount to cowardice—a sort of character failure to follow through on what to Klyce were obvious conclusions regarding the nature of nature and science. Dewey's response throughout the correspondence was to solidify his claim in the face of Klyce's hectoring criticism; that truth, reality, and other predicates were assigned as satisfactory solutions to problems of investigation (e.g., Dewey to Klyce, May 04, 1927, 04692).

In contrast to the ongoing dispute with Klyce, Dewey had very positive engagements with his erstwhile student Sidney Hook and his friend Joseph Ratner. Hook in particular provided much support to Dewey during these years. During the period of preparation for the 1927–1928 Types of Logical Theory, Dewey wrote to Hook regarding the function of the copula and for the first time claimed that all universals were hypothetical (Dewey to Hook, August 27, 1927, 05710).[55] Beyond this, Hook was invaluable for Dewey's ongoing construction of the 1927–1928 Lectures. Dewey would often write to Hook acknowledging his often slow and painful progress in putting the lectures together. In this correspondence, we see the germination of Dewey's distinction between generic propositions and universal judgments—a distinction that would concern Dewey up to and including the writing of the 1938 *Logic*. By 1929—the year after the presentation of the logic lectures and the year of *The Quest for Certainty*—Dewey had established the distinction between the two.[56] And again, in preparation for the 1929 Gifford Lectures (what would become *The Quest for Certainty*), Dewey used Bohr and Heisenberg to claim that every situation or event has with it an indeterminacy. Indeed, observation itself introduces indeterminacy into perceptions (Dewey to Hook, February 12, 1929, 05721). Prediction, it turns out, is always accompanied by the element of chance. Temporal-spatial ordering is logical, structured, and fixed, whereas the temporal quality that runs through events and situations immediately perceived is fluid, flexible, and relative to the observer. In other words, the twin continuities, if we may call the temporality that runs through events and situations a continuity, are distinct. Yet, for all that, they are related, for, as we shall see, they form a double continuity; a unity. What would remain for Dewey is to give an account of how these distinctive continuities are aligned and unified.

Part 4: Dewey's Logical Education, 1933–1937

Dewey's activity during this final period leading up to the 1938 *Logic* was that of refinement rather than revolution. He had in place almost all of the pieces he needed to begin writing in earnest. The immediacy of experience and the continuity of immediate havings and undergoings therein was established in the period between *Experience and Nature* and "Qualitative Thought"; the role of biology and social psychology in human conduct was already well established; the role of science in society was a feature of *The Public and Its Problems* (1927) and related works.[57] What was left to do involved establishing a proper schematic of relations between various propositions and judgments. Dewey began to abandon his earlier wholesale use of the term "existential propositions" in the 19271928 Types of Logical Theory, and limited these to a specific proposition involved in classification of material kinds. By contrast, Dewey turned to generic propositions as propositions of classes and kinds, and universal propositions as propositions denoting the relationships between these kinds. Universal propositions were rendered abstract and hypothetical. This, however, was only the beginning, for more distinctions had to be qualified in Dewey's account of propositions and judgments. It had long been Dewey's concern that philosophers and logicians mistook generic propositions for abstract and hypothetical universals, reducing the latter to the former. Dewey would begin to insist in this period that this was a chief failing of formal logicians in particular (e.g., LW 8, 161–62). Universal judgments or propositions were abstract; they concerned only the relations between kinds (extension) and not particulars of a kind (intension). Though this was first mentioned in the 19271928 Types of Logical Theory, it became an important consideration in Dewey's three papers to the *Journal of Philosophy*, beginning in January 1936.[58] Universals operated in a different functional domain than generic propositions; a domain of abstract, as opposed to concrete, operations. With this in place, Dewey's path was now clear to canvass the various functional operations of judgments in inquiry—a task he took up in chapters 9 through 14 of the 1938 *Logic*.

By 1934, Dewey was able to share a working outline of chapters to his logic with his interlocutors.[59] Many of the headings that would surface by 1938 were already in place. In the next four years, Dewey would consolidate his thinking, particularly on the issue of propositions and judgments, and these were revised in the 1938 *Logic* accordingly. Dewey also refined his account of the pattern of inquiry. In 1910, at the time of the first edition of *How We Think*, the pattern of inquiry established *seemed* fixed and linear, progressing from felt difficulty to problem articulation to hypothesis, then to testing via analysis and synthesis (induction and deduction), and, finally, to evaluation. Yet there was no doubt Dewey's intention was to render the pattern of inquiry flexible and self-correcting. Dewey took the opportunity in the second edition of *How We Think* to emphasize the *recursive* nature of inquiry; any stage of inquiry could be entered into or exited while maintaining the overall form (LW 8, 206).[60] Dewey also stressed the predictive nature of inquiry; inquiry acts as a forecast of anticipated events—the latter being changes in phenomena (LW 8, 208–9).

The year immediately preceding the publication of Dewey's *Logic* was busy, for this was a year of extensive travel, including the trek to Mexico to head the Preliminary Commission of Inquiry that examined the charges against Leon Trotsky. Not only was Dewey in near-constant contact with his interlocutors Bentley, Hook, and Ratner, but he also was busy with the publisher Henry Holt and Company, reading proofs and making last-minute corrections to the manuscript. Dewey apparently sent the first five chapters to a typist in March 1937 as he continued to work on the manuscript (Dewey to Alice Davis, 25 March, 1937, 06496). Dewey received the contract from the publisher on April 30, 1938, and delivered the manuscript to the publisher on June, 3, 1938.[61] Of the manuscript as a whole, he would tell Sidney Hook,

> I want to say this as strong as I can make it. I am not stuck on anything in the Logic—certainly not on its vocabulary—My own development was slow & tentative. I can claim only that I never permitted pride in what I had written in the past to slow it up. In fact I rarely look at what I've written in the past. When I do, its [sic] for some special reason & when I find something that I still like & hold to, Im [sic] tickled stiff. And I worked my way alone largely by means of habits formed in lecturing to a class—trying different modes of statement if by the grace of God I might hit some—& save 'em from philosophical perdition. (Dewey to Hook, September 1, 1938, 06032)[62]

Peirce

Dewey had several opportunities to comment on Peirce in these years. To begin with, Dewey reviewed the first volume of the *Collected Papers* of Peirce in 1931. In 1935, Dewey reviewed the fifth volume of the *Collected Papers*, and again, in 1937, the entirely of volumes 1 through 6.[63] In 1935, Dewey wrote a stand-alone paper on Peirce's theory of quality for the *Journal of Philosophy*.[64] The latter continued to move Dewey in the direction of Peirce's causal theory of reality. Dewey agreed with Peirce that objects (what Peirce called Seconds), which are first had in primary experience, are actual insofar as they do not dissolve in new experiences; when an experience is refined or recharacterized, the actual object remains, though it takes on logical qualities, features, and traits. Therefore, what changes in regards to the actual object concerns the qualities, features, and traits it takes on in the new, refined experience. Dewey's actual object thus plays the role of a real, out of which a new experience—a refined experience with its own qualitative characterization, immediate and logical—is had. The actual object plays an intermediate role in the establishment of the spatiotemporal chain built up in the refined experience, as it remains steady as the new experience, together with its qualitative and logical traits and features, is had. The refined object—the object of refined experience—becomes a logical object, together with its unique qualitative characterization of spatiality and temporality. A continuity between the actual object and the logical object is thus built up out of the qualitative resituating of the object in a refined experience—a double continuity in which a unity of two continuities, one of the traits and qualities of an actual object and the other the traits and qualities of the logical object, emerges. Dewey would underscore Peirce's significance in writing the logic in terms of the emphasis not only on continuity, but also on causality, as chapters 22 and 23 of the 1938 *Logic* makes clear.

Dewey's Correspondence

In regards to the development of Dewey's logical theory, the chief correspondents for Dewey in this period were Arthur Bentley, Sidney Hook, and Joseph Ratner. Dewey and Bentley first began to correspond in the mid-1930s.[65] Dewey acknowledged the help that Bentley's book, *Linguistic Analysis of Mathematics*, had had on him as he grappled with formal and syllogistic logic in his own project (Dewey to Bentley, May 22, 1935, 08597).[66] He also thanked Bentley for helping him make explicit the importance of criticism of the formal logics for important extraneous (metaphysical and epistemological) commitments in their accounts (Dewey to Bentley, August 15, 1935, 08603). Of even more benefit to Dewey was the correspondence with Sidney Hook. Dewey sent Hook his first complete draft of an outline for the *Logic* in 1934 and corresponded with him on updates. Additionally, Dewey continued to discuss the relationship between universal conceptions and generic propositions with Hook, and was engaged in this communication as late as February 1938 (e.g., Dewey to Hook, February 3, 1938, 06011). Dewey's correspondence with Ratner helped solidify his awareness of the basic distinction between universals and generic propositions; the former inductively arrived at kinds; the latter abstract relations between kinds (e.g., Dewey to Ratner, August 23, 1935, 05722). Dewey found that Oliver Reiser's work on philosophy of science was helpful in making distinctions between scientific and logical uses of propositions; a sentiment that Ratner shared, as they were both engaged with Reiser's text.[67] In correspondence with both Hook and Ratner, Dewey dropped the term "existential" and replaced it with the terms "singular" and "particular." This would prove important for Dewey's 1936 *Journal of Philosophy* articles in particular and for the 1938 *Logic* generally; the material that Dewey worked out in detail with Hook and Ratner in correspondence would figure heavily in chapters 13 and 14 of the 1938 *Logic*. Dewey would also refigure his account of the propositions of existence in this period: with the help of Hook and Ratner, and with guidance from L. Susan Stebbing's work on singulars, Dewey would limit singulars and particulars to the kind, existential proposition, leaving kinds that deal in relationships among individual cases generic.[68]

Conclusion

Dewey's logical education in the period 1916–1937 included not only his reading and writings on logic proper, but also his reading and writing on science, the theory of knowledge, experience, education, culture, art and social psychology, as well as teaching in the guise of Types of Logical Theory given at Columbia University, and his correspondence with various interlocutors, of whom Albert Barnes, Arthur Bentley, Sidney Hook, and Joseph Ratner emerge as the most important. Though Dewey had many of the ingredients for his 1938 *Logic* already in place by 1915, fundamental considerations remained to be articulated. Most of this would occur in the intervening years; some would wait until the 1938 *Logic* proper. In upcoming chapters, I discuss these considerations in terms of the four themes I develop in my earlier volume, *John Dewey's Earlier Logical Theory*. These themes are "Traits, Meanings, and the Indeterminacy of Situations," "the Existential Matrices of Inquiry (biological and social)," "Scientific and Social Inquiry," and "Propositions and Inferences in Inquiry." In terms of the four, we will see that Dewey made significant gains in his accounts of experience and propositions and inferences in particular, and modest gains in his accounts of the two others. The upshot was a more or less unified account of continuity; a double continuity that consisted of both the qualitative trait of temporality at the level of immediate experience (qualitative continuity) and temporal-seriality (logical continuity) in refined experience. This was a unified continuity that, while qualitatively distinctive in the different phases of experience, nevertheless, by way of the actual object, spanned the gap between these. Indeed, it would emerge in Dewey's account of logical operations that continuity as qualitative temporality *and* temporal-serial ordering was key to the connection of the gross and macroscopic and refined phases in experience as detailed in *Experience and Nature*: thus, the key to Dewey's logical theory turns out to lie in his metaphysics. The following chapters attempt to capture some of the specific considerations Dewey grappled with that led to the 1938 *Logic*.

Table 1. Dewey's Logical Theory circa 1915: Some Important Conclusions

Themes	Conclusions	Location
Traits, Meanings, and the Indeterminacy of Situations	• Instrumentalism, Realism • Inquiry into situations; events • Wholeness, incompleteness, continuity, focus, and content as qualitative traits • Double Movement of focus and content • Inquiry intermediate between beginnings and endings • No form-matter dualism • Continuity of reference from meaning to fact and back (double movement)	*Studies* (1903) *Essays* (1916) *HWT* (1910)
The Matrices of Inquiry	• Inquiry context-based, self-correcting • Genetic-historical accounting of inquiry • Biological and social account of impulses, desires, habits • Self-correcting phases and stages	*Studies* (1903) *HWT* (1910)
Scientific and Social Inquiry	• Scientific Inquiry distinguished from empirical know-how • No ontological difference in kind between the two	*HWT* (1910)

Propositions and Inferences in Inquiry	• Symbols operate in relation to one another
	• Inference as recognition of relations of signs
	• Induction and Deduction as inferences
	• Judgments as Propositions
	• All judgments are hypothetical
	• Types of Propositions
	  ▪ Practical
	  ▪ Abstract/Mathematical/Formal
	  ▪ Narrative
	  ▪ Descriptive
		HWT (1910)
		Studies (1903)
		Essays (1916)
		LJP (1915)

Chapter 2

Dewey's Logical Development 1916–1924

The year 1916 was a milestone in Dewey's logical development. This was the year of the publication of Dewey's *Essays in Experimental Logic*. *Essays* consisted of Dewey's earlier *Studies in Logical Theory* (1903), several previously published papers concerning the theory of knowledge and pragmatism, a lengthy introduction, and an essay first published several months previously that was to have ongoing importance ("The Logic of Judgments of Practice").[1] While *Studies* encapsulated his logical theory proper, the introduction invoked and articulated a theory of experience in which existence is embedded in experience, and logic resides and operates in experience. "The Logic of Judgments of Practice" extended the operation of inquiry to matters of value—matters, incidentally, that Dewey would return to in full force in *Theory of Valuation* (1939).[2] Dewey also emphasizes the problematic nature of inquiry—a feature of inquiry at work since Dewey's *How We Think* (1910) and beyond.

Truly novel, however, is Dewey's discussion of knowledge claims as regards to the "new realism" and "analytic logic" (MW 10, 335). The new realists (Dewey undoubtedly has the Critical Realists as well as the New Realism of Bertrand Russell in mind) take pragmatism's position to be idealist with respect to knowledge claims: these New Realists take what Dewey calls "logical objects" for timeless epistemic truths (MW 10, 338). Here, Dewey and the Critical and New Realists part ways, for Dewey takes these objects as instrumentalities rather than fixed and final substances (MW 10, 338). Dewey claims that New or Analytic Realism is a form of "presentative realism," in which logical objects are conflated with objects taken as in-themselves (MW 10, 347). These objects taken as in-themselves correspond in the main to the objects of British sense-psychology: sensations, sense-qualia, and mental intermediaries Dewey recognizes as phenomenalistic (MW 8, 16–17). The fixation of objects extends to meanings for the Critical and Analytic Realists. Whereas pragmatists view meanings as context-bounded and suggestions for actions, New and Critical Realists hypostasize them with the upshot of making them metaphysical essences (MW 10, 348–49). Finally, Dewey discusses the nature of the instrumentalist method; above all, this is to be genetic. Knowledge (and the products of inquiry) is to be understood as the natural history of its development (MW 10, 361). In this regard, Dewey makes the analogy with biology and sociology (MW 10, 361).[3]

In the introduction to *Essays in Experimental Logic*, we have Dewey emphasizing several concerns he believes are paramount for an instrumentalist accounting of logical theory: a theory of experience sufficient to account for the context in which inquiry operates and develops; an accounting of knowledge claims, including logical objects and meanings; an account of method and, most importantly, the genetic and historical character of this method; and, finally, responses to criticisms, especially the New Realism and Analytic Realism, inclusive of their various shortcomings. In "The Logic of Judgments of Practice," Dewey maintains that differences of logical form are due to differences of subject matters and that judgments as to the act an individual performs are never solely by and for themselves; rather, they are judgments of the course of action a subject matter will take. It should not come as a surprise that Dewey's other writings bearing on logical theory directly would have these as concerns. In this chapter, I discuss some of Dewey's related writings on logical theory in the period 1916–1924. I examine these against themes Dewey develops in light of certain criticisms and shortcomings he and his critics perceived in his logical theory circa 1916. These themes I label "traits, meanings, and the indeterminacy of experiential situations," "the matrices of inquiry," "scientific and social inquiry," and, finally, "forms and propositions in logical theory."[4]

Under the above rubrics, I discuss the recently published 1915–1916 Types of Logical Theory Dewey gave at Columbia University. I then turn to several of Dewey's articles and papers published or delivered in the period in question. I examine Dewey's 1916 lecture presentation "Logical Objects," 1916's "The Pragmatism of Peirce," Dewey's 1917 reply to Daniel Sommer Robinson, "Concerning Novelties in Logic: a Reply to Mr. Robinson,"[5] and 1924's "Logical Method and Law." There are as well certain claims of Dewey's bearing indirectly on logical theory, yet important for understanding his logical development during these years. Certain specific arguments Dewey makes concerning habit and continuity in *Democracy and Education* (1916), experience, scientific method and the role of science in *Reconstruction in Philosophy* (1920), and both habits and the continuum of means and ends in *Human Nature and Conduct* (1922) are pertinent. I also discuss Dewey's correspondence for the period in question.

Traits, Meanings, and the Indeterminacy of Experiential Situations

Dewey begins the introduction to *Essays in Experiential Logic* with the proviso that the key to understanding the *Essays* concerns "the temporal development of experience" and that inquiry is intermediate in an experience (MW 10, 320). What is at stake here (beyond a cogent accounting of inquiry) is Dewey's allegiance to a realist accounting of logical theory.[6] We see this primarily in Dewey's attempt in the introduction to distance his experimental logic from idealist models: absolutist and rationalist systems of thought make light of the "specific demand and work of intelligence" (MW 10, 332–33). Existential "fact" and the logic that investigates this cannot be separated other than for functional purposes, and this is just what idealist systems of logic mistakenly do. An experimental logic—a logic of inquiry based in experience—does not, however, commit this mistake. The task is to show that experience contains within itself logic, the intermediary of thought. In *Essays*, Dewey characterizes experience as "the immediately engrossing and matter of course," "a notation of the inexpressible as that which decides the ultimate status of all which is expressed" (MW 10, 325).[7] Experience is that which we inhabit; the here and the now.[8] An experience has its beginnings and endings; its sense of completeness or incompleteness, its finality. An experience has its (generic) traits, chief among these being a "double movement" between "focus and context" in regard to things or "*Res*"; and "continuity" (MW 10, 323).[9] But for Dewey's critics, this would not do. Experience is still far too ephemeral in such a description, and the Critical and New (including Analytic) Realists would continue to hammer Dewey on his vagueness and what seemed to them to be idealist proclivities. For it seemed as if Dewey were saying that experience (and "situation" and "event") was precisely that which was undefinable, unprovable as a sense-perceived object, yet made vital and even necessary for any accounting of logical theory.[10] Yet it seems, at least in Dewey's mind, that the vagueness of experience was a choice made under the influence of his interlocutor Scudder Klyce.[11] (We will see some of these criticisms indirectly manifest, for example, in the discussion of the contexts in which judgments and propositions operate, beginning with Robinson's exposition of *Essays in Experimental Logic* for the *Journal of Philosophy, Psychology, and Scientific Methods* in 1917.)[12] Here, I wish to examine what, if any, development in Dewey's theory of experience and associated matters (events, situations, meanings, and traits) took place between 1916–1924. I argue that there are (at least) four sources that demonstrate Dewey's advancement in matters of experience: the 1915–1916 Types of Logical Theory, the correspondence with Scudder Klyce, together with claims made regarding experience and continuity in *Democracy and Education* and *Reconstruction in Philosophy.*

The 1915–1916 Types of Logical Theory

Two sets of lectures on logic Dewey gave while at Columbia have been preserved and are now published. The first of these was given over two consecutive spring terms, 1915–1916. They have been titled "Types of Logical Theory" and are constituted of 8 sections.[13] This set consists of a historical development of logics from the Aristotelian to the pragmatic. The bulk of the manuscript consists of lectures from spring 1915, with a somewhat lessened amount from spring 1916. As some of these lectures were given at the very time Dewey was readying his *Essays in Experimental Logic* for final publication, we would expect to find his most recent thinking on display, particularly in regard to discussions of recent logical systems. In fact, we glean clues about Dewey's own use of experience at the time and specifically, the sort of experience *it could never be*. In what appears to be a discussion of William James and pragmatic logical theory, Dewey says of absolute experience,

> Admitting that reflection does involve a disjunction of immediacy and mediation, an appeal to absolute experience doesn't really solve anything. More positively what we have here indicated is simply a distinction of two types of modes of our own experience or any experience, i.e., what is indicated here is that all reflective knowledge is relative or instrumental

to a non-reflective type of experience. There is no reason for passing over to an absolute in order to find that non-reflective type where meanings and existence are identical. (TLT, May 16, 1916)

Dewey was aware of the various idealist criticisms against his logical theory (some of these surface in his previous year's correspondence with Scudder Klyce), and this admonishment of the idealist's absolute (Dewey has Josiah Royce and F. H. Bradley under discussion in the particular passage) is the result. Dewey is saying that the turn to absolute experience is unnecessary, as experience contains within itself its modes, one of which is logical inquiry, including the products of thinking; of reflection.[14] This is a sentiment that Dewey will develop most fully in the first chapter of *Experience and Nature*.[15] To claim an absolute experience is to do nothing beyond what ordinary experience already accommodates. A pragmatic accounting of experience (the context here is Jamesean pragmatism) does not require an absolute experience, for it is sufficient both for reflection and for the situation or event in which reflection operates.

Dewey's Correspondence

Dewey's correspondence with Scudder Klyce concerns the publication of *Essays* directly. Dewey's begins with an acknowledgement of his indebtedness to Klyce for the term "infinity" in place of "experience" (Dewey to Klyce, April 14, 1916, 03552). Klyce sent a series of lengthy missives on receipt of the *Essays*.[16] Much of the content of Klyce's letters is given over to issues of quantity versus quality, science versus philosophy, and various other dualisms. This letter, dated July 24, 1916, is particularly lengthy and involved. In it, Klyce determines that time (as temporal continuity) is the main problem in logic. Dewey's use of time in *Essays* comes in for criticism, chiefly because of its informality. Klyce also chides Dewey for not understanding how scientists quantitatively address time.[17] Klyce claims time (continuity), including infinity, as monistic; as one (Klyce to Dewey, July 24, 1916, 03554). Klyce claims we can know continuity scientifically (he is an example of such knowing), and do so consciously.[18] There is a fabric at the base of the universe; a fabric of continuity that consists of more than mere cause and effect. Dewey tried to get at this fabric, which Klyce intimates Dewey only hints at, in his *Essays*, but fails because he remains dualistic; he remains confused about logical theory and this because he has not yet come to terms with his emotions, his "oriental" or "buddhist" side (Klyce to Dewey, July 24, 1916, 03554). Dewey would do well, Klyce thinks, to operate on a logical theory that has time and space as real, with the formal terms "time" and "space" as unreal. So too, "experience": "experience" denotes a reality that is ineffable, while the term itself retains an arbitrary meaning (Klyce to Dewey, July 24, 1916, 03554).

The issue of time and space is bound up, for Klyce, with philosophical notions of idealism. In Klyce's estimation, Dewey is fearful of labeling time and space as real, though he treats them as such reflectively (Klyce says Dewey is "thinking of time and space as real" (Klyce to Dewey July 24, 1916, 03554). Dewey refuses to give them a formal place and hesitates, Klyce thinks, for primarily emotional reasons. Klyce seems displeased by Dewey's hesitancy and claims that the scientific terms are best, though they do not obtain their reality verbatim. Indeed, much of the vocabulary Dewey uses in *Essays* is foreign to "Occidental" logicians (for Klyce, Dewey is a closet Oriental in temperament), and would do best to "shift over to meaning or monism as being real" (Klyce to Dewey, July 24, 1916, 03554). The monism Klyce endorses is none other than that of time and space—of infinity—what Dewey is calling experience, yet, for Klyce, what Dewey still wants to carve up dualistically into logical and scientific terms and the situations or events out of which inquiry arises and back into which inquiry sets its logical products. For Klyce, all time is zero time—no "real" time of past or future, but instant, immediate time here and now.[19]

As regards Dewey's accounting of experience, temporal continuity, and time and space, Klyce's intentions are several-fold. Klyce would have Dewey shore up his account of experience above all, chiefly through abandoning any pretense to terms such as "experience," "situation," and "time and space" denoting some reality. It is enough that the scientific terms of these stand, and we use them as such. Furthermore, "experience," "time and space," and other scientific accountings must be understood as ineffable, instantaneous, and immediate. They are not to be conflated with the merely verbal terms we give these, nor are they to be conflated with past or future representations (themselves terms) of these. Above all, Dewey is to embrace a monism of continuity—a monism in which the only reality is the instantaneous and immediate reality common to Klyce's Oriental (Buddhist) visions of the world. Dewey *would* shore up his accounting of experience and time and space, particularly in *Experience and Nature*. He would, however, continue to resist the "monism" Klyce suggests for him (Dewey to Klyce, April 23, 1915, 03517).[20] Continuity, on the other hand, would become more and more important to Dewey as a chief trait of logical theory, and Klyce certainly helped to push him in this direction.[21]

Democracy and Education (1916)

Dewey's account of experience and the roles for traits and situations therein did not vary substantially until the publication of *Experience and Nature*. We don't see, for example, novel theoretical positions taken on the main attributes of experience—situations, events, traits of existence, organism-environment interaction, and so forth—until 1925.[22] There are, to be sure, changes in Dewey's thinking regarding other vital aspects of logical theory: habit, meaning, reflection, proposition, and judgment: but experience in logical theory remains most fully articulated in the introduction to Dewey's 1916 *Essays*.

By 1910, Dewey had offered a stage theory of inquiry that was open-ended and recursive, a model of inquiry sufficiently flexible to forgo stepwise, linear progression and allow for entrance and exit at any one of the stages. Though the theory was again presented (in altered form) in 1933, it did not find its way into the *Essays in Experimental Logic* of 1916. The beginnings and endings of inquiry were present in *Essays*: the qualitative indeterminacy or lack of a situation sufficient to occasion an inquiry, together with the reestablishment of (qualitative) wholeness. But the "guts"—the accounts of inferences, of judging—were not present in the form Dewey had set it down in *How We Think*. In the most important of the *Essays*, "The Logic of Judgments of Practice" (1915), Dewey stressed the process of making judgments of value. Valuing takes place along a continuum in which a "change of mode of behaviour from direct acceptance and welcoming to doubting and looking into—acts which involve postponement of direct . . . action which imply a future act having a different *meaning* from that now occurring . . ." occurs (MW 8, 30). When we pass judgment, we do so in regard to the connections with other acts. To make a judgment of value is to make a judgment of what to do, and this is the "future termination of an incomplete and in so far indeterminate situation" (MW 8, 30). The judgment, in other words, takes place in an existential context and involves not sense-perceptual objects, but situations; events (MW 8, 31).

Now Dewey discusses the indeterminate situation and its role in initiating inquiry at length in *How We Think* (MW 6, 262–63). But what he doesn't stress is that there is an *existential continuity* of events. A complete act of thought has its beginning and ending: it is a qualitative whole. But this seems to suggest that one situation or event is cut off from another. In "The Logic of Judgments of Practice," Dewey suggests otherwise. For in the latter work, values are traits. Traits are not of objects but situations; events. Traits of situations are directly related to the judgment of a situation such that a value arises in consideration of the existential quality of that situation (MW 8, 32). Values are not *ab extra*: they arise *as* considerations *of* an event. Inquiring into and considering a situation *is* valuing. And while values certainly seem to be individuals in that they accompany judgments of situations, they in fact are linkages in a series of meaningful interactions. Dewey makes this point abundantly clear in *Democracy and Education* (1916): when we think, we make connections between doing and the consequences that result from doing. "Thinking, in other words, is the intentional endeavor to discover specific connections between something which we do and the consequences which result, so that the two become continuous" (MW 9, 157).

Dewey follows in outline the complete act of thought as discussed in *How We Think*. However, in *Democracy and Education*, he stresses an aspect of thinking merely glossed in the former work: thinking itself is an experience (MW 9, 174).[23] Dewey broaches the topic of thinking as experience in his claim that every mind at every stage of development has its own logic and that the union of the psychological and logical is, properly speaking, a continuum.[24] But the focus here is on the role of mind in natural growth and development, not experience per se. Furthermore, experience is "a single continuous interaction of a great diversity (literally countless in number) of energies" (MW 9, 174.) And what links these energies is that "every conception and statement shall be of such a kind as to follow from others and lead to others" (MW 9, 174). Energies here denote activities: what we do when we have and undergo an experience. They also invoke the biological basis of the human as organism. Energies are activities of the organism as it responds to its environment. Energies include modifications the organism makes as regards its environment, including those modifications Dewey calls habit. And what we do when we undergo an experience in which thinking is predominant is to connect. We connect conceptions to propositions and propositions to existential phenomena; we connect values to values, ideas to ideas, and meanings to meanings. We form an unbroken chain of (continuous) doing and undergoing. Thus, while at one level, having an experience is a finished affair with a beginning and ending, and the sense of accomplishment a felt because qualitative whole, at another it is a moment, a link, a node in a series of experiences made possible in thought.

Dewey applies this insight to the question of the subject matter of education. As Dewey insists, subject matter is not to be divorced from the learner (MW 9, 192–93). The logical corollary to this is form and matter. Form, including the formal aspects of inquiry (principles, standards, ideas, concepts) and matter (as the existential-phenomenal material inquiry works with) do not come with ontological distinctions pressed upon them; they are distinguished for functional purposes. This was a central insight of *Studies in Logical Theory* (1903), and it will factor heavily in the 1938 *Logic*. Indeed, we might even say that this is Dewey's preoccupation as regards continuity in the *Logic*. Thus, Dewey can talk of the development of subject matter in the learner, as subject matter is material *already* shaped by know-how and existing discursive knowledge. And while know-how is not coeval with knowledge formed through inquiry into existing conditions, it is the basis for subsequent inquiry (MW 9, 192). This is also the basis for social knowledge, for we learn new habits through interacting not only with subject matters but with subject matters through others. What Dewey calls "Modes of purposeful doing" already invites and invokes intercommunication (MW 9, 193). A central goal of education is to connect refined knowledge ("information") to the learner's existing knowledge (MW 9, 194).

The series of habits developed and practiced takes place in the context of construction and reconstruction of actions and reactions. To this Dewey assigns the term "consistency" and equates it with "totality" and "continuity" (MW 9, 335). Habits, as with all else regarding thought, grow; they are adapted and reconstructed as the situation demands (MW 9, 335). They of course rely upon the totality of the series of dispositions and actions that constitutes the habit at a specific point in time, but they also include and gesture to their transformation, their change. The connection between past iterations of habit and the present (and future) instance *is* temporal continuity. When we assign causality to events, we mark them as temporally related. We draw the (temporal) inference. But there is a deeper, more naturalistically metaphysical and underlying continuity at work in thinking: this is what undergirds the connection of present habit to past habit, together with all the traits and characteristics of habit (tempers and attitudes, judgments, dispositions, actions, and of course values) in a pattern or series. This continuity consists in the to-and-fro, back and forth of the traits of existence that are present in any continuity discernable in the connection of past and present habit. Of course, it is the business of reflecting to reveal these connections, and this, too, is an aspect (the refined aspect) of experience (LW 1, 15–17). Together, these continuities emerge as a *double continuity*—a *unity* of dual continuities—as inquiry temporally orders events and situations. But in 1916, Dewey has not yet articulated this unity of dual continuities. This unity will only be revealed in the major works on experience; *Experience and Nature* and *Art as Experience*, together with "Qualitative Thought" (1930).

Reconstruction in Philosophy (1920)

Reconstruction in Philosophy appeared in 1920—four years after the publication of *Essays in Experimental Logic*. In the period 1916–1920, the introduction to *Essays* and chapter 4 ("Changed Conceptions of Experience and Reason") of *Reconstruction*, together with *Democracy and Education*'s "Experience and Thinking," served as Dewey's major statements on the topic of experience. Though Dewey's account of experience in *Reconstruction* shares many features of his account in *Essays* (and *Democracy and Education*), it surpasses these in (at least) two ways: one is the stress on "doing, suffering, or undergoing" (MW 12, 129), and the other is the situation of knowledge, reflection, and thinking as aspects of experience "secondary in origin" (MW 12, 129).[25] And while neither of these is absent (let alone denied) in either *Essays* or *Democracy and Education*), they are not foregrounded. These, incidentally, would become central pillars of Dewey's account of experience in *Experience and Nature* (LW 1, 15–17).

Dewey's stress on suffering, doing, and undergoing solves a particular problem that aggravated his account of logical theory since *Studies*: the ascent from having an experience (as qualities or traits) to meaning-making, including meaning involved and invoked in judgments and inferences. Dewey's insistence that there was no ontological gulf between these fell flat, to judge by his critics.[26] A stronger, more robust claim than the one Dewey provided in *Essays* was required.[27] Dewey is most forceful in the following passage:

> Note what a change this [the "civilized"] point of view entails in the traditional notions of experience. Experience becomes an affair primarily of doing. The organism does not stand about, Micawber-like, waiting for something to turn up. It

does not wait passive and inert for something to impress itself upon it from without. The organism acts in accordance with its own structure, simple or complex, upon its surroundings. As a consequence the changes produced in the environment react upon the organism and its activities. The living creature undergoes, suffers, the consequences of its own behavior. The close connection between doing and suffering or undergoing forms what we call experience. (MW 12, 170)

We see immediately that Dewey is using the language of *How We Think* and *Democracy and Education*—the language of organisms, environment, and adjustment/change. But he is insisting that experience is an activity involving the organism's own behavior. An experience, therefore, is something we have and are part of, in contrast to the classical empirical notion of passivity and absorption. This sets the stage for Dewey's next pronouncement—that knowledge (variously understood as reflection, thinking, and inquiry) is secondary to this primary experience, yet still itself a sort of experience. Certain important implications for philosophy follow. In the first place, the interaction of organism and environment, resulting in some adaptation that secures utilization of the latter, is the primary fact, the basic category. Knowledge is shown to be in a derived position, secondary in origin, even if its importance, when once it is established, is overshadowing. Knowledge is not something separate and self-sufficing, but is involved in the process by which life evolves and is sustained. The immediacy in "interaction" we may deem primary experience, whereas knowledge is secondary experience (what Dewey in *Experience and Nature* will discuss as "gross and macroscopic" and "refined" experience (LW 1, 15). Yet these are not understood by Dewey to be ontologically distinct kinds; they are both involved in "interaction." Admittedly, what Dewey gives us in *Reconstruction* is an all-too brief indication of the direction he is taking. Yet it serves as a beginning rebuttal of certain critics' claims that Dewey cannot explain the gap between sense-perceiving and meaning-making.

The Matrices of Inquiry: habit, language, culture

In the *Essays* of 1916, what counted as the context in and from which inquiry sprang was handled chiefly in *Studies in Logical Theory* (reprinted in *Essays*) and "The Logic of Judgments of Practice." The context was best typified, Dewey thought, in the genetic-historical accounting of inquiry (MW 2, 300, 308). In this, each instrument of logical theory is treated as an "instrument of adjustment or adaptation to a particular, environing situation" (MW 2, 310).[28] Dewey recurs to context in "The Logic of Judgments of Practice," chiding Russell for mischaracterizing objects of inquiry as primitive sense-perceptions (MW 8, 52). This failure of recognition, Dewey thinks, stems from the failure to distinguish among the traits in experience and the objects reflection forms in inquiring into the qualities of an experience. This in turn stems from a failure to recognize the functional (not ontological) distinction between the form and matter of the logical situation or event.

However, on the matter of the context of logical inquiry, Dewey does not advance far beyond his initial claims in *Studies*. For example, the gains Dewey makes in *How We Think*—gains that involve accounts of judgments and meanings stressing their interconnectedness and attitudinal bearing (MW 6, 272–74; 278), as well as their linkage to the context of a larger whole—while not absent from *Essays*, are downplayed in favor of the language of experience. There is little notable advance on these earlier themes. Dewey would further develop his account of habit—and language and culture—but not in *Essays*. Rather, this would be done in the landmark works of the Middle Period: *Democracy and Education* (1916) and *Human Nature and Conduct* (1922). Aside from these and along the way, Dewey would recur to discussions of habit in certain prominent articles, most importantly "The Pragmatism of Peirce" (1916).

Democracy and Education (1916)

I have discussed habits in regard to experiences, and the importance of the linkage of past habits to present ones as temporal continuity. The habits Dewey has in mind are active and dynamic: in the context of Dewey's statements, they are marks of "an intellectual disposition" (MW 9, 53) and form the basis of intelligent responses to the environment. Of course, not all habits are alike, and Dewey breaks ground in distinguishing certain habits from others in the context of his discussion of training and education in *Democracy and Education*. Dewey first discusses habits in regard to the adjustment of the organism to its environment. When an organism responds to some stimulus, it adjusts itself and, in doing so, responds to its environment. But not all activities of the organism are thoughtful: indeed, many if not most are formed un- or subconsciously (MW 9, 34). These are habits that "move" or "control" us (MW 9, 34). These habits are ones in which we have no "idea" of the thing, for to have an idea is to have some control, some meaning, "to be able to respond to a thing in view of its place in an inclusive scheme of action" (MW 9, 35).

Elsewhere, Dewey distinguishes between our understanding of habit as "habituation" and habits as "*Expressions of Growth*" (MW 9, 51). Here, Dewey defines habit as "a form of executive skill, of efficiency in doing," and "an ability to use natural conditions as means to ends." This is an "active control of the environment" (MW 9, 51). In contrast to this, certain habits strike us as "*relatively* passive," and Dewey recurs to the image of the seal in wax in articulating his claim (MW 9, 51). Yet Dewey's aim is not to assert two distinctive kinds of habits, but rather two rival understandings of habit, one active, one passive, which on further inspection turn out to be one and the same. For all habits (Dewey is speaking of the human organism) have their intellectual side, their "inclination" to settle an uneasy or unsettled situation, their "modes of thought," and their "forms of skill and desire" (MW 9, 53). Dewey's point is an educational one: when habits are shorn of their intellectual side, or severed from reason, they degenerate into blind and routine ways of acting. They become "unthinking" habits (MW 9, 54). Characteristically, only the "full use of intelligence in the process of forming habits" can ameliorate this situation (MW 9, 54).

In human organisms at least, habits are to be educated. This means they are to be directed by intelligence—itself a disposition. Intelligent habits are to direct all (further) habits. Left alone, or otherwise uneducated, habits degenerate into fixed and customary ways of acting. They are self-subsisting, yet cut off from the rich context of other habits, including the intelligence that directs them to further outlets. Intelligent habits provide a linking function: they serve to connect habits to habits, which supplies habits with a mode for operating—a (legitimate) aim and end of action. "Intelligent" is thus not merely an adjective that applies to certain kinds of habits (e.g., thinking habits; reflective habits), but one that applies to all habits active in the human organism. As there are distinct functional kinds of experience (gross, reflective), so there are distinct functional kinds of habits (active, passive). These are not fixed kinds, and habits vary as to the degree of intelligence therein. Continuity of habit, provided through intelligent dispositions, is the link that ensures a habit remains active and dynamic rather than passive and routine.

The Pragmatism of Peirce (1916)

This paper was not the first publication Dewey had written on Peirce.[29] It was the first concentrated discussion, however, and would prove fruitful in regard to not only his (ongoing) esteem for Peirce's method of inquiry, but also his own theory of continuity.[30] And while Dewey works from Peirce's earlier writings, such as the *Popular Science Monthly* papers of 1877–1878, he also engages his later works, especially the *Monist* papers of 1905–1907. In both the earlier and later series, Dewey notes a conscious relationship between pragmatism and the formation of habit (MW 10, 73). Habits for Peirce are "ways of acting" and imply their general kinds, or universals (MW 10, 73). Thus, Peirce is committed to a program of realism. In Peirce's pragmatism, habits are therefore "generalized methods" (MW 10, 74). We move along a doubt-inquiry model, from an irritation to a resolution of belief or habit through scientific method (MW 10, 74–75).

Dewey attributes to Peirce a causal theory of meaning and reality. That is to say, Peirce first argues for real things that have their effects upon us. These effects are beliefs. Thus real things "cause" beliefs through their effects.[31] "Beliefs are then consequences which give the general term reality or "rational purport" (MW 10, 75). "And on the assumption of the scientific method, the *distinguishing* character of the *real* object must be that it tends to produce a single universally accepted belief" (MW 10, 75). The importance of the methods of inquiry cannot be underestimated here: without a scientific approach to the fixation of belief, the causal chain of events that leads from the real to doubt to inquiry to belief cannot be maintained, and the demonstration of reality cannot be ascertained (MW 10, 76).

The acceptance of this theory of meaning places a great demand on Peirce's theory of habit. For habit, as an "attitudinal response," must bear the burden of all the action that arises from "a change in existence" (MW 10, 77). The habit must be so connected to the initial existential event that it can seamlessly respond. This of course augurs for a fundamental continuity running through the causal chain: there is no recourse to a mere stimulus-response mechanism here; the chain runs back and forth from and to the real object and the habit or belief of that real. For a real to be real as articulated in Peirce's theory of habit and meaning requires an indelible linkage between various aspects of the universe (the real, the stimulus, the response/habit of the organism) together with a

feedback loop of sorts, running from habit to the real and back again.³²
This sort of continuity is doubtlessly metaphysical, though Dewey does
not develop this theme on Peirce's behalf.³³

I argue in chapter 4 that Dewey, too, adopts a causal theory of
meaning and reality. I suggest that causality, for Dewey as for Peirce,
consists in a continuity that bridges both the qualitative, generic traits
of existence *and* the serial-temporal ordering of history and the sciences.
I suggest that neither is temporally prior to the other, because the temporality of causation depends on the qualitative features of existence, and
these features are themselves not temporally ordered until they are refined
in and through inquiry (though logical or temporal causation will tend
to place the results of the descriptive metaphysical account of causation
first). But for now, I claim only that Dewey thought Peirce's method
of inquiry a causal theory and this causal theory unobjectionable. This
was a causal theory that did not fall prey to the classical objection to
causal theories of truth: that belief follows inexorably on there being a
causal matter-of-fact of the case. That is to say, we can be committed to
a belief about the world, there can be causal affirmation of that belief,
yet we can hold that belief wrongly. For to hold a belief rightly, for
Peirce, is to have gained it through the method of scientific inquiry,
not through tenacity or authority or the a priori. This condition must
be in place before a rightly held belief can be pronounced. Dewey, I
believe, would concur.

Human Nature and Conduct (1922)

Human Nature and Conduct is the *locus classicus* of Dewey's mature theory
of habit. Originally a series of lectures presented at Stanford University
in 1918, Dewey worked the nascent material into a stand-alone publication on the role of the social in human behavior. In 1916, Dewey
claimed habits are not ontological kinds, and habits vary as to the degree
of intelligence therein. Continuity became key in elucidating a proper
accounting of habit. We see this claim significantly developed six years
later with *Human Nature and Conduct*. I discuss the continuity of habit
in the context of the means-ends accounting of deliberation Dewey gives
us in the latter half of the book. But first, I discuss the context in which
habits reside: the customs of the speech acts of social groups.

While it is abundantly clear at the time of *Democracy and Education* that habits are more than a mere complex of behaviors suitable for psychological study, the account Dewey gives in *Human Nature and Conduct* serves to drive the point about social context home. Dewey claims:

> We often fancy that institutions, social custom, collective habit, have been formed by the consolidation of individual habits. In the main this supposition is false to fact. To a considerable extent customs, or widespread uniformities of habit, exist because individuals face the same situation and react in like fashion. But to a larger extent customs persist because individuals form their personal habits under conditions set by prior customs. An individual usually acquires the morality as he inherits the speech act of his social group. (MW 14, 43)

Social psychology, Dewey claims, "puts the cart before the horse" (MW 14, 46). For it assumes there is a social or individual mind that, once formed, looks for instances of relational behaviors. Instead, the converse is the case: "The problem of social psychology is not how either individual or collective mind forms social groups and customs, but how different customs, established interacting arrangements, form and nurture different social minds" (MW 14, 46).

Drawing on his account of habit from *Democracy and Education*, Dewey claims habits are "conditions of intellectual efficiency" (MW 14, 121). They serve to place limits on thinking. Yet they are more than this. For habits are also "positive agencies" that serve to refine our perceptions, our discriminations, and "the presentations by our imagination" (MW 14, 122). Habits do the work of consciousness in perceiving, in recognizing, in conceiving and judging (MW 14, 123) without the necessity of a separate accounting of consciousness over and above them.[34] Habits also do the work of supplying old content in new inquiries: they supply the "recognizable subject matter" that inquiry then takes as its point of departure (MW 14, 126). Through habits, objects—logical objects—form in new inquiries from old subject matters brought about by new problems. Objects "represent habits turned inside out. They exhibit both the onward tendency of habit and the objective conditions which have been incorporated within it" (MW 14, 127). Habits link our experiences together through linking these objects. Dewey uses the language of "figured framework" to describe the temporal linkage of objects (MW 14, 128). Habits—and not consciousness apart from habits—do the work of this linking. Habits come to look a great deal like Peirce's "generalized methods" (MW 10, 74).

There is another linkage; this one between habit and impulses. Our tendency to react against the environment in unsettled situations is of course guided by and through habit. But this conceals an even deeper relationship: impulses are themselves the reactive results of failed habits. Habits, as ways of conducting oneself, operate in routinized settings in which standard situations call upon standard ways of conduct. When, however, a standard way of conduct fails, the habit breaks down and an impulse is triggered and released. The impetus of the impulse is the point of departure for the development of a new habit (MW 14, 128). Delving even deeper, Dewey suggests, in a manner foreshadowing his later discussion of the traits of existence in *Experience and Nature*, that the unity of actual events with ideals in thinking is an example of a trait—a generic trait—of continuity (MW 14, 129).

The social context in which habits arise is equally the context in which satisfaction arises (MW 14, 146).[35] This is the impetus for what Dewey calls the "fulfillment conditioned on thought" (MW 14, 146). Goodness for Dewey involves habits; for example, a habit that is judged good owing to its meaning in being experienced. It is first felt, then judged. We grasp it first in its immediacy and we reflect upon it. It is "the meaning that is experienced to belong to an activity when conflict and entanglement of various incompatible impulses and habits terminate in a unified orderly release in action" (MW 14, 146).[36] The immediate meaning of good is not the terminal point, however. This point is only reached in and through deliberation (MW 14, 150).

Dewey strengthens his thinking circa 1900 from ideals as the point of departure in striving toward the good to aims as already embedded in human action (MW 12, 154).[37] Aims "are not, as current theories often imply, things lying beyond activity at which the latter is directed. They are not strictly speaking ends or termini of action at all. They are terminals of deliberation, and so turning points *in* activity" (MW 14, 154). Aims are "ends-in-view," or "consequences" (MW 14, 155). They are products of deliberation and not fixed, self-enclosed finalities" (MW 14, 159) existing outside and beyond the limits of thinking. Dewey characterizes "ends-in-view" as "endless ends": ends that have no other end than beginnings for yet other ends (MW 14, 159). Aims or ends-in-view that demonstrate their practical worth in solving problems involving deliberation are "principles" (MW 14, 164).

Principles are the intellectual corollary to habits in action (MW 14, 164). They have their modus operandi as hypotheses in future events (MW 14, 165). They are "instrumentalities," and not fixed and final tenets for all possible cases. Principles operate as "ends-in-view," or "ideals," to use Dewey's earlier terminology.[38] They guide us through deliberation, but they do not remain inert and impermeable; for as the situation changes, so might the principle; and as habits break down, so do principles. The logic of "ends-in-view" should not puzzle us: for this is just the logic of inquiry, of hypothesis formation, derivation of consequences, and from the derivation of consequences, the testing of consequences and the gathering of particulars into general kinds or classes. It is hypothesis formation, deduction and induction. The principles serve as hypotheses, anticipated consequences of thinking and acting serve as the derivation of consequences, and the testing of these consequences and selection of proper consequences serve as the inductive gathering of particulars into a general kind that then serves as a leading principle for further cases. All of this Dewey labels the continuum of means-ends-in-view (MW 14, 168), with the stress on continuity.

The continuity here is inclusive of means-ends-in-view and a scientific characterization of the deliberation of goods. We begin, of course, in and with experience and the felt meaning of immediacy that is a disturbance; a "felt difficulty" as Dewey characterizes it in *How We Think* (MW 6, 236). From there, we form a hypothesis. Not just any hypothesis will do, and preferred principles are generally offered as these hypotheses, to be tested in inquiry. Each hypothesis has its deductive consequences, and these will take the shape of anticipatory consequences in what Dewey calls "suggestion" in thinking (MW 6, 239). Suggestions are tested as evidence in an inductive taking-up of particulars into a general class or kind. Suggestions that don't fit are jettisoned, and suggestions that do are given pride of place in this inductive venture. The upshot, of course, is that the suggestion has instrumental value, as it has been tested and found to solve the particular problem that initiates the inquiry. It stands as an ideal, which is pressed into service in future cases. The continuity of means and ends-in-view is the continuity of scientific inquiry, involving the stages of thinking as Dewey discusses it in various places, notably *How We Think* (MW 6, 239).

Scientific and Social inquiry

The continuity of inquiry—scientific and social—was early insisted upon in Dewey's logical theory (MW 2, 308–9). The possibility of a genetic-historical accounting of science is the possibility of a continuity of scientific method (logical theory) and ordinary thinking. In *Studies* (1903), Dewey claimed that a genetic-historical accounting of science brings science into the ambit of "the conduct of life" (MW 3, 308). This sentiment is carried forward in *How We Think* (1910): science takes the "repeated conjunction or coincidence of separate facts" and reorders them in a "single comprehensive fact" (MW 6, 296). By 1916 and *Essays*, the matter was set in the debate about the role and scope of truth and reality. The bugbear, of course, is metaphysics; specifically, a fixed and final accounting of truth and reality, whether in the form of absolute ideas or essentials. The scientific method is the antidote to this metaphysics, and the result of this antidote is (scientific) demonstration through "operations of getting, using, and testing evidence—the process of knowledge getting" (MW 10, 360).

As we see, several issues are bound up in the claim that scientific and social inquiry are continuous. First is a claim about the proper method in which to undertake science and, indeed, thinking: is science something distinctive and apart from (ordinary) thinking? Dewey's answer is yes, but functionally and not ontologically so. Second is a (related) claim about the nature of facts: do they come stamped with the authority of their self-evidence upon them, or is this authority a product of their (further) arrangement? Dewey sides with the latter. Third and perhaps most important is a claim about the metaphysics of truth and reality: is it to be fixed and final or naturalistic and fallible? Dewey's answers circa 1916 did not satisfy his critics.[39] For what was most at stake in Dewey's accounting of inquiry was, for Dewey's critics, begged: the supposed need for the presence of fixed causal laws already available to the scientific knower. Dewey would be forced to fall back on his account of continuity once again, strengthen it to overcome this objection, and present his final conclusions in the 1938 *Logic*. However, at least some of the work required to do this occurred in the period between 1916 and 1924. I look at four works in particular: the first is (again) *Democracy and Education*. The second is (again) "The Pragmatism of Peirce." The third is *Reconstruction in Philosophy*, and the final is an essay written in 1924 titled "Science, Belief, and the Public."

Democracy and Education (1916)

We have seen the role continuity plays in respect of habit. Continuity also plays a role in the functional distinctions set up between science and ordinary thinking. Dewey calls science in *Democracy and Education* the "perfected outcome of learning—its consummation" (MW 9, 196). What is known is what is certain. Thus, science plays a role in the ascertainment of certainty. But whereas in a Platonic universe, knowledge is godly, absolute, and transcendent, in a naturalist accounting, it is fallible. And the difference Dewey chalks up to experience (MW 9, 196). There is, as Dewey puts it, a difference between the certainty of a subject matter and our certainty in experience (MW 9, 196). Certainty, it turns out, is a matter for our satisfaction in respect of the conditions of inquiry satisfied, and not the satisfaction of the Gods.[40] Our satisfaction, then, is tied to the methods of inquiry and testing. Reference to this assurance, Dewey claims, is *"rational* assurance, —logical warranty" (MW 9, 198).[41] Dewey notes there is a "double relation" in scientific inquiry: a relation of "leading to and confirming" (MW 9, 198).[42] In the to-and-fro of inquiry, particular facts and confirming conceptions both support and alter one another.

The upshot of this to-and-fro can best be seen, Dewey thinks, in the example of water.

> The everyday conception of water is more available for ordinary uses of drinking, washing, irrigation, etc., than the chemist's notion of it. The latter's description as H_2O is superior from the standpoint of place in use in inquiry. It states the nature of water in a way which connects it with knowledge of other things, indicating to one who understands it how the knowledge is arrived at and its bearings upon other portions of knowledge of the structure of things. Strictly speaking, it does not indicate the objective relations of water any more than does a statement that water is transparent, fluid, without taste or odor, satisfying to thirst, etc. It is just as true that water has these relations as that it is constituted by two molecules of hydrogen in combination with one of oxygen. But for the *particular purpose* of conducting discovery with a view to ascertainment of fact, the latter relations are fundamental. The more one emphasizes organization as a mark of science, then, the more he is committed to a recognition of the primacy of method in the definition of science. For method defines the kind of organization in virtue of which science is science, (MW 9, 198–99)

I note several important claims here. First of all, there is no ontological distinction to be made between the discourses of science and ordinary uses of water: there is no foundationalist claim about the reality of water, nor about the language use regarding water. "Water is water" and "water is H_2O" are both functional claims, borne of experimental inquiry. Second, if one wants to discern facts, one should follow the scientific inquiry with its observations, testing, and confirmation. For this will net us facts better than ordinary inquiry. Third, and perhaps most important, if it is relations we want to build up—relations, that is, between facts and conceptions—scientific inquiry is best, for it defines (i.e., consists in) just those relations. Continuity in respect of the functional relationships among facts and conceptions here and elsewhere does yeoman work in setting Dewey up for a fuller response (in *Experience and Nature*, in *Art as Experience*, and in the 1938 *Logic*) to the criticisms that scientific inquiry presupposes fixed and final canons of thinking.[43]

The Pragmatism of Peirce (1916)

We have discussed Dewey's appraisal of Peirce's notion of habit. Here, I emphasize that this habit is social. Habits are generals for Peirce and generals are real (MW 10, 73). Dewey interprets Peirce's claim that "the pragmaticist does not make the *summum bonum* to consist in action, but makes it to consist in that process of evolution whereby the existent comes more and more to embody those generals . . ." as the aim of habit "becomes, through action as embodiment of rational purports . . . generalized as widely as possible" (MW 10, 74).[44] The context here is ethics and ethical inquiry; but the terminus of this inquiry and *a fortiori* the terminus of the generals, is to as wide a dissemination as possible. And contrasting Peirce favorably to James, Dewey remarks that Peirce's accounting of scientific inquiry is more dependent on the social factor (MW 10, 77). Dewey notes, "The appeal in Peirce is essentially to the consensus of those who have investigated, using methods which are capable of employment by all. It is the need for social agreement, and the fact that in its absence "the method of tenacity" will be exposed to disintegration from without, which finally forces upon mankind the wider and wider utilization of scientific method" (MW 10, 77). Of course, Dewey agrees with Peirce's sentiment and distinguishes Peirce's pragmatism from James's partly on this basis.

Reconstruction in Philosophy (1920)

"Philosophy starts from some deep and wide way of responding to the difficulties life presents, but it grows only when material is at hand for making this practical response conscious, articulate, and communicable" (MW 12, 110). So claims Dewey at the beginning of the third chapter of *Reconstruction in Philosophy*. While largely rhetorical on the matter of the linkage of science and social inquiry, Dewey nevertheless does offer some valuable insights into the relationship between the two. Dewey takes the genetic-historical account of the development of science to heart: prior to scientific inquiry, sages read social relationships into nature (MW 12, 116); laws and their ordering of observations are demonstrably feudal; for laws are the governors of phenomena (MW 12, 116). The earliest scientists (astronomers) disabused us of this governance. Laws, it turns out, don't order events; events give rise to laws in inquiry. "Modern science took its first step when daring astronomers abolished the distinction of high, sublime and ideal forces operating in the heavens from lower and material forces actuating terrestrial events" (MW 12, 116).

The upshot for Dewey is how to inquire in the surest manner.

> The material of direct handling and observation is that of which we are surest; it is the better known. Until we can convert the grosser and more superficial observations of far-away things in the heavens into elements identical with those of things directly at hand, they remain blind and not understood. Instead of presenting superior worth, they present only problems. They are not means of enlightenment but challenges. (MW 12, 117)

What this means is to practice a democracy of inquiry. Dewey's political rhetoric is at full play here. Facts of the matter (Dewey has in mind the earth, the sun, and the moon) do not exist in a hierarchical ordering; they exist in what Dewey characterizes as a democratic relationship. This means they do not have metaphysical superiority over one another on the basis of their purported ranking in an existing social order. "The net result may be termed, I think, without any great forcing, the substitution of a democracy of individual facts equal in rank for the feudal system of an ordered gradation of general classes of unequal ranks" (MW 12, 117). Admittedly, this democracy of individual facts is challenged in the epistemological turn of the seventeenth to the twentieth centuries; the turn to ideals that once formed the raison d'être of cosmology (MW 12, 119–20). But these ideals prove chimerical: for they serve to inhibit the human effort to enact change. And this human effort turns out to be both concept- and value-laden. Inhibiting the human effort to exact change in the world is tantamount not only to arresting scientific growth, it is to place human ends in the realm of an essentialist metaphysics. Encouraging the human effort to exact change in the world, on the other hand, is to reestablish the humanity of science. This is the upshot of the democracy of individual facts. When we proceed with scientific inquiry humanely considered, we do not set up a hierarchy of facts, some material and others ideal, by which facts reign over human needs and wants. We bring the material and the moral (the valuable) together, in scientific inquiry (MW 12, 179). Ordinary thinking turns out to be thinking about values, with the assistance of scientific inquiry. These turn out to be, in other words, aspects of one another.

Science, Belief, and the Public (1924)

I end this section with a brief examination of an article Dewey published in the *New Republic* (1924).[45] Dewey is clearly foreshadowing his later *The Public and Its Problems* (1927) in this article, for he outright insists that "The public, the popular mass that the enlightened could once refer to as canaille, has taken an active part; but the conditions which have enabled the public actively to intervene have failed in providing an education which would enable the public to discriminate, with respect to the matters upon which it is most given to vehement expression, between opinions untouched by scientific method and attitude and the weight of evidence" (MW 15, 49). It is not that science remains to accomplish its revolution; it is rather that schooling of the public has failed to instill the "rudiments of the scientific attitude in vast numbers of persons," such that they may distinguish scientific fact from mere opinion (MW 15, 49). The cause for this falls in part on the intellectual classes—those that pay lip service to public schooling, yet remain skeptical regarding the ability of the working classes of the public to reason (MW 15, 50–51).[46] At the root of this, Dewey claims, is a "fear of independent thinking" (MW 15, 51). It is the authority of tenacity in matters of educating the public that serves to sideline scientific thinking in these contexts. And without the intervention of the public through education in matters of scientific inquiry, the scientific authorities, while attending to their own business, will do so apart and away from the public that is to use their results and learn from their advances.[47] Education is to serve as a bridge to bring together the divided camps of science and the public. The key to education's serving as a bridge lies in turn in the adoption of the scientific attitude on the part of the scientific community and the simultaneous abandonment of the attitude of elitism with respect to the public's intelligence.

Forms and Propositions in Logical Theory

It is Dewey's accounting of the internal logic of logical theory that frustrated his critics the most. The so-called Critical Realists, as well as New Realists such as Bertrand Russell, were not impressed with Dewey's claims in either *Studies* or *Essays* and relentlessly attacked him in the second decade of the twentieth century.[48] As far as they were concerned, Dewey was not attempting logical theory. Indeed, for them, his was an idealist enterprise in epistemology: an enterprise that eschewed formal methods such as symbolic and the newer mathematical logics. In particular, they attacked his theories of judgment, inference, and propositions. Dewey steadfastly refused to accord inferences and propositions a status beyond that of tools: operations performed in inquiry, with no formal symbolic essence (MW 10, 340). Neither Dewey nor his critics were satisfied with the results of the debate, and Dewey continued to adjust his accounts of forms, judgments, and propositions in the years between 1916 and 1938.

The cornerstone of Dewey's response to the critics turned out to be a thoroughgoing continuity of qualities and traits, together with the temporal continuity inquiry provides. This thoroughgoing continuity would provide the existential-cultural context within which the tools or techniques of inquiry, as forms, judgments and propositions, reside and operate. Dewey had, of course, always endorsed this continuity, even if more suggested than articulated. This is clear as early as *Studies* (MW 2, 305–6). But it took on renewed interest in both *Essays* (with Dewey's accounting of experience in the introduction) and in non-logical works such as *Democracy and Education*. One of the chief issues concerned the relationship between continuity as a generic trait of existence, and the formal operations in inquiry with their buildup of serial-temporal continuity. Spelling out this relationship required Dewey to significantly alter his theory of propositions. Whereas Dewey discussed existential and universal propositions in *Essays* (e.g., as "contingent," "hypothetical," and "factual" propositions (MW 8, 17–21), by the time of the 1938 *Logic* this gave way to a more robust and delineated accounting of propositions according to their various functions. Some of this work began in earnest in the period of 1916–1924, as we shall soon see.

The 1915–1916 Types of Logical Theory

Dewey provided these Lectures at approximately the same time he was assembling the various papers that formed *Essays* (1916). The bulk of the lectures are given over to a descriptive accounting of the history of logical theory from Aristotle to William James. However, Dewey frequently interspersed comments and considerations throughout. Particularly relevant for us are those comments directed at critics of pragmatism and, especially, Dewey's realist and idealist foes. Also relevant are discussions of central topics to the internal workings of inquiry. Dewey treats several of these throughout the lectures, most notably terms and propositions, judgments, induction, and deduction. It is to these we look for clues to Dewey's logical reconstruction of forms and propositions in his later works.

In a section on modern logic, Dewey uses the examples of Locke's claims regarding sensations and perceptions to engage Russell's notion of atomic facts and propositions. He highlights the failure of "molecular" (i.e., irreducible) propositions to function in the wider context of inference.[49] Of Russell, he says, "Molecular propositions are necessary to inference; no amount of atomic propositions will give inference so long as they remain atomic. He makes atomic propositions irrelevant to inference. The logical apparatus is the statement of the conditions under which atomic propositions take their form. It would look as if atomic propositions were the conclusions of inferences rather than the bases" (TLT, May 10, 1915).[50] Dewey thinks Russell mistakes "descriptive" and "narrative" propositions (such as "nouns, adjectives, verbs, prepositions and conjunctive forms") for atomic ones (TLT, May 10, 1915). Whereas Russell thinks these can be distilled down into truth functions capable of quantification, by themselves these remain merely descriptive. However, in a scientific account of inquiry, they take on a different function. They "represent the subject matter of our descriptive accounts of things" through translating this "over into the kinds of syntax which makes these propositions readily available for inference" (TLT, May 10, 1915). Thus, "inference represents transfer of applicability from one statement to another situation. Ultimately it means substitutability. Inference means the control of situations through the substitutability of factors" (TLT, May 10, 1915).

Dewey locates the problem with Russell's account of molecular propositions in its implied dualism between the irreducible logical syntax that describes situations and the situations themselves. Russell's syntax does not grow out of the situations; it bears down upon them. This leaves it a mystery how the syntax is to relate to the situation.[51] An organic accounting of inquiry, on the other hand, avoids this dualism. Through descriptive and narrative propositions, a syntax can be constructed that guides (further) propositions involving subject matters. This guidance is a matter of function in inference. Dewey does not tell us how descriptive and narrative propositions function in an existential situation: he merely suggests that they do.[52] However, he recognizes that an accounting of this must be provided. Dewey will continue with the functional characterization of narration and description provided here: these resurface in chapter 12 of the 1938 *Logic* as part of a larger accounting of the spatio-temporal matrix of inquiry.[53]

In another section of the lectures, Dewey discusses the distinction between judgments and propositions. The context is logical theory in the school of idealism. Idealists prefer "judgments," whereas realists prefer "propositions" (TLT, May 3, 1916). But, as Dewey considers, "either school might have used the other term" (TLT, May 3, 1916). For the problem both contemplate is "existence-meaning": the role "reflection" plays between what we experience ("existence") and our thinking of it ("meaning"). Propositions turn out to be inferential tools in a functional accounting of inquiry.[54] Judgment turns out to be the activity of inferring (TLT, May 3, 1916). Both propositions and judgments have their raison d'être exhausted in their functions. And propositions, it turns out, have as many functions as there are inferences to be made in an inquiry.

Dewey further develops his account of existential propositions in the lectures. The point of departure for these is Aristotle.[55] Dewey suggests Aristotle's logic operated with existential propositions, though not so named.[56] For Aristotle, there were three classes of knowledge.

> These prior notions are of three . . . classes: (1) existence already known, (2) definition that is known, (3) sometimes both must be known.

1. Of everything which is, it must be true either to affirm it or deny it. This the existential proposition. Obviously, the table is white, or it is not white.

2. Triangle is example of definition.

3. Unity involves both existential and definitional knowledge. (TLT, May 3, 1915)[57]

Existential propositions, then, are claims about facts of the matter. Dewey will characterize existential propositions in a separate lecture as "bound up with the conditions of the existence of a thing" (TLT, May 10, 1915).[58] Existential propositions "give control" (TLT, May 10, 1915); and they do so with "reference to other kinds of knowledge" (TLT, May 10, 1915).[59] Doubtless, Dewey is thinking of knowledge in the abstract; knowledge of relations of relations, which would include mathematical knowledge and the various inferences therein.[60]

Dewey has much to say about inferences utilized in inquiry, and specifically, induction and deduction. On induction, Dewey compares Aristotle favorably with the Critical and Analytic Realists (Dewey calls these "neo-realists" here), for Aristotle's account of induction has an actual correspondence to the world (TLT, April 10, 1916), whereas the modern-day realists efface this correspondence, doubtless through a veil of irreducible propositions.[61] Dewey is of course critical of the attempt to eradicate the correspondence of generalizability and existential facts.[62] Oddly enough, Mill serves as a strong example of this tendency. Dewey spends much time on Mill's theory of induction in the lectures. By making empirical induction distinct from scientific induction (probabilistic conclusion), Dewey thinks Mill drops other tools of inference out of the accounting of inquiry. These tools of inference dropped out are hypothesis formation and deduction. Yet they resurface in Mill's account *malgré lui*. For it turns out that Mill's undercharacterization of induction actually conceals operations of hypothesis formation and deduction.[63] Dewey expends several pages demonstrating the hidden roles hypothesis formation and deduction play in buttressing Mill's impoverished account of scientific induction. Dewey's conclusion is "All induction does not depend on deduction in the sense of depending on a universal truth, but in the sense that depends on hypotheses. All experiments are guided by some kind of hypothetical thought" (TLT, March 31, 1915).[64]

Mill's account of deduction serves as the locus for Dewey's own pronouncements on the subject. For Mill, "Deduction is a process of interpreting the general proposition arrived at by induction . . . All our knowledge comes through induction. The object of his whole logic is to find rules for the process of reasoning from particulars to correspond to the syllogistic rules of formal logic" (TLT, March 31, 1915). For Mill, hypothesis formation seemingly drops out of the picture, for the qualities of particulars of the generalized kind are simply deduced in terms of the kind's consequences. The way this works, according to Dewey, is that the particulars in each kind are related to one another, and in this relating, "particular occurrences" are noted and inferences drawn from one occurrence to another (TLT, March 31, 1915). Deduction thus denotes the method according to which these inferences are drawn. But what ends up happening is sense-qualia are taken for occurrences instead of products of inquiry. And so deduction ends up confirming instances of sense-qualia shared among various particulars. It becomes a question-begging procedure in inquiry.[65] Dewey's criticism of Mill, as regards the case of induction, comes down to a claim for the hypothetico-deductive method, in which hypotheses generate deductive consequences that are then tested and confirmed as particulars in a (larger) genera. This is roughly Peirce's accounting of scientific inquiry. And by 1915, it is Dewey's as well.

Dewey's Correspondence

In a revealing letter to Scudder Klyce, dated April 23, 1915, Dewey discusses his rationale for emphasizing the importance of existential propositions in logical theory. The context of the letter concerns, first, Bertrand Russell and his recently published *Our Knowledge of the External World as a Field for Scientific Method in Philosophy* (1914),[66] and, second, Dewey's recent (1915) "The Logical Judgments of Practice." In the latter, Dewey introduced several functional kinds of propositions, notably "contingent" and "practical" propositions. These were set in (functional) contrast to "mathematical propositions" of the Russellean variety.[67] Unlike in the case of contingent and practical propositions, mathematical propositions "do not enter into the constitutions of the subject-matter of the proposition" (MW 8, 17). Dewey introduces the term "existential proposition" in the letter to Klyce as having the same functionality as propositions of contingency and practicality: these do enter into the constitution of the subject matter.

Formal logicians of Russellean guise all agree, Dewey says, that universal propositions (here inclusive of mathematical propositions) are non-existential. Furthermore, they agree that existential propositions "are particular, and yet they are limiting cases of the universal" (Dewey to Klyce, April 23, 1915, 03517). Dewey gives the example of

"All U is either M or non-M."

This is the law of the excluded middle. Yet both M and non-M are cases of U, and as such, they have something in common. What unifies the proposition? Dewey's answer is the copula. The copula, it turns out, is not a "member" of the proposition, but a function: indeed, it is the "name for the whole-specificied [sic]-from-the-standpoint-of-the-purpose-of-the-proposition (or the meaning of the assertion)" (Dewey to Klyce, April 23, 1915, 03517). The copula, then, performs the function of unification of the terms or members of the proposition.[68]

Terms or members of a proposition, contra Russell, turn out to be *functionally* distinctive features of inquiry rather than "symmetrical transitive relations" (Dewey to Klyce, April 23, 1915, 03517); relations which Russell sets up as *ontologically* distinctive logical forms. The problem with Russell's characterization of logical forms is demonstrated when one tries to set up a wholly thought-centered system of relations of names (Dewey gives the example of the series of ordinal numbers). All ideal numbers are implied in correspondence with one another (when you name one number, you potentially name all numbers in correspondence with that number). But specific numbers (i.e., of a thing) require specific choices and actions, and this is experimental (Dewey to Klyce, April 23, 1915, 03517). For this, existential propositions are needed to get us from the actual, specific choice involved in naming numbers to the admittedly conceptual relationship of the set of ideal numbers. The upshot is we cannot do without existential propositions; propositions that operate in concrete, actual circumstances. Even as seemingly benign a prospect as picking out specific numbers in an ordinal series proves this. For in so doing, we select experimentally the specific number in a conscious act of choice. And this requires a separate proposition to handle the selection and ordering of the number.[69] Dewey reinforces a point first made in "The Logic of Judgments of Practice" (MW 8, 17–18): existential propositions are determinate factors in the completion of inquiries.

Logical Objects (1916)

"Logical Objects" is a presentation delivered to the Philosophical Club at Columbia University on March 9, 1916. The content of the presentation corresponds to claims Dewey made in the introduction of *Essays in Experimental Logic* concerning "distinctive objects of knowledge" (MW 10, 338). These objects are discussed in the context of realism and, in particular, Dewey's claims against his realist critics.[70] Dewey's account of these in *Essays* is brief; here, he expands on this. Logical objects turn out to be protean: they are objects consisting of words such as "between," "if," "or" (MW 10, 89). They consist of "numbers," "subsistences," and "essences" (MW 10, 89). They are "logical entities" (MW 10, 89). They have been treated as physical, as mental, and as metaphysical. They have affinities with Cartesianism and lately have been held up as ideal forms by contemporary mathematical philosophers (MW 10, 89–90). Against these views, Dewey puts forth his own: ". . . logical entities are truly logical, while "logical" denotes having to do intrinsically with the occurrence of inference. In other words, logical objects are things (or traits of things) which are found when inference is found and which are only found then" (MW 10, 90).[71]

Inference, unsurprisingly, turns out not to be a purely mental affair. For inference is concerned with action and behavior. And these take place in the world. Therefore, inference is about the world (MW 10, 90). Dewey is, of course, nesting logical objects in an accounting of inquiry broadly considered. Inquiry begins in an indeterminate situation and ends in a determinate one. In between, objects are formed in inquiry concerning the relationships between various hypotheses and their consequences in action. The inference turns out to be "the specific change induced in his behavior . . ." (MW 10, 91).[72] Inference also turns out to be a matter of functional relations: Inference is ". . . the use of things as evidence of other things . . ." (MW 10, 92). Dewey stresses the instrumental import of inference: it is a tool; an operation (MW 10, 92).

The rest of the presentation is given over to a comparison with Russell's account of logical objects. For Russell, there are "molecular propositions," which are inclusive of the terms "as," "if," "or," and "and" (MW 10, 94).[73] These terms are not, therefore, extraneous operations of inquiry, but rather entities built into propositions themselves. Whereas for Dewey, such terms are extraneous operations between and among terms that unite otherwise disparate members into a whole. These logical objects, for Dewey, are derived *from* inferring (relating) and not *by* inferring. The difference is great. In derivation *from* inferring, the relation of the proposition's terms is sealed by the inference, which is an empirical ascertainment of the relationship between terms through experimentation. Whereas in derivation *by* inferring, the inference itself provides for the conclusion of the relationship between the terms. For Dewey, logical objects are ascertained in inquiry; for Russell, they are basic to the propositions themselves. The upshot for Dewey is that logical objects are not terms or facts preexisting in molecular propositions; they are means operative in inquiry that cannot be considered as logical *unless and until* they actually operate in an inquiry (MW 10, 95).

Concerning Novelties in Logic: A reply to Mr. Robinson (1917)

The impetus for this response is an article published in the *Journal of Philosophy, Psychology, and Scientific Method* by Daniel Sommer Robinson titled "An Alleged New Discovery in Logic."[74] Dewey's response was published in the following issue of the same journal. Robinson appears as an apologist not for Russell, Dewey's chief locus of criticism in *Essays*, but rather F. H. Bradley. Nevertheless, Robinson thinks the criticism he brings forward trenchant enough to damage Dewey's responses to Russell. The issue concerns the applicability of practical judgments. Is practicability a "differentia of all judgment" or a "characteristic which distinguishes one form of judgment from other forms"? (MW 10, 418). Can it be used both ways? Robinson claims that Dewey doesn't say, though he needs to. For if all judgments are practical, do we assess this practically by degree (which Dewey denies) or by character (with which Dewey agrees)? But if the latter, how do we judge the practicality of the judgment unless we are certain that characteristics constitute practicality? Another and related concern is Dewey's request to justify judgments not according to "logical stability," but through another method that doesn't abstract from the subject matter (MW 10, 419). Robinson doesn't think Dewey has the right to ask logicians to give up their tried and true method of abstracting form from subject matter, because, as Robinson avers, discovery (i.e., induction) is not the same as determining judgment (deduction) (MW 10, 420).[75] Finally, Robinson accuses Dewey of using the terms proposition and judgment, synonymously when they are clearly distinct kinds (MW 10, 420–1).

Responding to Robinson gave Dewey the opportunity to clear up misconceptions regarding this theory of practical judgments. In his reply,

Dewey is quite shrill and at times rhetorical. But he has the virtue of being clear on where he stands. Whereas Robinson thinks that differences in logical form are immune to subject matters, and form and matter are completely independent of one another, Dewey thinks otherwise, claiming, "I hold that all differences of logical form are due to differences in type of subject-matter" (MW 10, p. 99).[76] And whereas Robinson thinks Dewey holds to a "twofold use of the term judgment," Dewey disagrees, claiming that a proposition is a judgment and a judgment a proposition; a proposition "about the course of action to pursue (the proposition in which a deliberative decision is embodied) is always a judgment as to the course which an objective subject matter may take, a judgment as to changes made possible by changes that are going on independent of the agent" (MW 10, 102–3). There is no getting away from it; every proposition put into operation is a judgment; a judgment, that is, about a subject matter's direction.[77]

Every proposition and a fortiori every judgment operates in a larger existential situation. Every proposition and every judgment takes its bearing in and from that situation, such that it is a factor in the outcome of that situation (MW 10, 103). The psychical and the physical converge in this operation; indeed, Dewey claims, they were never apart to begin with. Only on a psychical accounting of propositions does it seem natural to conclude that judgments and propositions are different logical kinds and that propositions are mere terms in an act of judging (MW 10, 103, footnote). Another way to put the point is this: unless and until a determinate situation is established from an indeterminate one, all propositions and judgments are tentative and, thus, incomplete (MW 10, 105). Dewey admits his language regarding the finality of judging could have been clearer and that he should have talked about judging in terms of completeness. The solution is to consider judgments in terms of the continuity with their subject matters (MW 10, 106). Particular judgments in this regard take part in a system of judging that is complete when an indeterminate situation is rendered a determinate one.

Reconstruction in Philosophy (1920)

The year 1916 was a watershed for logical theory. Experience and continuity, for example, while discussed in *Studies* (1903) and many of Dewey's more philosophically centered papers in the intervening years, only made an effectual appearance in *Essays* and related papers and presentations of 1916. Dewey's momentum after 1916, however, seemed to stall: little in the way of logical theory strictly speaking was produced in the period 1917–1924. There are, however, two broad exceptions.[78] The first of these, which I discuss here, is *Reconstruction in Philosophy*.[79] Much of *Reconstruction in Philosophy* is admittedly rhetorical; designed to persuade readers of the need to cast off older ways of thinking and adopt the newer, scientific understandings of culture and conduct, it is derivative of much Dewey wrote in the second decade of the twentieth century. However, in chapter 7, which deals with logical theory, there is a novel occurrence. This concerns above all Dewey's movement of his logical theory closer to Peirce.

Dewey reminds his readers that the organizing factors and functions of scientific systems are themselves hypotheses. The context in which he makes this claim, oddly enough, concerns a theory of truth. Dewey claims:

> Here it is enough to note that notions, theories, systems, no matter how elaborate and self-consistent they are, must be regarded as hypotheses. They are to be accepted bases of actions which test them, not as finalities. To perceive this fact is to abolish rigid dogmas from the world. It is to recognize that conceptions, theories and systems of thought are always open to development through use. It is to enforce the lesson that we must be on the lookout for quite as much for indications to alter them as for opportunities to assert them. They are tools. As in the case of all tools, their value resides not in themselves but in their capacity to work as shown in the consequences of their use. (MW 12, 163)

The sentiment is avowedly Peircean: it is with hypotheses that we begin formal inquiry, and generalized kinds, whether individual propositions, theories, or entire systems, are fair game. That Dewey would consider this claim in the context of *truth* should strike us as weighty. For it serves to invoke and involve the Peircean notion of truth as Dewey himself understood Peirce to be claiming.

Dewey contrasts two rival ways of approaching truth: nominalism and conceptualism. Now, pragmatism sets its rival project against conceptualism, or idealism. But, it turns out, pragmatism sets its rival project against nominalism as well. For nominalism (Dewey has Locke in mind), while according efficiency and instrumentality to the ends of inquiry, made a fetish of names when what was called for was "a genuine objective standard for the goodness of special classification" (MW 12, 168).[80] Forgetting this, Dewey claims of the nominalists, is to render classifications of kinds into something mental. Nominalism, it turns out, shares with idealism the fetish for abstractions. Effects in the world, rather than classificatory apparatus, is what constitutes objective standards (MW 12, 168). This anti-nominalistic bent Dewey shares with Peirce. Whereas Peirce's anti-nominalism is decidedly stronger than Dewey's (Dewey after all agrees with Locke in making the instrumental nature of classification key, whereas Peirce never would), on the question of what constitutes an objective standard, Dewey sides with Peirce.

Truth, then, is the term accorded to the hypothesis that works. "The hypothesis that works is the true one; and truth is an abstract noun applied to the collection of cases, actual, foreseen and desired, that receive confirmation in their works and consequences" (MW 12, 170). This "truth-as-confirmation" is not personal; it (at least) "includes public and objective conditions" (MW 12, 170). Truth is what we name the condition at which we arrive when our hypothesis is confirmed; yet truth, as this condition, is equally fallible and therefore subject to falsity. For truth lasts as long as the objective conditions that go into it as a judgment of a situation. When these conditions no longer hold (a novel situation of which the operating premise fails to grasp), then truth no longer holds. This *is* the Peircean account of truth.[81]

Logical Method and the Law (1924)

Dewey wrote "Logical Method and the Law" for the *Cornell Law Review*.[82] The article accomplishes two feats: first, it serves as an argument for experimental methods to be utilized in juridical matters. Second, it proves a *précis* of Dewey's latest thinking on logic; particularly his thinking in chapter 7 of *Reconstruction in Philosophy*. The context is the role of logic in legal cases. The subcontext is the relationship between universals and particulars. It is to this I turn in claiming Dewey offers to his logical theory something novel. Dewey recognizes the tension inherent in case law: on the one hand, it conforms to a system; on the other, it deals in particular cases. Dewey neglects neither pole of the tension. What he does, though, is claim that in the final analysis, generalized logical systems are subservient to the particular decisions made in particular cases.

> It is most important that rules of law should form as coherent generalized logical systems as possible. But these logical systematizations of law in any field, whether of crime, contracts, or torts, with their reduction of a multitude of decisions to a few general principles that are logically consistent with one another while it may be an end in itself for a particular student, is clearly in last resort subservient to the economical and effective reaching of decisions in particular cases. (MW 15, p. 67)

The logic Dewey advocates is a "functional logic," which is developmental in that it derives from selecting (empirical) material without a thought to logical theory (MW 15, 68). Multiple methods are tried, but the method that best works is the one selected.[83] This, however, has not been the case with law. Historically, law operates syllogistically in terms of its logical theory. That is, it is a purely deductive enterprise. Opening premises (the major premise of a syllogism) are very often absolute claims that are taken for granted and require no further testing. Dewey challenges this.[84] Opening premises have their operating force in their purposes or consequences. Dewey recurs to the example of "expectancy tables of insurance companies" in buttressing the claim that "all men are mortal" (MW 15, 70). "The 'universal' stated in the major premise is not outside of and antecedent to particular cases; neither is it a selection of something found in a variety of cases. It is an indication of a single way of treating cases for certain purposes or consequences in spite of their diversity" (MW 15, 70). Here, we see Dewey treating the "universal" premise as a hypothesis that is to be tested in terms of its purposes or consequences.

The question Dewey poses is how do we arrive at premises? Arrival at premises takes place only in a highly refined form of inquiry. Problem finding and problem solving do not generally occur in such a refined context. Dewey maintains (once again) that premises arise out of the establishment of inquiry into a confused situation (MW 15, 72). And they do so gradually. "The problem is to find statements, of general principle and of particular fact, which are worthy to serve as premises"

(MW 15, 72). So for inquiry generally, so for the logic of judicial decisions. These, too, ought to abandon the deductive, syllogistic approach to deliberation and alight on an experimental method, a "logic of prediction of probabilities" (MW 15, 74).[85] This, of course, hearkens to Peirce, who famously argues that hypotheses are predictions of consequences, and universal propositions are all hypothetical. Opening premises have their force in their predictive capabilities, and not in their seeming absoluteness. They operate to establish a defining statement of the situation, as well as its resolution. They lead to deductive consequences regarding features and attributes of particular cases that are then gathered together in a general claim or statement of class or kind. This class or kind serves as the opening premise for a further defining statement of the situation, wherein a novel or indeterminate situation is encountered.

Conclusion

Dewey makes both rhetorical and substantive gains in his logical theory during the period 1916–1924. Dewey's rhetorical gains include an overall strengthening of his positions on each of the four themes brought forward at the outset of this chapter. Specifically, Dewey strengthens his claims for the importance of continuity as a trait of (logical) inquiry, and this is evident in all of the themes. Beyond this, Dewey moves further away from a vague and ambiguous accounting of experience that lent itself to criticisms of absoluteness, toward a naturalized one. This we find in Dewey's correspondence and the Types of Logical Theory. This helps him in responding to common but mistaken perceptions of his scholarship as idealist. As well, Dewey strengthens the import of habit and its role in bringing together impulses and desires in a continuum of thinking. We see this most clearly in *Democracy and Education* and *Human Nature and Conduct*. Dewey's sympathy with Peirce also increases during this period ("The Pragmatism of Peirce"), especially as regards scientific method. Finally, and in tandem with *Essays*, Dewey strengthens his position against Russell's sense-psychology as well as his account of "molecular propositions." We see this in the Types of Logical Theory and *Reconstruction in Philosophy*.

But there are substantive gains in this period that may be less clear, and it will do to note these before moving to our next period. To begin with, Dewey not only strengthens his rhetoric involving experience and continuity, but he also clearly identifies thinking (reflection) as involved in what it means to experience. In *Reconstruction in Philosophy*, for example, Dewey casts the differences in experience in terms of primary and secondary. This of course, Dewey will make much of in *Experience and Nature*, especially in his functional distinction of experience as either "gross and macroscopic" or "refined." But the impetus for this later account is first to be found in the pages of *Democracy and Education* and *Reconstruction in Philosophy*. Making this identification allows Dewey to posit continuity as a trait, not only of existence, but also of inquiry. And this is manifest through habit and the relationship habits have with one another. Continuity turns out to be not only a naturalistic metaphysical trait of existence together with other, similar traits (rhythm, completeness), but also a trait of temporal succession common to all inquiry. Continuity begins to be articulated as double.

Dewey's account of habit undergoes modifications during this period. We see this particularly in *Democracy and Education* and *Human Nature and Conduct*. In the former, habit is not only in continuity with itself, but it also emerges as a way of acting. In the latter, habits are methods. Indeed, they are generalized methods for problem solving. In the period in question, habits are enriched, having the characteristics of activity and generalization. These generalized methods serve as principles in future inquiries. This accords as well with the claims Dewey makes regarding Peirce's notion of habit in "The Pragmatism of Peirce." Habit for Peirce is mind, and mind is irreducibly relational. The proper nomenclature for reflection, thinking, mind, and other "mental" activities is habit, which stresses the active nature of inquiry: problem finding, problem solving, and behaving and acting in a situation that is composed of person(s) and environment.

Dewey makes advances in his discussions of scientific and commonsense inquiry in this period. *Democracy and Education* is one key example: Dewey's discussion of water as water and as H_2O serves to point up the lack of a foundationalist discourse undergirding scientific as opposed to commonsense discourses. Another is his genetic-historical claim regarding the "democracy" of attitudes scientific inquiry sets up for everyday understandings of the world: unless and until scientific inquiry investigates the world about, the world will remain mysterious, and an ongoing temptation to hierarchize elements (e.g., the heavens) will persist. Through scientific inquiry we literally bring hitherto unfathomable aspects of the universe down to earth. The link between scientific inquiry and common sense, then, emerges as a continuity in which patient investigation and testing leads to novel understandings that bring aspects of the world together, and serves to de-hierarchize natural (and social) orders.

It is Dewey's accounts of propositions and judgments that undergo the most transformation in this period. The relationship between universal and existential propositions—a feature of the introduction to Dewey's *Essays*—emerges at several points in his lectures and correspondence of 1915–1916. Dewey already established that existential propositions were claims about facts of the matter in debate with Russell in the pages of *Essays*. But there, the precise relationship between universal and existential propositions is left open. In Types of Logical Theory, Dewey makes the latter depend (in part) on the former. Existential propositions give control through reference to other kinds of knowledge. And these kinds concern not only the existence of things, but things in the abstract: relations of relations. In Dewey's correspondence with Scudder Klyce, he tries to demonstrate that we need existential propositions to get us to the specific choices involved in picking out abstract features (Dewey's example is a number from the infinite set of ideal numbers). Unlike the relations of ideal numbers to one another, in selecting a specific number, one requires a proposition that operates in an actual, not ideal, circumstance. Dewey reinforces the connection between universal and existential propositions in each of his papers, "Logical Objects" and "A Reply to Daniel Sommer Robinson."

In *Reconstruction in Philosophy* and "Logical Method and the Law," Dewey strengthens his earlier claim in "The Pragmatism of Peirce"; principles are hypotheses. We begin with general principles inductively arrived at, and we proceed upon that basis. General principles (kinds) are put in place when an inquiry is begun. These are fallible: they have their (deductive) consequences tested in particular cases. If they fail to accord with particular cases, they are jettisoned or reconstructed. All principles, therefore, are fair game for reconstruction. In *Reconstruction and Philosophy* and beyond, Dewey begins the long work of bringing his logic of inquiry into line with Peirce's theory of abduction (hypothesis testing), deduction, and induction. This sets the stage for the broadly Peircean framework in which logical theory rests in 1938. It also sets the stage for an increasingly realist (and anti-nominalist) theory of reality; a theory that will bear fruit in two of Dewey's major works in the second period (1925–1932): *Experience and Nature* and *The Quest for Certainty.*

Table 2. Dewey's Logical Theory circa 1916–1924: Some Important Conclusions

Themes	Conclusions	Location
Traits, Meanings, and the Indeterminacy of Situations	• Thinking as an aspect of experience • Continuity as a trait of existence *and* inquiry • Existential trait of temporality • Logical trait of serial-temporal succession • Anti-nominalism • Primary and Secondary Experience	*Reconstruction* (1920) *DE* (1916) "The Pragmatism of Peirce" (1916) *Reconstruction* (1920)
The Matrices of Inquiry	• Habits as generalized methods for problem-solving • Habits as serial-temporal • Habits as serially ordered and continuous	*DE* (1916) *HNC* (1922)
Scientific and Social Inquiry	• Continuity between scientific and commonsense inquiry	*DE* (1916) *Reconstruction* (1920)
Propositions and Inferences in Inquiry	• Central importance of existential propositions • Role of existential conceptions for abstract conceptions • Induction, deduction, hypothesis • Toward a causal theory of reality	*TLT* (1915) Correspondence "The Pragmatism of Peirce" (1916)

Chapter 3

Dewey's Logical Development 1925–1932

Dewey's logical development in these years encompasses two major events. The first is the publication in 1925 of *Experience and Nature*. The second is the presentation in 1927–1928 of Dewey's Types of Logical Theory at Columbia University. Both of these events are milestones in Dewey's logical thinking. The first represents a tremendous leap in Dewey's articulation of the role of experience in inquiry, together with the contexts within which scientific inquiry operates. The second represents a leap in Dewey's articulation of the logical forms involved in reflection, the further development of propositions of existence and universality, and further discrimination regarding induction and deduction. Between and beyond these, however, are other articles and books Dewey writes that bear indirectly on logical theory as regards the four themes discussed in the previous chapter. Finally, Dewey's correspondence sheds light on certain issues germane to our themes, particularly as regards his developing understanding of causality, space and time, and the forms and propositions in inquiry.

By the beginning of 1925, Dewey had made small but significant progress in various aspects of his logical theory beyond his *Essays* of 1916. To begin with, Dewey had strengthened his rhetoric regarding the importance of experience, continuity, habit, the Peircean method of inquiry, and the criticisms of sense-psychology common to Analytic Realism and classical empiricism, including Bertrand Russell and J. S. Mill. Beyond this, Dewey furthered the actual development of his accounts of continuity, habit, and logical forms and propositions. Continuity is now considered doubly, as a trait of existence *and* a feature of inquiry.

Habit is now the basis of logical relation—of relations of reflection to reflection and reflection to existential situations or events. There are existential and universal propositions operative in all inquiry, though the precise relationship between the two remains only partly articulated. Altogether, these advances in Dewey's logical theory serve to refine the overall claims made in *Essays*.

Between 1925 and 1932, Dewey made tremendous advances in two of the thematic areas discussed in chapter 2: "traits, meanings, and the indeterminacy of experiential situations" and "forms and propositions in logical theory." He made lesser, albeit important, advances in "the matrices of inquiry" and "scientific and social inquiry." In terms of the first theme, Dewey's text *Experience and Nature* is the most important. Indeed, aside from Dewey's 1927–1928 lectures on the Types of Logical Theory, this is the single most important work for logical theory in the period 1916–1937. In terms of the second theme, Dewey's 1927–1928 Types of Logical Theory lectures show the most development as regards propositions and forms, induction and deduction, and other tools of inference. Other texts, however, are also important. As regards the first theme, Dewey's second introduction to *Experience and Nature* (1929), together with the articles "The Development of American Pragmatism" (1925), "Meaning and Existence" (1928), and especially "Qualitative Thought" (1930), are key. As regards the second theme, "The Applicability of Logic to Existence" (1929) and *The Quest for Certainty* (1929), as well as Dewey's review of the *Collected Papers of Charles Saunders Peirce*, Volume 1 (1931), are valuable. In terms of the remaining themes, for "the matrices of inquiry," Dewey's *Experience and Nature*, together with "Conduct and Experience" (1930), proves useful. For "scientific and social inquiry," *Experience and Nature* and *The Quest for Certainty*, along with Dewey's 1927–1928 Types of Logical Theory lectures and *The Public and Its Problems* (1927), prove of benefit. Dewey's correspondence is also valuable, and is discussed as regards "scientific and social inquiry" and "forms and propositions in logical inquiry."

Traits, Meanings, and the Indeterminacy of Experiential Situations

By 1924, Dewey had the ingredients in place for a much fuller statement about the traits of existence, their role in distinctive functional (though not yet ontological) aspects of experiences, and the roles that continuity and interaction play in bringing these functional aspects together. At this juncture, Dewey was operating with a theory of continuity that consisted of both traits of existence and the temporal succession brought about in and by inferences in inquiry. However, this *double continuity* was not as yet fully articulated. Bringing these two accounts together in a fuller accounting of continuity was a task necessary for a further, fuller accounting of logical theory, and it is this task (as well as many others unrelated to logical theory) Dewey accomplishes with *Experience and Nature* and the various articles and responses to critics that follow in its wake. While Dewey had broached the subject of the continuity between immediate and refined meanings (e.g., *Human Nature and Conduct*, MW 14, 146), he hadn't yet set out a full account of the role of qualitative traits in that continuity. He would do so in *Experience and Nature*. Additionally, Dewey developed a fuller account of meaning, and especially the distinction between immediate or qualitative meanings and mediate or logical meanings. The account of meanings Dewey begins in *Experience and Nature* is carried through and completed in his 1930 essay "Qualitative Thought." Together, these prove important in the connection of immediate with reflective experience and set the stage for Dewey's accounting of existential continuity. I discuss three main topics in this section: the traits of existence; the meanings of experiences and especially how experiences relate to one another in terms of meanings; and the existential continuity built up as a result of this.[1] Here, I discuss Dewey's landmark text *Experience and Nature*, together with related articles including "The Development of American Pragmatism," Dewey's contribution to the second volume of the *Studies in the History of Ideas* (1925); "Meaning and Existence" (1927); the second introduction to *Experience and Nature* (1929); and "Qualitative Thought" (1930).

Experience and Nature (1925)

Experience and Nature is Dewey's mature statement regarding his naturalistic metaphysics. As such, it contains his most complete discussion of experience and experiencing yet produced. For the first time, Dewey writes a text that brings together both the functional (relational) and ontological (existential) domains of experience, and in so doing, demonstrates once and for all that they are two sides of the same coin. But the journey is a difficult one, with perhaps Dewey's least effective prose, raising as many if not more questions than answers, to which Dewey would respond in the several years following its 1925 publication. Central to Dewey's logical theory are unresolved questions regarding the traits of existence, meaning(s), and continuity, and it is to these I steer my discussion henceforth.

The Traits of Existence

I begin with the traits of existence. Dewey uses both the discarded, original opening chapter of 1925 and its replacement of 1929 to emphasize the wholeness of experience (e.g., LW 1, 371; 384). (I discuss the replacement introductory chapter separately.) Experience is also its history (LW 1, 385), suggesting the temporal-successive dimension, as experience takes certain objects as final. Philosophy is its method (LW 1, 371–72), and this method is "denotative," involving "pointing, finding, showing, and the necessity of seeing what is pointed to and accepting what is found with good faith and without discount" (LW 1, 372). The genuine philosophical method, at least in the first introduction, is therefore "empirical" (LW 1, 380). All properly *philosophic* methods are denotative, as they take their cue in and from experience; but not all *scientific* methods are (LW 1, 380): positivistic scientism, in which the method of the physical sciences becomes the arbiter of all inquiry, is a good example of a non-denotative yet ostensibly scientific approach.[2]

Following on *Essays* and *Reconstruction in Philosophy*, Dewey tells us that structures, which we take as the basic furniture of the world, are characters of events (LW 1, 64). These structures are populated of qualities permanent and stable, but in no case are they to be thought of as fixed and final essences. Eventfulness, if Dewey were to characterize the situations in which we consistently find ourselves in having and undergoing experiences, would be the chief characteristic or trait of these. And this forecloses the possibility of a perfectly stable world. Indeed, I am part of the event, as is the world I experience. For my experience of the world is as much me as the world's and the world's as mine. This is the operating premise of Dewey's account of interaction and will bear fruit when Dewey comes to discuss continuity as regards the body-mind.

Events have qualities that are the results of interaction of organism and environment. In such an interaction, qualities "appear"; "they are had" (LW 1, 111). It is the business of reflective inquiry to collect these in a history of events (LW 1, 112). These events are first emergent; they have a quality about them that is immediate. Dewey calls these "immediate, qualitatively integral objects" (LW 1, 116).[3] These objects bear traits or qualities of existence (LW 1, 124). All of this Dewey has discussed in contexts as various as *Essays*, *Democracy and Education*, and *Reconstruction in Philosophy*.[4] Here, though, Dewey goes further: for the specific traits of existence can be further characterized. Chapter 2 isolates two of them in its title: stability and precariousness. Between chapter 2 and the final chapter, Dewey isolates many more. Several of these are identified in the final chapter. These include "qualitative individuality and constant relations, contingency and need, movement and arrest" (LW 1, 308).[5] Indeed, at least thirty distinguishable generic traits have been identified in *Experience and Nature*.[6] While most of these are straightforwardly generic (existential), some have to do with inquiry, or refined experience. Having and undergoing an experience guarantees at least some qualitative traits; but refining that experience through inquiring (what Dewey calls "reflection") is the "precondition of secure appropriation and attainment" of those traits (LW 1, 309). Having an experience can only be shown; demonstrated through the experience.[7] Other than the trait of continuity, which of the traits have priority over others in an accounting of experience (primary or secondary) is not my concern; my concern is with traits generally understood, and with the specific trait of continuity (and its paired opposite, discontinuity).

It is important to underline the significance of Dewey's claim. Every experience had and undergone contains traits of existence that are themselves immediately had along with the experience, but must be refined for their final acceptance. Dewey has long told us that experiences consist in beginnings and endings: for example, in *How We Think* (1910), Dewey told us that inquiry begins with a "felt difficulty" (MW 6, 236). By 1925, beginnings are variously characterized as a problematic, unsettled, or indeterminate situation, and endings as a closure, a settlement of an unsettled or indeterminate situation. Situations are events, and events are interactions of organism and environment, experienced. Experiences are therefore events; situations. And experiences have traits, which require refinement for final acceptance. The new element in Dewey's story is, of course, the generic traits of existence. These are ontological qualities or features of every situation or event. The resolution of an unsettled event turns on the presence of these, and these determine whether or not a situation is settled or not. Generic traits of existence are traits "that are sure to turn up in every universe of discourse"; whereas logical traits, such as the traits imbued on objects and things as a result of inquiry, do not meet this condition (LW 1, 286).[8] There are, therefore, generic traits and logical traits, and what distinguishes them is (in part) the former's ubiquity or absence in our discourses.

What counts as settlement as regards these traits of existence? Dewey tells us that the role of refinement in settling the unsettled is "as means to a final, consummatory end of immediate possession, suffering, and enjoyment" (LW 1, 269).[9] This final end is an aesthetic end. Dewey sometimes characterizes it as a "qualitative whole" or "terminus" (e.g., LW 1, 198). When we look at the traits closely, we see they are often (though not always) arranged dialectically (precarious and stable; individuality and constant relations; contingency and need; movement and arrest).[10] Their union is what constitutes satisfaction, and their imbalance is what determines the characterized unsettling of an event or situation. Dewey makes this clear in discussing the stable and precarious: "The union of the hazardous and stable, of the incomplete and the recurrent, is the condition of all experienced satisfaction as truly as of our predicaments and problems" (LW 1, 57). The union is an effected balance or reconciliation in which each of the poles limits the pretensions of one-sidedness of the other, while being limited in turn. The experience that is consummatory is the experience in which the traits of existence are reconciled to one another through the overcoming of a natural dialectic through inquiry, or refinement. This claim Dewey will carry forward from *Experience and Nature* through to *Logic: The Theory of Inquiry*.

Meanings

Dewey's account of meanings is perhaps the opaquest feature of *Experience and Nature*. It certainly leads a number of scholars to question Dewey's overall accounting of experience. Part of the problem is due to the inadequacy of the first (1925) introduction. It does not sufficiently distinguish between functional kinds of experience. The second (1929) introduction remedies this. But there are other issues as well. These devolve on Dewey's insistence on there being both immediate and refined meanings, and his sometime equivocation on these, especially in chapter 7. Nevertheless, Dewey's account of meanings *is* a significant advance over his discussion in *Essays*. There, Dewey elides the distinction between meanings immediately had, and those built up in and through inquiry (e.g., MW 8, 69–70). This discussion begins in earnest in other works, for example, *Human Nature and Conduct* (1922). There, goodness is first felt as an immediate meaning and then taken up in reflection. Goodness is "the meaning that is experienced to belong to an activity when conflict and entanglement of various incompatible impulses and habits terminate in a unified orderly release in action" (MW 14, 146). But it is in *Experience and Nature* that Dewey first gives a detailed account of the distinction, together with the continuity of traits of existence to logical traits in inquiry. And he does this in and through his accounting of meaning. As problematic as Dewey's account remains, it is a significant step beyond his earlier ones.

It will do to discuss Dewey's account of immediate meanings first. (I save the discussion of meanings in the revised chapter 1 for later.) Dewey tells us that all qualities "appear"; they are "had" (LW 1, 111). Emergent events are the beginning (and endings) of knowledge (LW 1, 113). Events have a final quality, which we connect or relate to other events (LW 1, 113). These qualities, or (as Dewey will later call them) traits of existence are the basis of meaning-making through relations (LW 1, 115–16; 124). But these are not (yet) meanings. For the condition for meanings is communication; discourse (LW 1, 133; 144). Language has two faces. One face is obviously "a form of action and in its instrumental use is always a means of concerted action for an end," while the other face is "consummatory . . . an immediate enhancement of life, enjoyed for its own sake" (LW 1, 144).[11] Meaning, however, arises when marks and noises (to use a favorite phrase of Richard Rorty) become words or speech (LW 1, 145). For Dewey it is here, at this juncture, that meanings come into existence.

This is also the juncture of Dewey's infamous line, "language, being the tool of tools, is the cherishing mother of all significance" (LW 1, 146). Unfortunately, to stop here would be a grave disservice to Dewey's overall account of meaning. For language as tool use does not deny immediacy. However, immediacy is "transient to the point of evanescence," and it has to be "fixed by some easily recoverable and recurrent act within control of the organism, like gesture and spoken sounds, before things can be intentionally utilized" (LW 1, 147). Particular existence (Dewey's example is the comfort derived from a creature accidentally warming itself by a fire) is only made meaningful through language. But this does not deny the particular existence and the comfort (in this case) there derived. Meanings are "generic" or "universal" (LW 1, 147). They are generic insofar as they are common to a speaker, a hearer, and a thing to which speech refers. They are universal (G. H. Mead might say "generalized") insofar as they are common to many.

As we might have guessed, Dewey is no nominalist when it comes to meanings. He rejects the Lockean view of meanings as induced particulars. It is no "expression of a ready-made, exclusively individual, mental state" (LW 1, 145). Meanings are relations, interactions, communications. And these are objective features of the world (LW 1, 148). In naming, we name an event. But we do not name the event immediately; instead, we use discourse to pick out its features. And these features are qualities that lead to further features—what Dewey calls "the potential consequences of existence" (LW 1, 150). Picking out features in discourse, then, turns out to be relating events according to features in light of a fuller understanding. There is no sense in which we immediately name a feature and then conclude (or intuit) that the feature is the pure particularity or essence of something.

So far so good. Things begin to get problematic for Dewey when he discusses the qualities of situations or events in chapter 7. For organic creatures such as ourselves, qualities are had; they are qualities of an interaction of organism and surrounding environment (LW 1, 200). Sense is not feeling; feeling is primary, whereas sense "has a recognized reference" (LW 1, 200). Sense is also different from signification. Signification (in very Peircean language) "involves use of a quality as a sign or index of something else" (LW 1, 200).[12] The sense of something, on the other hand, "is an immediate and immanent meaning; it is meaning which is itself felt or directly had" (LW 1, 200). Sense as a meaning which is itself felt or had is different from Locke or Russell's sensations; for sense turns out not to be a fixed and static thing; rather a relation. A relation of what? A relation of felt-ness to an interpreter. It is appropriate, therefore, to call immediate meaning an immediate relation—a felt sense that is the first of perhaps many relations. Unfortunately, Dewey is less than clear in these passages, and, consequently, many have misunderstood Dewey on this point. They take the immediate *qualities* had as immediate *meanings*, and conflate these with his later talk of generic traits of existence.[13] While the generic traits of existence are to be found in all events or situations, they are not to be thought of as irreducible particulars in the Lockean/Russellian sense. They are qualities that may serve as further qualities (senses) that in turn form the basis for interactions. But they are meaningful only as a result of interaction, and not beneath or beyond it.[14] It is through traits, as Dewey tells us, that we search for the meaning of things (LW 1, 309). But this fact does not inhibit a generic accounting of existence from the same scrutiny that every interaction or relation undergoes. This sets up the metaphysical conclusion that "[t]he universe is no infinite self-representative series, if only because the addition within it of a representation makes it a different universe" (LW 1, 310).

We are now at the juncture of meanings and continuity. For we can now trace the development of relations from immediate to mediate meanings. We can make sense of Dewey's otherwise odd claim that

> Empirically, things are poignant, tragic, beautiful, humorous, settled, disturbed, comfortable, annoying, barren, harsh, consoling, splendid, fearful; are such immediately and in their own right and behalf . . . Any quality as such is final; it is at once initial and terminal; just what it is as it exists. It may be referred to other things, it may be treated as an effect or as a sign. But this involves an extraneous extension and use. It takes us beyond quality in its immediate qualitativeness. (LW 1, 82)

This regards not generic traits of existence, but meanings; qualities meaningful of an interaction first had. (Immediate "things" had will become "situations" in light of Dewey's further claims in "Qualitative Thought" [LW 5, 247].) Qualities as such, of course, are in themselves final; but qualities are as of yet meaningless until further reference to other meanings. "Quality in its immediate qualitativeness" is not meaningful unless and until it is related. Dewey will discuss this further in *Logic: The Theory of Inquiry* as part of his discussion on immediate knowledge in chapter 8.

Continuity

Continuity is double; that is to say, continuity operates on two dimensions. It is, first of all, naturally metaphysical. This characterization of continuity applies to the terminus; the qualitative whole of a (consummatory) experience, as Dewey discusses it in chapter 9 (e.g., LW 1, 269). But it is also historical-temporal and a result of inquiry. Temporality is a (qualitative) feature that applies to both the natural and qualitatively metaphysical *and* refined product of inquiry. So it should come as no surprise that Dewey characterizes temporality as having two functions: quality and order. The first conforms to the understanding of immediacy, in that it is a "Quality as quality, direct, immediate, and undefinable" (LW 1, 97). Whereas the second is a refined product. "Order is a matter of relation, of definition, dating, placing and describing. It is discovered in reflection, not directly had and denoted as is temporal quality" (LW 1, 97). Dewey makes this distinction again in the discussion of order versus quality; "Temporal order is a matter of science; temporal quality is an immediate trait [not meaning] of every occurrence whether in or out of consciousness" (LW 1, 97). Just what kind of trait is temporal quality? We can only conclude it is a generic trait of existence. "Every event as such is passing into other things, in such a way that a later occurrence is an integral part of the *character* or *nature* of present existence" (LW 1, 92). While *nature* is an unfortunate term in this context (for it begs the question), the upshot of Dewey is clear: beyond the temporal ordering of inquiry, there is a naturalistic and metaphysical trait of events passing to other events that presumably makes for the possibility of temporal orderings. Temporality, or temporal quality, refers to the generic trait of existence; temporal order to the logical trait assigned to the situation as a result of investigation, or inquiry.

This points up the wisdom of Dewey's claim that "every existence is an event" (LW 1, 63). For change applies to things in events and not merely to the products of inquiry into events. (We would not be able to measure change were it not for the fact that things in events change.)[15] Indeed, we should not be surprised at this, for both "mind and matter" belong to events (LW 1, 66). Events are basic; "mind and matter" are functions. But when we investigate events, when we inquire, we convert the temporal quality of the event into a sequential order (LW 1, 84) through assigning to it propositions in (scientific) discourse, and with these propositions, we draw inferences. Indeed, causality *is* sequential order (LW 1, 84). The beginnings and endings of events to which we apply our propositions in inquiry are the anticipated outcomes of our inquiry; our "ends-in-view." Our antecedents and consequents, in inquiry, are the "ends-in-view" of our investigation into natural events. Qualitative features of events stand out. They are noted, first as felt-sensed (as immediate) and then as distinct because signified features assigned to propositions in inquiry. They play their role in a series of further, deliberate events (e.g., testing) and are granted meaning as a result of their success. Some of these features will be denoted as antecedent; some as consequent. They will play their role as ends-in-view toward a final accounting or deliberation of a specific inquiry. These further, deliberative events are the events of sequential temporal order. For they are the events of a historical chain of antecedents and consequents leading to a (complete) characterization of a phenomenon's existence. But they are, in turn, indebted to temporal qualities that are converted into this sequential order; qualities that, as features of existence, have their non-sequential dimension (LW 1, 119). There is a continuity basic to events that is picked up when those individual features are noted and placed in the context of an inquiry, and this basic continuity is developed and articulated through signification and inference, forming the causal-historic-temporal order with which science and scientific method operates. This continuity itself has dual or double aspects, for it is both naturalistically metaphysical *and* refined, and both are included and involved in any temporal ascertainment of phenomena.[16] In the 1938 *Logic*, Dewey will discuss the first aspect in the context of chapters 2 and 3, the biological-cultural matrices of inquiry, and the second in the context of causations and sequences and the context of objects (e.g., LW 12, 122).

The 1929 introduction to *Experience and Nature*

Dewey rewrote the introduction to *Experience and Nature* in 1929 because he felt the original too misleading (LW 1, 4). It did not sufficiently demonstrate to the reader the extant relation between experience and nature that is made manifest only in method (LW 1, 5).[17] To begin with, Dewey reverses the introductions of his nomenclature; the *denotative method* is not immediately introduced; we are first presented with *the empirical method* (e.g., LW 1, 13–14). Yet the empirical method is in essentials the denotative method. It is that method that operates on two scales: one for experienced subject matter and the other for the special sciences (LW 1, 14). This method accepts and endorses a functional (not ontological) contrast: "the contrast between gross, macroscopic, crude subject-matters in primary experience and the refined, derived objects of reflection" (LW 1, 15). The distinction between "gross and macroscopic subject-matters" (which I henceforth discuss as gross and macroscopic experience[s]) and "refined and derived objects of reflection" (which I henceforth discuss as refined experience[s]) is just the distinction "between what is experienced as the result of a minimum of incidental reflection and what is experienced in consequence of continued and regulated reflective inquiry" (LW 1, 15). We might consider the first sort of experience as that which is unalloyed by reflection and closest to what we might consider "intuitive"; whereas the second is the product of science (Dewey invokes Darwin, Einstein, and Eddington in his discussion of this). The denotative method is introduced *after* the empirical method (LW 1, 16). The denotative method is that method that is properly a matter of *refined experience*, which involves testing and verification of scientific objects (LW 1, 16–17).[18]

Two characteristics of experience that bear on Dewey's logical theory need to be conveyed; the first is their establishment under *method*; the second is the *functional* distinction between the two. There is no experience *ab initio*; without some method already in play and in and through which experience is characterized, there can be no experience in which features or characteristics are picked out for the organism's satisfaction. To have and undergo an experience is to have some method of arrangement, order, categorization, and classification operative. And within that method, the two sorts of experience (what I am characterizing as gross and macroscopic and refined; primary and secondary) are functionally, not ontologically, distinct. This means there is no ground that gross and macroscopic has unique to that distinction. (Dewey discusses this with a scientific example in *The Quest for Certainty*, LW 4, 138.) What grounds experience is actual transacting. What arises in having and undergoing an experience—having and undergoing an event—is qualitative traits of existence. But these turn out to be traits not merely of experiences gross and macroscopic or primary, but refined or secondary. To have an experience, whether it is functionally distinguished as primary or secondary, is to have and undergo features of experience that are first qualitative, and on reflection, refined. This is important because it suggests that all experiencing has a logical feature—or trait—about it; there is a logic to experiencing that is always already operative even as we experience immediately the empirical brute-ness of the world.

The Development of American Pragmatism (1925)

This article is Dewey's first contribution to the second volume of Columbia University's *Studies in the History of Ideas*. What is noteworthy regarding this article (aside from its significance for locating Dewey historically among the prevailing pragmatist thinkers) is the further attribution of characteristics of a theory of meaning to Peirce; a theory of meaning that is in most respects also Dewey's.[19] Dewey's account of Peirce comes from two main articles: "How to Make Our Ideas Clear" (1878) and "What

Pragmatism Is" (1905).[20] After discussing Peirce's forward-looking theory of meaning as it is first developed in "How To Make Our Ideas Clear," he turns to "What Pragmatism Is" and quotes a passage in which Peirce claims the meaning of a proposition lies in its applicability to human conduct (Peirce, in LW 2, 4–5).[21] Of this, Dewey claims, "in order to be able to attribute a meaning to concepts, one must be able to apply them to existence" (LW 2, 5). Yet, and following Peirce, "The greater the extensions of the concepts, the more they are freed from the restrictions which limit them to particular cases" (LW 2, 5). Meanings imply existential applications, yet also range beyond "the achievement of a particular end" (LW 2, 5). Meanings are characterized of both existence and range. Of Peirce and in contrast to James, Dewey claims a "fixed meaning" is the object of philosophy (LW 2, 9). This meaning is a hypothesis, based in turn on our existing habits or meanings, that extends the applicability of these to future events. We must, in order to extend, fix the meanings of such hypotheses as God and matter until a resolution to the hypothesis is determined (LW 2, 9). This latter consequence will bear fruit for Dewey in chapter 23 of the 1938 *Logic*. Dewey's conclusion is that Peirce, writing as a logician, followed a logical continuity that was different from the humanism of James.[22] In 1925, James's humanism figured as an advance over Peirce (LW 2, 10). In 1938, as we shall see, it is Peirce's logical continuity (for a theory of logic) that will be an advance upon James's.

Meaning and Existence (1928)

The context for this essay is a review of *Experience and Nature* by Everett W. Hall titled "Some Meanings of Meanings in Dewey's Experience and Nature."[23] In the essay, Hall charges Dewey with (among other things) bifurcating meanings into "added" and "vague, immediate, non-articulated meanings" (LW 3, 402). Specifically, Hall accuses Dewey of restricting meaning to the linguistic (LW 3, 409). But this implies there is no reality that is not linguistic; no reality, in other words, that is meaningful (LW 3, 409). Hall's intervention is to admit there are realms of meanings; meanings within language and meaning within experience. As Hall says, "There can be no realm of existence from which all meaning can be excluded" (LW 3, 411). Dewey responds to Hall in "Meaning and Existence."[24] Dewey's response is that "feelings" are "prerequisites" to meanings (LW 3, 85). But Dewey denies that feelings are meanings (LW 3, 85). Dewey sets out a continuum of meanings, immediate and instrumental (LW 3, 86). Immediate meanings are immanent meanings. (Dewey uses the example of sounds standing as signs when they stand for something beyond themselves.) They are the consequents of "the repeated successful outcome of referential or evidential meanings" (LW 3, 87). The thing signified takes its place as an instrument in "a larger temporal whole[s]" (LW 3, 87). Finally, the "fulfilling or consummatory meaning" of a case becomes the "immanent meaning" for subsequent cases (LW 3, 87). Meanings operate along a means-ends continuum, with immediate meanings as hypothetical in subsequent inquiries, emerging as instrumental and final in the resolution of those inquiries. There is no case in which situations or events as yet inquired into have meanings on the face of them. With this response, Dewey begins his differentiation of immediate meanings from objects and things; a differentiation that was only partly articulated in *Experience and Nature* and only fully resolved in "Qualitative Thought" (1930).

The Quest for Certainty (1929)

The *Quest for Certainty* is the publication of Dewey's Gifford Lectures, presented in April and May 1929. The book is wide-ranging but at its heart constitutes an impassioned criticism of modern epistemology and support of its rival: experimental inquiry.[25] Dewey discusses the issue of continuity in the context of scientific and immediate objects. In what is no doubt a reference to the 1929 introductory chapter of *Experience and Nature*, Dewey comments on the "double status" of experienced objects: "They are individualized, consummatory, whether in the way of enjoyment or of suffering. They are also involved in a continuity of interactions and changes, and hence are causes and potential means of later experiences (LW 4, 188).[26] There is an incompatibility, Dewey notes, between the "traits of an object in its direct individual and unique nature and those traits that belong to it in its relations or continuities" (LW 4, 189). The only way to remove this compatibility is "by actions which temporally reconstruct what is given and constitute a new object having both individuality and the internal coherence of continuity in a series" (LW 4, 189).

We should pause and reflect on what Dewey is saying, for this a genuine advance in his thinking on inquiry as set out in *Essays* (1916). As with *Experience and Nature*, Dewey notes a discrepancy in the characters of those objects immediately had and those refined through inquiry. The resolution of the discrepancy is through inquiry. Inquiry constitutes the "actions" discussed in the above paragraph. In inquiring, we temporally reconstitute the qualities and characteristics of objects, and when we do so, a new object emerges in inquiry's stead. This new object is a reconstructed object, for it contains the preliminary traits and characteristics of the experienced object immediately had, yet it has other and new traits; traits of a (new) logical object. These new traits are relations; relations to other objects. But Dewey also says the new object has "both individuality and . . . internal coherence" (LW 4, 189). The reconstruction of this object has brought the immediacy of the older, experienced object together with the new through its situation in a temporal series. And just what are the conditions for "actions which temporally reconstruct?" (LW 4, 189). These are none other than "Acts of analytic reduction of the gross total situation to determine data," together with "formation of ideas or hypotheses to direct further operations that reveal new material"; "deductions and calculations that organize the new and old subject-matter together"; and "operations that finally determine the existence of a new integrated situation with added meaning . . ." (LW 4, 189). In short, they are the hypothetico-deductive operations of inquiry.[27]

An object had (we may think of a taken-for-granted object, such as an everyday object in our field of perception) has its qualities; its traits or characteristics. Such an object is meaningful because it is "individualized, consummatory, whether in the way of enjoyment or of suffering" (LW 4, 188). Yet it is also meaningful because it is "involved in a continuity of interactions and changes, and hence are causes and potential means of later experiences" (LW 4, 188). The operations of inquiry, through hypotheses, acts of inference such as judging, discrimination and reconstitution in a new situation, and evaluation, transform that object into a new one; an object that is mediate and logical, or scientific. Yet in so doing, the mediate object retains its earlier traits; the traits that made it immediately meaningful. The temporal-because-successive re-situation in a (continuous) history of events is made possible through inquiry, while the product of inquiry (the mediate or scientific object) retains its earlier, qualitative continuity of traits (first experienced as immediate) within.

Qualitative Thought (1930)

Dewey published "Qualitative Thought" in the journal *Symposium*, in January 1930.[28] What makes "Qualitative Thought" stand out from Dewey's other essays on experience, and particularly *Experience and Nature*, is the time and attention given to thinking out the consequences of the object/thing/situation/event nomenclature, inclusive of their respective traits and meanings. In *Experience and Nature*, Dewey had often used object and thing in place of situation and event (e.g., LW 1, 97; 116). This was an unfortunate practice, for it lent credence to the claim that objects and things had their immediacy stamped on them, and that the generic traits of existence of an object and thing were there to be felt and undergone as surely as they were in a situation or event.[29] C. Everett Hall's criticism of Dewey's supposed various meanings was emblematic of this credence. In fact, Dewey's considered opinion (e.g., LW 1, 74; 82) confined such traits to situations and events. But one can forgive readers perplexed by the inconsistency. By design, "Qualitative Thought" has none of this inconsistency. "Situation" and "event" stand in for Dewey's unfortunate usage of "object" and "thing" in denoting the "complex existence" held together by "a single quality" (LW 5, 246). A single quality—a single trait of existence—is enough to hold together a situation or event. A situation or event without a single quality or trait, on the other hand, is nothing—mere indeterminateness. And the existence cannot, therefore, be taken as generic.[30]

The essay is also notable for expanding on Dewey's notion of situation and the role that propositions play therein. In *Experience and Nature*, Dewey stressed the experience of the situation as primary. Here, he elaborates and, in so doing, develops further characteristics of situations germane to his discussion of the existential matrices of inquiry in the 1938 *Logic*, as well as to his account of propositions. It bears on logical theory inasmuch as the acknowledgement of qualitative events is required for further, logical formation; for if these remain unacknowledged, an unbridgeable dualism between unanalyzable phenomena in intuition and their properties emerges (LW 5, 246). The solution to this "property dualism" is to demonstrate a functional distinction between situations and objects. Dewey draws the distinction this way: "By the term situation in this connection is signified the fact that the subject-matter ultimately referred to in existential propositions is a complex existence that is held together in spite of its internal complexity by the fact that it is dominated and characterized throughout by a single quality" (LW 5, 246). The single quality is equivalent to the immediate featuring of the situation. Empirically, Dewey has told us, *things* are what they are as immediate (LW 1, 97). So, for example, we have and undergo an experience of an event that has a final, single quality. This is having an experience that is primary—"gross and macroscopic" (LW 1, 15–17). In refining that experience, in inquiring into it, we confirm the having of that final, single quality as a feeling (LW 5, 248). This feeling is an articulated one, meaning it is a logical trait or quality of a logical object. By itself, however, the event (Dewey is no longer using the term "thing") remains unarticulated. The situation, in which we participate and from which we experience, is the subject matter of (further) refinement (LW 5, 247). With *Experience and Nature* and "Qualitative Thought," together with other articles bookended in between, Dewey is able to give a definitive account of experience; an account that rids itself of the nebulous "thing" and "object" of prior accounts in favor of event and situation.

We may also note that existential propositions refer to situations, not (logical) objects (LW 5, 246). Existential propositions serve in situations; events. Existential propositions do not have meaning in themselves (LW 5, 254). Logical objects, or objects of thought, are objects *of* quality; a quality "that is first directly and unreflectively experienced and had" (LW 5, 254). If Dewey is correct, then refinements of situations and events are qualitative, and the existential propositions (though not the universal conceptions) that go into them are qualitative. The logical adequacy of an existential proposition, therefore, is not how well it relates to abstract concepts, but rather how well it relates to its situation or event. Indeed, this corroborates Dewey's claim in *The Quest for Certainty*; mediate or scientific objects contain within them the qualitative traits of immediate experience.

The Matrices of Inquiry: habit, language, culture

All three of habit, language, and culture undergo slight transformation in the period 1925–1932. Of the three, habit is the least developed; Dewey's last and great statement on the nature of habits (*Human Nature and Conduct*) is referenced only implicitly in *Experience and Nature* (LW 1, 213–15) but not otherwise further developed. Indeed, Dewey seldom returns to habit after 1922, and when he does (such as in chapters 2 and 3 of the 1938 *Logic*), it is in service of different subject matters. Language and culture, on the other hand, are more thoroughly developed, and particularly in regard to their roles in sign and symbol-formation and philosophy, respectively. Once again, *Experience and Nature* is the *locus classicus* of these developments. But beyond this, there is one text important for the development of habit as having a bearing on Dewey's 1938 *Logic*; this is Dewey's (1930) publication in *Psychologies of 1930* titled *Conduct and Experience*.[31] It is to these two texts that I now turn.

Experience and Nature (1925)

We have discussed language as regards meaning and the context of "immediate meanings" thus far. Dewey characteristically emphasizes the role of pragmatics in language; it is language use that concerns Dewey above all. His account owes a great deal to the work of G. H. Mead and Max Meyer.[32] Dewey emphasizes the gestural activity of language in his denotation of the "signaling act" (LW 1, 139–40). The context here is one of signaling, pointing, and gesturing toward. That which is signaled is made a "cross-reference" that "brings about a partaking in a common, inclusive, undertaking" (LW 1, 141). The heart of language, Dewey concludes, is not expression of an antecedent something; rather, it is "communication; the establishment of cooperation in an activity in which there are partners, and in which the activity of each is modified and regulated by partnership" (LW 1, 141). Language, Dewey says, "is a relationship" (LW 1, 147). Specifically, it is a relationship in which immediate meanings are able to be shared, leading to greater and fuller experiences inasmuch as these are further reconstituted in (social) inquiry as significant meanings. It is this account of language that will find its way in Dewey's discussion of the same in chapter 3 of the 1938 *Logic*.

A similar claim with regard to culture makes its way into the 1938 *Logic* as well. As is well-known, Dewey's explication of culture was heavily influenced by certain anthropologists at Columbia and elsewhere.[33] And though Dewey takes pains in *Experience and Nature* to claim that "philosophy is not to be merged in an anthropological view of culture," this is, of course, precisely his attitude by 1949 (LW 1, 331).[34] Indeed, the final chapter of *Experience and Nature* bears this out. The milieu in which philosophy operates as "a criticism of criticisms" is none other than culture. Though Dewey mentions culture infrequently in that chapter and never pauses to give an operational definition of it, culture, as the continuum of (signified) relationships established in and through communication (language), counts as the context in which philosophy operates (LW 1, 298–99). And of course, the clear objective of philosophy is to break down barriers to this continuity of communication; barriers that, in Dewey's time (and perhaps in ours as well), consisted in ontological distinctions between "science, morals, and esthetic appreciation" (LW 1, 304). The continuity of communication is none other than the cultural matrix of inquiry, which Dewey will discuss at length in chapter 3 of the 1938 *Logic*.

Conduct and Experience (1930)

Dewey published this paper at the behest of his colleague Carl Murchison in 1930. The paper is notable for bringing the claims of *Experience and Nature* to bear on the recent scholarship in psychology. Also notable for Dewey's logical theory is the importance Dewey assigns to the field to recognize the import of continuity as regards behavior. Doubtless hearkening back to the long-established claim (first made in "The Reflex Arc Concept in Psychology," 1896) that behavior is to be understood not as an arc but as a circuit, Dewey informs the audience that stimuli and responses depend on the experimenter's inquiry in order to be placed in a temporal chain (LW 5, 221).[35] The behavior of the subject in an experimental inquiry goes beyond the mere picking out of stimuli and responses, and consists of a series of traits that lead us in turn "into a content that has a temporal spread" (LW 5, 221). If we are to understand this behavior, experimenters must recognize the context in which such traits are found and discriminated; otherwise stimuli and responses will appear as isolated acts, and "Their whole scientific point is lost unless they are placed as one phase of this contextual behavior" (LW 5, 221).

The upshot for Dewey is that behavior is serial. Though this is a claim Dewey makes as early as "The Reflex Arc Concept in Psychology" of 1896 (e.g., EW 5, 108–9), Dewey casts this in terms of his established claim regarding continuity in *Experience and Nature*: there are temporal successions that inquirers make and use when they situate phenomena in regard to each other through scientific inference using propositions; and there are serial events whose continuity is immediately had, and through inquiry, transformed into temporal succession (LW 5, 222–23). The problem with the causal structure invoked in stimulus-response behaviorism is its readiness to rest merely on the artifacts of inquiry (stimulus, response) and deny the seriality of events. This is tantamount to committing the psychologist's fallacy; of taking a part for the whole, and abstracting that part (in this case, the phenomena of stimulus and response) into a complete theory of behavioristic psychology. Stimuli are evidence of changes in the environment; changes in the transacted event. "A stimulus is always a *change* in the environment which is connected with a *change* in activity. No stimulus is a stimulus to action as such but only to a change in the *direction* or intensity of action" (LW 5, 224). Inquiry into an event yields stimuli and responses; but these are indicators of real change occurring at the level of event, which is that immediately had and undergone as an experience. Logical objects and concepts such as stimuli and responses therefore map the existential traits of events; they do not exist outside or beyond them other than for functional and discursive purposes.

Science and Social Inquiry

The continuity in scientific and social inquiry was well established by 1924, thanks in part to Dewey's insistence on the experiential basis of both in texts such as "The Pragmatism of Peirce" (1916), *Democracy and Education* (1916), *Reconstruction in Philosophy* (1920), and *Human Nature and Conduct* (1922). What Dewey lacked was an account of the role of the qualitative traits of existence and their role in the immediacy of meanings of an event or situation. This Dewey would supply in *Experience and Nature* (1925) and has here been discussed under the rubric of "meaning" as regards that text. Beyond this, two further interventions for science and social inquiry were provided in this period: the subordinate relationship of science to art and the subordinate relationship of pure (physical) to applied (social) science. The first intervention is put forward in Dewey's treatise *Experience and Nature* (1925). The second intervention is put forward in Dewey's major work of political theory, *The Public and Its Problems* (1927). There is also a discussion of pure and applied science in Dewey's 1927–1928 Types of Logical Theory. Beyond this, certain claims of Dewey's in *The Quest for Certainty* (1929), as well as Dewey's "Science and Society" (1931), prove valuable.

Experience and Nature (1925)

One of the outstanding features of *Experience and Nature*, and one that caught the attention of many sympathetic readers (now as then), is Dewey's characterization of the relationship of science to art. For Dewey has science in the role of an instrumentality to art (LW 1, 276). Indeed, science is said to be "the intelligent factor in art" (LW 1, 276). What often gets overlooked is what Dewey says next:

> The connection of means-consequences is never one of bare succession in time, such that the element that is means is pat and gone when the end is instituted. An active process is strung out temporally, but there is a deposit at each stage and point entering cumulatively and constitutively into the outcome. A genuine instrumentality *for* is always an organ *of* an end. It confers continued efficacy upon the object in which it is embodied." (LW 1, 276)

Inquiries, as active processes, are temporal affairs. But, as Dewey tells us, each stage of inquiry leaves a deposit; and each deposit accumulates toward an outcome.[36] (The outcome is assuredly the settlement of an unsettled or indeterminate situation.) Art, which, when undertaken, yields a "consummatory object," betokens the resolution of an unsettled or indeterminate situation. But this "object" must in turn become an instrument; an instrument for "further consummatory experience" (LW 4, 274). It must be resituated in a further set of temporal affairs.

The way Dewey sets up the relationship between science and art is along a means-consequence continuum, with science supplying the means and art the consequence (in the guise of a qualitatively had, consummatory experience, itself taken up as meaning) (LW 1, 278). Science converts what are "relations of succession" (Dewey also calls these "causal bonds") into social meanings (LW 1, 277). These meanings are then converted into means and consequences (LW 1, 278). Consequences, Dewey says, belong "integrally" to the conditions out of which they arise (LW 1, 278). Consequences are meanings. Though they are transformed into further meanings by way of science, in their relationship to the conditions of immediacy (experience as primary; gross and macroscopic), they become means to a further, consummatory experience. Their value is suggested by their role in bringing these experiences about (LW 1, 278). Thus, and echoing Dewey's earlier claim (LW 1, 97), all refining, all inquiry, is qualitative insofar as it consists partly of qualitative relations in the guise of immediate meanings that are causal bonds.

> Thinking is preeminently an art; knowledge and propositions which are the products of thinking, are works of art, as much

so as statuary and symphonies. Every successive stage of thinking is a conclusion in which the meaning of what has produced it is condensed; and it is no sooner stated that it is a light radiating to other things—unless it be a fog which obscures them. The antecedents of a conclusion are as causal and existential as those of a building. They are not logical or dialectical, or an affair of ideas. (LW 1, 283)

This gives Dewey the wherewithal to claim that the separation of science and art perpetrated by philosophy in the name of abstraction is a false one.

The Public and Its Problems (1927)

The Public and Its Problems is Dewey's first extended foray into matters of political philosophy. Notable for Dewey's logical theory is his separation of the methods of physical science from those of social science, together with the importance Dewey attaches to experimental inquiry as the proper method in undertaking problems of the public. Nowhere else is Dewey's antagonism to borrowing methods properly belonging to the physical sciences for use in social contexts as focused as it is here. Historically, Dewey says, the social sciences began to utilize the absolutistic logics common to the physical sciences, with the result that fixed stages were brought into accounts of social development (LW 2, 357–58). But, as Dewey claims, "every such logic is fatal to free experimental social inquiry," for accounts of social development were forced into the earlier rubrics common to the physical sciences, with the results being static because of an absolutistic accounting of social development.[37] The "backwardness" of social science and art is not attributable to their intrinsic qualities; rather to its taking up (or being forced to take up) the logic common to mathematics and the physical sciences (LW 2, 358).

The assimilation of social science to the physical sciences is tantamount to the assimilation of social logic to physical logic: in both cases a "physical absolutism" predominates (LW 2, 359–60). Dewey draws a functional distinction between the operational methods used in solving problems of a physical nature (Dewey uses the example of the nervous system in chemistry) with problems of a social nature (Dewey uses the example of mental disturbances). Separate logics are required for physical and social problems. Whereas inquirers solving physical problems (the problems of mathematics and physical science) very often work at a remove from phenomena and existential conditions, this is not the case with inquirers solving social problems (LW 2, 360–61). Issues of causation, for example, are issues of abstract and universal conceptions for physical science; issues involving formulas of correlation, of change, and "a certain historical career of sequential events" (LW 2, 361). The case is different with respect to concepts involved in the solution to social problems (Dewey gives us the examples of "individualism" and "collectivism"), in which concepts are applied in a hard and fast manner to existential situations involving relations among peoples with the results that situations are made to fit the concepts, and not concepts the situations (LW 2, 361).

The logic of method Dewey recommends for the social sciences is to be different from the method for the physical sciences. In both cases, method is experimental. But what counts as the context in which method operates is distinctive. Close observation of the consequences is crucial in each, yet what counts as observing and what as consequences differentiates the two. Though Dewey does not say so in *The Public and Its Problems*, the apparatus common to conducting operations in inquiry will look different for each.[38] The conceptions formed and propositions used for inquiry in the social sciences will be different than for inquiry in the physical sciences because the beginnings and endings of inquiry differ, and the consequences of inquiry must differ to be of benefit to those endings. Perhaps most importantly, social problems, experimentally treated, will be problems that involve *social* inquiry; and this inquiry is common in the sense of being shared and available to all (LW 2, 362). (Dewey of course, has the entire public in mind here.)

Dewey subordinates the uses (though not the methods) of physical science to social science, insofar as physical science is used as a means to ameliorate social problems. Social problems resemble more closely the commonsense situations in which nonscientific inquiry operates. While specific inquiries in physical science certainly have their qualitative beginnings and endings, their satisfaction and termini in a qualitative whole, these satisfactions are consequences that are put in place in a broader, social inquiry as means for further, social satisfactions. From the standpoint of social inquiry, physical inquiry is a means to the furtherance of solutions to social problems. The satisfactions of solutions to social problems count as the ends for which physical inquiry is to be put. As such, social inquiry is closer in spirit to commonsense inquiry, but only insofar as it deals directly with the interrelationships among peoples in various communities and social groups.

1927–1928 Types of Logical Theory

Dewey's 1927–1928 lectures on the Types of Logical Theory offer a treasure trove of insights into the development of his logical theory at the end of the third decade of the twentieth century. The lectures were given at Columbia University beginning in October 1927 and extending to the winter and spring terms of 1928. They are organized by date. Altogether, there are some forty-five lectures, and they span some 470 pages of double-spaced text. However, they come with a (tremendous) caveat: they are not Dewey's own handwritten or typed lectures. Rather, they are notes taken down by a student, Marion E. Dwight. As such, they are written in third-person singular, and paragraphs often begin with "Dewey says" or "Dewey wants." Despite this great shortcoming, the lectures are coherent, and it is evident that the student was meticulous in capturing the fine details of Dewey's presentation.[39]

We might be surprised to find Dewey claiming that thinking is not itself a logical matter, yet he makes this claim in the lectures in the context of the analysis and validation of material: "The process of thinking as an actual occurrence or process is not of itself a logical matter, although the more we know about it, the greater presumably is the element of control of the process, i.e., of introducing the logical factor. The processes of thought may be called psychological. It will then have to be admitted that the account of how people actually think is not a very highly developed branch of psychology" (TLT, November 7, 1927). In fact, this is an old claim, often repeated, and is earlier developed in texts such as *How We Think* (1910) and *Democracy and Education* (1916). Habit does much if not most of the work of thinking; only in unsettled or indeterminate situations are operations of judgment (inference) called upon in the selection, analysis, synthesis, and evaluation of materials. What is striking here is Dewey's claim that two processes of thinking in this particular lecture ("induction and deduction") are not a logical matter. These, too, it turns out, are habituated and psychological. These, too, belong to the nexus of social inquiry.

What goes for induction and deduction goes for "directive judgments" (TLT, March 7, 1928). These are judgments of acts to be performed that modify or transform existential situations in inquiry. They are the judgments that, properly speaking, operate with existential propositions. Of these, it is said,

> In the case of anything that could be called a directive judgment, there is clearly an element of application which comes in; there is to be an act performed through which the existing situation is to be modified somewhat. Take a scientific inquiry where the modifications are themselves directed toward the discovery of a principle for which the scientist has in mind no application at all. This is the distinction between Pure and Applied Science . . . There is a possibility that the law, or general formulae or universal principle is in its logical statement simply a method of action. (TLT, March 7, 1928)

Notice the definition of "Pure Science"; it is an inquiry in which a principle that has no existential role is determined. Dewey will return to this in the simultaneously written *The Public and Its Problems* (1927).

Dewey also returns to "Pure Science" in his discussion of "scientific" and "popular" concepts as regards his treatment of universals. The scientific concepts "do not merely sum up and record what has been previously found out; they are of such a nature that they define the field of their application" (TLT, March 7, 1928). Scientific concepts as Dewey discusses them here connote both abstract (mathematical) and universal concepts; the latter being those used principally by the sciences in formulating inquiries into the physical universe. As Dewey puts it, "popular concepts" often contain what is "irrelevant and misleading," and may "omit features really crucial in determining any subsequent subject matter," whereas "the scientific idea of a concept" contains those logical traits that "enable the inquirer to determine the nature of the subsequent phenomena with which he is occupied" (TLT, March 7, 1928). The distinction between scientific and popular concepts is not drawn in terms of general kinds; rather, characteristics. And these characteristics are logical traits, or traits common to operations such as judging, as in the case of the scientific concept. Popular concepts do not contain the logical traits of operations necessary to determine analytically and synthetically the nature of situations or events. And they assuredly do not have the power to reconstruct these events. This, above all, is what distinguishes scientific from common concepts.

The Quest for Certainty (1929)

Dewey offers a discussion of the role of scientific inquiry in the broader social context that resembles his earlier discussion in *The Public and Its Problems* (1927). Here, though, Dewey speaks in the language of *Experience and Nature*—the language of value. Consequences, the upshot of values are the outcomes of inquiry—existential, but also logically objective situations in which are found reconstructed objects. While physical operations have refined values borne of "definite selective operations," social operations (here we may think broadly of all forms of social communication) often do not (LW 4, 216). Yet, as Dewey points out, this cannot be a reason to distinguish, other than for functional purposes, the two operations. The result of this false distinction is the failure to modify the methods of physical operations for social contexts (LW 4, 216). Setting the object that we value now and for the future requires us to temporally situate it in a means-consequence relationship, in which the consequences (the valued object) require antecedent objects (those developed in prior inquiries) as their point of departure. Establishing what the most valuable consequences are, however, is a game of probability that requires the means of those selective operations of inquiry. As Dewey puts it, "What is needed is intelligent examination of the consequences that are actually effected by inherited institutions and customs, in order that there may be intelligent consideration of the ways in which they are to be intentionally modified in behalf of generation of different consequences" (LW 4, 218). And this is the move of the experimental method from strictly scientific to moral affairs.

Science and Society (1931)

"Science and Society" was first published in a collected volume of essays titled *Philosophy and Civilization* in 1931.[40] Dewey reverses the traditional thinking on the importance of the pure and applied sciences, for he has the "outward forms" of the civilization of the Western world due to applied, and not pure, science (LW 6, 53). This reversal sets the tone for the entire essay insofar as technology, and not pure science, is made the proper basis of the alleviation of human sufferings and the amelioration of social problems. Dewey argues for a view of science as neutral throughout, claiming that science as a method and body of knowledge "adapts itself passively to the purposes and desires which animate . . . human beings.

It lends itself with equal impartiality to the kindly offices of medicine and hygiene and the destructive deeds of war. It elevates some through opening new horizons; it depresses others by making them slaves of machines operated for the pecuniary gain of owners" (LW 6, 54).[41] If science is an instrument, "indifferent to the external uses to which it is put," then we are at once brought to consider the relationship of human and social consequences produced by science (LW 6, 55). This, Dewey says, is the most important problem confronting existing social life.

Given the neutrality of science, the issue becomes one of who uses science and for what ends. Private, pecuniary interests no doubt have, and are operating with, science as a tool for their own gain. Science left in the hands of such interests will be used against cooperatives and communities in the manner of enforced social control (LW 6, 58). Only a strong public, democratically operating, using its collective will to craft social-scientific methods that "deliberately and systematically . . . control its social operations and consequences" will wrest science from the grasp of private interests and restore the use of technologies to the public (LW 6, 60). And this requires a sea change in intelligent method. It means casting off older and absolutistic understandings of society and morals and leaving absolutistic logics that Dewey discusses as obstructing legitimate public inquiry in *The Public and Its Problems* behind (LW 6, 60–61) in favor of experimentally driven inquiries into anticipated consequences.

Forms and Propositions in Logical Inquiry

As early as *Studies* in 1903, Dewey had established the judgment as the basic form of logical theory, and propositions as the working elements in judging. Operations such as induction and deduction, salient elements of the hypothetico-deductive method, of which Dewey makes much in the openings of *Experience and Nature*, are already established by 1910 (the year of *How We Think*). Specifically, the reciprocal nature of these in a further logical operation involving testing is made manifest. As well, various functional kinds of judgments, such as those of narration-description and practice, were a mainstay of Dewey's logical theory by the time of *Essays* (1916). Dewey also had contingent, hypothetical, and factual propositions outlined by that year. As well, all practical judgments were hypothetical until fully evaluated, and operated as if-then propositions. This had been established as early as 1915 with "The Logic of Judgments of Practice."

By 1925, Dewey had minimally operative notions of existential propositions and universal propositions (conceptions). However, these were as yet underdeveloped, for they received mention in various texts but were not fleshed out. By 1925, Dewey was able to talk of factual propositions as existential, though the move to align existential propositions with generic judgments was to wait until 1927 and beyond.

Much more work was required to flesh out the full significance of existential propositions and their relationship to universal conceptions and to inquiry more generally. Propositions required more discrimination, and functional distinctions between various uses in inquiry remained as yet unarticulated. The role of propositions specifically, and judgments more generally, in matters of physical science required further establishment. This was particularly the case with respect to the newer conclusions in celestial and quantum physics, which posited a greater role for the observer than otherwise. For Dewey, this represented a means to bring his account of psychology closer to matters of scientific knowledge—and specifically laws, theories, and data. The bases for the establishment of both the roles of propositions in inquiry and the approximation of psychology to scientific knowledge begins in earnest in the period 1925–1932 and, interestingly enough, with Dewey's correspondence to various interlocutors, most notably, Scudder Klyce and, later, Sidney Hook, Joseph Ratner, and Samuel Barnett. These discussions helped Dewey to frame his discussion regarding the role of propositions as regards spatio-temporal relations, as he responded to the newer, non-Newtonian physics of Max Planck, Niels Bohr, and Werner Heisenberg. This discussion preceded a fuller discussion in *The Quest for Certainty* (1929). Dewey also discusses scientific knowledge in some detail in his 1927–1928 Types of Logical Theory lectures. But it is his theory of propositions and their role in the operations of judgments that is most notable with respect to these lectures. Indeed, it is in these lectures that Dewey first begins to develop the intricate relations between propositions and propositions and propositions and judgments, particularly as regards the operations of existential and universal propositions (conceptions) and deduction and induction.

Attempts at a development of a philosophical account of science were not novel for Dewey, but they certainly were never "pure" in the sense of deductive-nomological. Dewey was wont to run the account of scientific explanation together with the justification of and for science, for these were mutually self-supporting. Indeed, this was just the strategy of

Studies (1903). That philosophy of science described a scientific method that was (loosely) coherent in terms of operations and aims was never in dispute for Dewey. What was in dispute (or, in any event, required detailed discussion) was the account of origins, and the role for specific operations (i.e., propositions in judgments). And it was these to which Dewey turned his energies. The most famous of origin stories concerned the role of biology and anthropology in the evolution of scientific method, and were mainstays of such articles as "Some Stages of Logical Thought" (1900); "Logical Conditions of a Scientific Treatment of Morality" (1903), *Studies in Logical Theory* (1903), and, perhaps most famously, *Reconstruction in Philosophy* (1920). Dewey allowed his psychological account of (logical) objects to do the work of description and explanation of phenomena; phenomena were products of inquiry, and not epistemic primitives such as senses, sense-qualia, or particulate matter. In *Reconstruction*, Dewey begins to move from a strictly psychological and logical analysis of the role of method in science to an account of the phenomena of science itself, and criticizes Newton for his reliance on a theory of matter as epistemologically primitive (e.g., MW 12, 168–70). This would become a mainstay of his characterization of seventeenth-century science from that point forward. However, while Dewey is content to discuss the failings of Newton owing to seventeenth-century science's reliance on sense-psychology, his contribution to the philosophy of science as regards fusing accounts of explanation and justification does not extend beyond *Essays* (1916) until the period 1925–1932.

Dewey's Correspondence

That Dewey read a number of salient treatises on scientific knowledge by eminent physicists and biologists is clear from the footnotes to his various works. Less well-known is Dewey's correspondence discussing these works. In the latter half of the 1920s and onward, Dewey began a lengthy correspondence with interlocutors on issues germane to the physical sciences; issues regarding temporality, space-time, the role of the observer in physical experimentation, and, perhaps most importantly, what to make of the novel conclusions of celestial and quantum physicists for logical theory. Chief among these interlocutors was Scudder Klyce and (especially) Sidney Hook. Hook's correspondence with Dewey bears the most fruit in this regard, though it must be said that Klyce helped to keep Dewey appraised of significant events in physical and natural science during the 1920s, as his letters were very often filled with discussions (not all of them easily interpretable) regarding the sea change occurring in physics and evolutionary biology.[42] By 1927 Dewey seldom responded to Klyce, and the responses he gave were often of exasperation at having been so badly misunderstood. His responses to Hook in particular, however, show he was paying attention to these debates. By 1929, and in conjunction with the final assembly of the Gifford Lectures that would become *The Quest for Certainty*, Dewey had worked out his basic approach to contextualizing for his own thinking Werner Heisenberg's stunning discovery of the indeterminacy of locating a particle, given its velocity.

In preparing for his Gifford Lectures, Dewey wrote to Sidney Hook on February 12, 1929, that he was struggling with the characterization of the proper objects of physical science. The struggle was due to temporal and spatial constraints, but also to Dewey's admitted lack of knowledge of contemporary physics (Dewey to Hook, February 12, 1929, 05721). After canvassing Newton's mistaken assumption that matter rested on a sense-psychological empiricism, he turned to the topic of certainty. Heisenberg is mentioned as one who, with his principle of "indetermination," provided "the proof that velocity and position cannot both be measured for the same thing, but . . . can . . . only if we fix one, assign a certain range within which the other falls" (Dewey to Hook, February 12, 1929, 05721). The range, Dewey says, is " 'of the same order of magnitude' " as Planck's . . . quantum . . . constant" (Dewey to Hook, February 12, 1929, 05721).[43] This serves to substantiate Dewey's use of Heisenberg's principle of indeterminacy as a foil against the spectator theory of knowledge. But there is more. What Dewey finds most interesting in his encounter with Heisenberg is that "All physical laws are nort [sic] statistical as far as I can see, and the definition of physical law is the prediction of the probability of an observation" (Dewey to Hook, February 12, 1929, 05721). This is exactly right; every prediction is a chance—the chance of a further observation turning out to be as intended. This augurs for the element of chance in the universe; an element Dewey has already suggested is to be found among the generic traits of existence common to all events and situations.[44]

Dewey finds similar, "necessary complementary conclusions" in Bohr's paper of 1928, which he claims he had read only recently. Dewey casts his net far, here. Invoked are "causation . . . continuity,' waves etc, following . . . falling . . . on the side of reason . . . and discrete [sic], space and time, quanta, on the side of observation" (Dewey to Hook,

February 12, 1929, 05721).[45] In terms of Dewey's functional characterization of experience, the first set (those on the side of reason) must refer to products of refined inquiry, while the second set (those on the side of observation) must refer to primary experience. Of course, Dewey thinks continuity falls on both sides, as he maintains in *Experience and Nature* (e.g., LW 1, 97). And Dewey thinks time and space are operations of ordering and control. So it might seem unclear as to what Dewey is driving. We must look further. Dewey continues, "Every observation opens up a closed—or necessary thought-system and introduces indeterminateness—this is Heisenbergs [sic] point—to observe an electron is to throw a beam of light on it and that introduces indeterminateness and probability" (Dewey to Hook, February 12, 1929, 05721). Observation introduces indeterminateness and probability: this is Dewey's conclusion. When we immediately experience something (a "that," to put it in terms of Dewey's 1905 essay "The Postulate of Immediate Empiricism"), we introduce indeterminacy into that situation, or event (MW 3, 164). It is not the case that we immediately perceive an object and then refine it through producing logical objects of inquiry that then match the perception. This is the failing of classical empiricism, and the failing of Newtonian mechanics. Instead, we introduce change into the observation even as we immediately experience the situation or event. The game of prediction is one of maximizing the likelihood that our future observations concur with our present. Thus, discrete spaces and times are observable spaces and times constructed through the phenomenon of the quantum; whereas (logical) continuity is the spatio-temporal ordering of these discrete spaces and times such that prediction of the likelihood of future discrete space-times is evinced. Discrete spaces and times are phenomenal artifacts of an existential situation or event, whereas continuous space-times (as represented in a temporal ordering such as a series of events) is quantitative and measurable.[46] Reality, as Dewey discusses it in the letter to Hook, turns out to be defined as "the subject-matter of an operation that determines a correlation of scientific objects (thought) with the operation that determines qualitative objects (obs[e]rvation)" (Dewey to Hook, February 12, 1929, 05721).[47] The correlation of scientific objects connotes the series of space-times (causation); observation the qualitative objects (discrete space-times of events or situations).[48]

We might think that Dewey is arguing for an account of spaces and times and the quantum phenomena therein as being coeval with the existential event or situation. But this would be a mistake. For to admit this would jeopardize Dewey's functionally distinguished senses of experience. In a follow-up letter to Sidney Hook dated April 1929, Dewey makes the following claim:

> The way I figure Heisenberg's is this—anything <u>known</u> (observed) involves theinteraction [sic] with the act of knowing so that what is observed is <u>going on</u>—it is becoming not over with. It has neither (fixed) position nor (fixed) velocity. These are <u>both</u> measurements of ours. But by taking either we can measure predict the probability of the other within a certain no. which is "of the same order of magnitude" as Planck's quantum constant, thus indicating that the pure discrete character of the quanta is a phenomenen [sic] of observing—the real minimum visible so to speak. (Dewey to Hook, April 07, 1929, 05722)

Note it is the "discrete character of the quanta," *not* the event or situation itself, that is the phenomenon of observing. Quanta are *phenomenal artifacts*, and not to be confused with the qualitative whole of the event or situation had and undergone, and in which they are characterized.

The other important feature of the correspondence concerns Dewey's developing theory of propositions and judgment. In the months prior to presenting his 1927–1928 Types of Logical Theory lectures, Dewey was in correspondence with several individuals with whom he discussed the details of his upcoming program. To begin with, the (ongoing) debate between Klyce and Dewey that reached its nadir in 1927 gave Dewey an opportunity to refine his nomenclature on issues germane to logical theory. Chief among these was the distinction Dewey made (in *Experience and Nature*) between truth and meaning (LW 1, 97). This was a source of no little annoyance to Klyce, who, in Kantian fashion, argued they were not abstractly one. But neither were they distinctive. Indeed, they were matters of the identity of "the many" in a qualitative whole. And the many were "quantitative differences in the proposition" (Klyce to Dewey, May 2, 1927, 04691). Dewey's retort was to deny he had said such a thing and to admit that identity was not a mere abstract conception, but burrowed down into the heart of the material of method (Dewey to Klyce, May 18, 1927, 04696). Truth was a confirmation and the "product" of this confirmation a predicate conferred to the satisfactory solution of an investigation. This confirmation was not coeval with the various relationships, taken abstractly, into that investigation. But truth *was* a predicate, and thus a meaning all of its own (Dewey to Klyce, May 18, 1927, 05696). In the letter written on May 4, 1927, Dewey chided Klyce for assuming that he (Dewey) should have created an account of knowledge in the abstract—a set of principles a priori—and that his entire project was set against this (Dewey to Klyce, May 4, 1927, 04692).[49]

Dewey discussed the development of the Types of Logical Theory with Sidney Hook in August 1927—two months prior to beginning the course. In the letter, he admits being behind on their production, and discusses what he is most interested in—the categories of relation. He wants to consider whether the categories of relation are themselves "connected with the judgment continuum" and whether the categorical judgment (all-some) is dependent on the disjunctive (either-or) and hypothetical (if-then) judgments, instead of the Kantian mainstay, in which the categorical judgment is primary and the disjunctive judgment is the product of the other two (Dewey to Hook, August 27, 1927, 05710).[50] The copula, "is," serves kinds, or generic propositions (and not abstract propositions, which Dewey claims the idealists traffic in). The copula is therefore dependent upon kinds (Dewey to Hook, August 27, 1927, 05710), which are in turn dependent upon existential changes. Dewey will make more of this in his lectures, as we shall soon see. Dewey also reinforces the hypothesis that the *only* universal is the *hypothetical* universal (Dewey to Hook, August 27, 1927, 05710). To my mind, this is Dewey's first explicit claim that universals are *solely* hypothetical. While Dewey came close to making this claim in "The Logical Judgments of Practice" (e.g., MW 8, 21), he did not put it forward as a hypothesis for testing until 1927.

1927–1928 Types of Logical Theory

In these lectures, Dewey broached multiple topics in logical theory. Whereas the 1915–1916 lectures were historical, dealing with specific figures and their various logical developments, the 1927–1928 lectures were, for the most part, topical and thematic.[51] And whereas Dewey's voice came through only here and there in the earlier lectures, Dewey's voice is foregrounded in the later ones. As I mentioned earlier, the caution in using these lectures concerns their secondhandedness; for they were taken down by a student (Marion E. Dwight) and are not a typescript or copy of Dewey's actual presentation. But the lectures are so meticulously described, we can with much confidence assume she was paraphrasing Dewey well. I am dividing the material in the lectures into six themes that bear directly on advancements in Dewey's overall logical theory. These themes are Physical Science; Judgments; Existential Propositions in Judging; Universal Conceptions in Judging; Abstract and Mathematical Conceptions in Judging; and the Logical Operations of Deduction and Induction.

Physical Science

Much of Dewey's considered thought regarding the revolution in physics took place during and after these lectures. Many of Dewey's nascent thoughts on Bohr, Planck, and Heisenberg made their way into Dewey's correspondence and *The Quest for Certainty* (1929) though oddly enough, not the lectures. We do know from Dewey's correspondence that he was reading Eddington, Bridgman, and Barry on physics in 1927, though there isn't much to show for it in the lectures. However, there is one telling example of Dewey's reading of quantum physics, and it is located in the context of a discussion on abstract thinking and its role in causal relations. Causality is a temporal relation. It is not a concern of and for existence. Rather, it is a matter of ordering and control in and through inquiry.[52] The logical object of space and time is an object settled in a temporal and spatial series; this is the causal or logical object. The causal object must not be conflated with the "real object" of existence—the object of the existential situation.

> The real object does not end in space as the object of thought does; for example, a table as an intellectual object has a sharp cut special and temporal delimitation which does not belong to its existential character. An interplay of ions and molecules is what is really there and has no relation strictly to ends or purposes of ours. Moreover, the actual existential table is changing all the time, although it remains fixed in thought and is a familiar term for eternity. We are bound in thinking to take a thing out of its existential context and give it a contour, an intellectual context of its own. This explains why we do it. (TLT, January 16, 1928)

Of course, the interplay of ions and molecules *is* a scientific description that is causal-temporal. I do not think Dewey is denying this. What he is trying to say is that the existential of the table is off limits to our immediate aims and purposes; aims and purposes that concern our role as experiencers in a world that cannot be grasped as a whole. Nor should we interpret this claim as a reductive one, in which the molecular and ionic description of the table is the correct one and all others incorrect (or less real). As Dewey maintains in *Democracy and Education* with the example of water and H_2O, the scientific description does more for us in the way of practical bearing, but does not replace the use for the other description (MW 9, 198).[53]

Judgments

What was unique about judgments, and what Dewey stressed throughout, was their *role-given* nature. Depending on how we wish to use them, judgments can be universal, particular, abstract. But they can also be refined as judgments of command (imperatives) and request, judgments of desire, judgments of inquiry or inquiring-into, and judgments of advice and council (TLT, January 9, 1928). What matters in regard to judgments is their *class*: and this turns on the *function* they serve. If what we want to do is direct a certain course of events, then judgments of the class "directive" come into play: likewise, for examining the relationships between ideas or concepts; we will want abstract judgments for this. Much of what Dewey has to say about judgments concerns specific characteristics and attributes arising as a result of their functions in logical operations. The two most important distinctions as regards these functions for Dewey in the 1927–1928 lectures concerned propositions and judgments and the terms existential, generic, and universal.

Existential Propositions and Generic Judgments

In the 1915–1916 lectures, propositions were cast as inferential tools in a functional accounting of inquiry. Judgment was cast as the activity of inferring (TLT, May 3, 1916). Both of these have their raison d'être exhausted in their functions. Dewey uses the term "existential propositions" once in the 1927–1928 lectures. It occurs rather late, in the context of a discussion of generic judgments.[54] We will want to discuss the context first in order to make sense of the claims Dewey is making for the uniqueness of these propositions. In the later lectures, Dewey discusses generic *judgments*. These are judgments of, and involving, kinds (TLT, March 1, 1928). They are the products of grouping things together as wholes (TLT, March 1, 1928). They are outside and beyond the "temporal subject-matters" that are constitutive of logical objects. Kinds, of course, operate in universal judgments (think of "All men are moral"). But kinds are the products of operations that group cases or things together (TLT, March 7, 1928), and not the universality implied in abstract relations. Kinds change inasmuch as the range of their attributes vary: all things being equal, the kind that is able to capture more attributes is the correct one. But for that, they are necessary for further inquiry. For they are conclusions about specific cases and things required for operations of "identification and discrimination" (TLT, March 7, 1928). And this allows judgments about relationships within kinds and across kinds. Kinds operate in what Dewey calls the "Material phase" of logic: the phase "concerned with controlling the subject-matter, i.e., securing the kind of data that furnishes a safe, economical, and efficacious basis for inference ("induction") (TLT, March 7, 1928). Thus, kinds operate in the larger operation of induction (we will discuss induction shortly).

Existential propositions operate as those statements made in the context of generic judgments or the judgments of kinds. Dewey gives us an example of a statement (proposition) with two kinds: paper and white.

> Take "This paper is white." The notion that that judgment is itself an inference, if only an unconscious one, is reached in this way. All the eye gives us is a certain sense-impression of color. But "paper" also involves certain tactile qualities to the touch, such as smoothness, and a certain use, such as being fit for writing. The theory says in effect: On the basis of a given quality, that of "white," we infer certain other qualities which are included in the fact of being paper. The emphasis then is clearly upon the antecedent conditions of the proposition "This is paper." (TLT, April 11, 1928)

Dewey's emphasis, on the other hand, is not on antecedent conditions but on what follows "This is paper" (TLT, April 11, 1928). For an existential proposition to be of value, Dewey claims, "There must be conditions such that when one quality is sensibly present, other qualities are directly present" (TLT, April 11, 1928). The existential proposition operates to signal the inference across all cases of the kind. For any case of the kind, paper, the same visual quality (within the accepted realm of various degrees of the quality) should be present. It implies a conditional (were-should) universal. If the conditional universal fails (if the quality of the paper falls outside of the acceptable visual range), the existential proposition fails ("this paper is white"). If enough existential propositions fail, if no qualities can be attributed to a kind, then the kind itself is in jeopardy. Dewey's unwritten rule, referenced here, is that existential propositions refer to singulars (This is of X), whereas generic propositions refer across the kind (All of X are of this kind), and universal conceptions refer to the feature or characteristic held by the kind (All X's have feature or characteristic Y). This is suggested first (and very briefly) in the 1927–1928 Types of Logical Theory lectures.

Universal Conceptions and Universal Judgments

Dewey defines universal judgments as those "rules used in judging one case by another" and as "the statement of laws and principles" (TLT, March 7, 1928). Universal judgments are lawful not because they carry within them some mysterious power; rather because "the very word suggests or implies rules of action" (TLT, March 7, 1928). Universal judgments are commonly referred to as "laws and principles" (TLT, March 7, 1928), but rules are already "rules of action" (TLT, March 7, 1928), and therefore are not fixed and final. Universal judgments are related to "generic judgments," which are closely associated with "Directive judgments" (TLT, March 7, 1928). Other associated judgments, directive in character, include "commands," "judgments of advice and council," "certain judgments of interrogation, i.e., of question and answer," "judgments of desire," and "all judgments that are formed in the operation of deliberation, when trying to reach a decision as to what to do" (TLT, March 7, 1928). In terms of their relationship to "directive judgments," they operate as principles to direct those judgments to an application. The class of judgments, universal, directs the class of judgments, directive. Directive judgments operate such that "there is to be an act performed through which the existing situation is to be modified somewhat" (TLT, March 7, 1928). Directive judgments are themselves existential or generic; they operate in situations. Universal judgments operate at a remove from situations, but they are not free-floating. They are the result, the "logical necessity" of a kind. If "identification and discrimination" are the common traits of kinds, the common traits of the universal are "constancy and invariance in the process of change" (TLT, March 14, 1928). When kinds are induced (as the "concluding object of one judgment"), any further judgment using that kind requires that kind to be the "ground upon which the concluding object of one judgment is made the instrument of knowing or judging another" (TLT, March 14, 1928). And this relationship, of ground to consequence, is the universal. This is a temporal and serial relationship, though reaching down to the situation's ontological core, to the traits of "constancy and invariance" in situations. It takes the traits as represented in logical objects by inquiry and resituates them in a temporal nexus. "As a proposition (if . . . then), it is a statement of a rule used in judging subject-matter in so far as that judgment is dependent upon the use of conclusions of prior judgments in such a way as to assimilate one case to another in some respect" (TLT, March 14, 1928).

The basic situation in which science operates is one of continuity and change (TLT, March 7, 1928). Logics ancient-to-modern did not recognize this, and took the kinds developed in logical theory as both basic and fixed. This is the chief failing of the Aristotelian syllogism. Dewey follows his claim in the 1915–1916 lectures that Aristotle's syllogism is the basic affirmative proposition of a universal (TLT, March 10, 1916). Dewey then suggests that the syllogism is not merely an inference, but a set of operations propositionalized; a set that operates (as a leading hypothesis) in a further judgment. The syllogism is a particular in relationship to a whole, the whole being not the abstract principle (the major premise of the syllogism), but the "whole species to which it belongs" (TLT, October 31, 1927).[55] As a proposition, the syllogism is dependent on the judgments that go into it (categorical/hypothetical, disjunctive). But, as a proposition, the syllogism becomes a leading hypothesis in a further set of judgments and not a fixed and stand-alone logical certainty.

Consider the standard first figure syllogism:

>All men are mortal
>Socrates is a man
>Socrates is mortal

It is not merely the conclusion that we take into a further judgment, but *the whole set of premises and their inferences*. And we take this syllogism as a working hypothesis. Of course, Dewey had been trying since 1903 to articulate this sentiment. But he lacked the proper nomenclature to do so. In *Studies* (1903), he claimed that the hypostatization of fixed methods (e.g., the syllogism) was the result of taking the conclusions of inquiry in one context for inquiry in all contexts (MW 3, 312). He tried to establish the basis of the inference as an event.[56] Now, with the advent of functional classes and kinds of propositions, Dewey is able to make his case for the (un-Aristotelian) operational nature of the syllogism, and does so through reconfiguring the Aristotelian notion of the syllogism as the inferential relationship of a particular to a whole to a relationship of a proposition that operates in a (further) whole. This whole is the whole of a situation, and this is the connection to Dewey's earlier claim in *Studies*. The whole, or situation, cannot be defined. "The only way 'situation' could be defined would be a denoted illustration: the thinking for example of a physician begins with a sick patient having certain habits of life, diet, etc. in a concrete environment. This is the whole which defines the particular situation, the whole problem begins with the concrete situation" (TLT, December 19, 1927). The whole, or situation, cannot be defined in principle; it can only be drawn out through example. With the reconstruction of the theory of the syllogism, Dewey is able to counter a leading objection from formal logicians; that he cannot account for what appear to be the axioms of syllogistic reasoning.[57] For now, he does not have to. He can admit of their fixity for a given particular situation, yet insist they be operationalized whenever they are used in subsequent judgments. The syllogism returns, modified for pragmatic purposes, to the domain of logical theory.

By 1915, Dewey had established the hypothetical nature of practical judgments (MW 8, 20–22). What he hadn't done was extend the range of practical judgments to scientific judgments, or judgments involved in the ascertainment of causal explanatory claims regarding nature. This he would do self-consciously in the 1927–1928 lectures. Dewey does so recurring to his oft-used example of the sweetness of sugar. In *Experience and Nature*, he had already pointed up the hypothetical significance of the example: "sugar is sweet" makes no ontological claim about the world. Instead, it makes an experimental one. The sweetness of sugar is the affirmative evaluation of a hypothesis that *if* this is sugar, *then* it is sweet. Here Dewey moves beyond his initial claim. Universal claims are claims to truth. Truth claims are not found in themselves (*pace* Aristotle), but in the sets of relations they have to other propositions. The truth of the statement "This is sweet" "can be determined by the consequence, by the performance of the interaction stated in the first proposition" (TLT, April 16, 1928). Universal conceptions are hypothetical judgments; and hypothetical judgments are judgments of practice. Other than for functional purposes, distinguishing scientific judgments from practical judgments is false.

Abstract Conceptions and Mathematics

By 1927, abstractions are clearly and distinctively operations.[58] To say there *is* an abstraction is, strictly speaking, incorrect. For abstraction denotes an activity, not a product. Thinking itself is abstraction, and "abstraction is the very heart of thinking" (TLT, December 19, 1927). For to think "is to liberate something from its actual existential setting, to so take it out and away from the conditions under which it exists as to take it a subject-matter of thought" (TLT, December 19, 1927). Dewey gives the example of a person burning himself. When the nascent judgment "I burned myself" is made, "he has extracted a meaning and set it above the existential flux" (TLT, December 19, 1927). Abstraction is not "a mental fact of the bare removal of a common element found in a considerable number of cases" (this is part of the operation of inducing). Dewey then recurs to the example "sugar is sweet." "Sweet" implies the abstraction has already been performed (TLT, March 21, 1928). Dewey refines his definition by claiming, further, that "Abstraction is transferring a thing into a new medium and conceiving it as operating in a new context" (TLT, March 21, 1928).[59] In the summary outline of Dewey's lectures, Dwight notes: Abstraction "is the act of changing the status of a thing from the realm of physical existence to that of the intellect, and therefore making it an intellectual force, as well as a physical one . . ." (TLT, summary).

All judgment, Dewey thinks, is abstraction, insofar as all judgments are hypothetical and put to the test in further judging. A judgment is subordinated in the act of change, and that subordination of the judgment ("of existing conditions") to the "change to be brought about through the judgment" is abstraction (TLT, January 16, 1928). We take a judgment of something out of its initial environment, and we place it in a new one; and in so doing, we are abstracting. (Dewey calls this process one of "redisposition." [TLT, January 16, 1928].) In terms of antecedents and consequents, the first judgment is consequent and the second, antecedent; in terms of causality, the judgment of existing conditions is the effect, of which the new judgment is the cause. In terms of means and ends-in-view, the linkage of the two judgments supports the distinction between this and the "real" end, which is existential, not symbolic. In other words, the end-in-view (the immediate aim or goal of the settlement of a situation) is an abstraction, whereas the "real" end is existential-situational. All of these need to be established for a complete understanding of the situation, and each of these requires the operation of abstraction.

Abstraction, therefore, is the operation of anticipating consequences. It is not entirely coeval with the formation of hypothesis, although the formation of hypotheses requires thought, and therefore, abstraction as the operation that moves us from one context to another. It is not entirely coeval with deduction, as deduction is (crudely) the inference from principles to particulars; yet it is the operation that allows us to move from the context of the whole to the part; and it is not entirely coeval with induction, as the gathering together of particular cases to a general kind or class; yet it is the operation that allows us to move from the context of the particular case to the general. In any situation where thinking is required, abstraction operates. Consequences, whether hypothetical, deductive, or inductive, are all indicative of the operation of abstraction. Strictly speaking, there is no "product" of abstraction other than the specific products of hypothesis formation and testing that abstraction helps produce. Abstraction is an operation of intelligence, not a product such as the logical products of conceptions, kinds, or classes.

We see this in Dewey's discussion of mathematics. There is a rigorous, though functional, distinction between mathematical operations (e.g., 2 + 2) and the product of these (4) for a given context or situation (TLT, April 11, 1928). Dewey cashes these out in terms of "the logical features" and the "physical or psychological features" of thought. The earlier and Aristotelian understanding of mathematics as obeying the rules of deductive, syllogistic logic has since the nineteenth century given way to an understanding that foregrounds operations involving physical changes (TLT, October 31, 1927). The terms and meanings of mathematical systems do not obey syllogistic reasoning, for syllogistic reasoning can only presuppose objects of knowledge, and not investigate them (TLT, December 7, 1927).[60] Mathematics is a symbol-system of *operations* (TLT, December 7, 1927). As such, it shares characteristics with other symbol-systems, including natural languages. This was a conclusion greatly influenced by the contributions of Bertrand Russell and others working with the formal characteristics of symbol-systems. The transposition of physical-scientific statements and theories into mathematical-symbolic terms is ultimately a transposition of meanings (TLT, December 7, 1927).[61] Dewey follows Bradley (and Hegel) in limiting the power of the syllogistic system to the inferential arrangements of conclusions and premises, rather than a pronouncement on the existence of this or that thing (TLT, March 21, 1928).[62] In recurring to his oft-used example of "paper is white," he disconnects the substances of things from their logical operations: likewise with 2 + 2 = 4; "plus" is an operation, an indication of an act to be performed. Without any change in the logical form of the judgment, we can say 3 + 1 = 4.

Mathematical operations are anticipated consequences and, as such, belong to the domain of abstractions: mathematics, aside from the particular products (numbers, results, etc.), is an operation.[63] It is not a distinctive category, as are generic judgments (kinds, classes) or universal conceptions (if-then claims and propositions). Making it so constitutes a category error. Operations, including mathematics, are what we do using generic judgments (containing existential propositions) and universal judgments (hypothetical claims as conceptions), and not a separate class or kind of judgments (or propositions). This is a clear distinction from Dewey's earlier (and vague) division between abstractions and universal propositions; a division that downplayed the operative force of the former and made the question of the difference between the two a matter of speculation. Here, the distinction is clear and forceful.

Deduction and Induction as Operations in Judging

Dewey had long thought of deduction and induction as twin operations in inquiry. As early as "The Present Position of Logical Theory" (1891), Dewey bemoaned the dichotomy of induction and deduction into separate, logical realms (EW 3, 131–32).[64] As with analysis and synthesis, Dewey saw these operations as twins; inferences made in the context of a whole inquiry (e.g., EW 3, 87–88; EW 3, 132–33). In *How We Think* (1910), Dewey took the pair of induction and deduction to be operations of a "double movement," "from the given partial and confused data to a suggested comprehensive (or inclusive" entire situation; and back from this suggested whole . . . to the particular facts, so as to connect these with one another and with additional facts to which the suggestion has directed attention" (MW 6, 242). Induction is a "phase" of inquiry that moves us from "fragmentary details" to a "connected view of the situation"; whereas deduction "begins with the latter" and moves us "back again to particulars, connecting them and binding them together" (MW 6, 244). Dewey would maintain his view of induction and deduction as twin functions through the course of his logical theory, up to and including the 1938 *Logic*.

Aside from the 1938 *Logic*, deduction and induction receive their most extensive treatment in the two editions of *How We Think* (1910; 1933) and the 1915–1916 and 1927–1928 Types of Logical Theory. Altogether, approximately thirty typed, double-spaced pages are given over to the topics in the latter lectures. Dewey distinguishes induction and deduction, together with suggestion (hypothesis formation) and meaning, as "Kinds of reasoning" (TLT, October 17, 1927). Deduction is concerned with logical forms, with "methods of statement" or propositions (TLT, October 17, 1927). Induction is "material" and is a logical term for reaching conclusions regarding kinds (TLT, October 31, 1927). Kinds allow us to secure subject matters (TLT, October 31, 1927). Deduction is historically understood as formal and "is concerned with the exposition of the relationship between the subject-matter (kinds) from which we reason and the conclusion drawn, thus serving to test the validity of the conclusion and thereby indirectly the adequacy of that from which we reason" (TLT, October 31, 1927). Deduction moves from subject-matters (kinds) to conclusions-as-consequences, testing the validity of the relationship. Induction is the "material phase" of logic and is concerned with "controlling the subject-matter;" deduction is the "formal phase" of logic and is concerned with "controlling the inference," or the "relationship between the subject-matter . . . and the conclusion" (TLT, summary). In Dewey's estimation, induction and deduction would operate thusly:

Induction:

X belongs to some kind (e.g., particulate matter)

P is a kind that encompasses all X (e.g., body)

X belongs to P

Deduction:

All P's are X's

Y is a P
———
Y is an X

As Dewey never tired of saying, induction is not merely a movement from part-to-whole, nor is deduction merely a movement of whole-to-part (TLT, October 31, 1927). Induction is rather the implication that thinking is "incomplete" and "that you have to get your data and a certain kind of data; and a certain kind of technique is involved in that procuring and assembling and collecting of data before you can go on to draw a conclusion" (TLT, October 31, 1927).[65] And deduction "implies you have reached a certain conclusion rounding out your belief of the subject matter, and you are then utilizing this completed or comprehensive view to state the logical relations which exist between all the elements and factors that enter into it" (TLT, October 31, 1927). The two, together, form a "complete incorporation in each other" (TLT, October 31, 1927).[66]

Furthermore, induction and deduction are not temporally separated events. "There is a constant interaction of the two functions. There is a vague sense of the whole constituting the problem which controls even the selection of data" (TLT, October 31, 1927). This whole is driven in part by the unsettled situation and the hypotheses formed in anticipation of a settled whole. Recurring to claims made in *Studies* (1903) and *Reconstruction in Philosophy* (1920), Dewey claimed taking deduction as the formal operation characteristic to the whole or entirety of inquiry, together with the self-limiting nature of the powers of observation, doomed the ancient Greeks to an incomplete scientific method. The powers of deduction, while able to isolate conclusions-as-consequences from premises, could not usher in the development of new instruments, and because they could not do this, the ancient Greeks could not change what they observed to see their observations differently (TLT, October 31, 1927). The ancient Greeks were merely able to " 'educe'—to draw out the essence of something from its observed material—whereas when we have new instruments to provoke differing observations which alter the conditions of physical nature, we are able to induce" (TLT, October 31, 1927). The upshot for Dewey is that inquiry consists of two functions: one is the specifically inferential, which terminates "in the discovery of new elements or discovering in them new meanings," and the second "the function of testing or checking up constantly on the question of whether the conclusion is one adequately supported or, from the other way around, whether the considerations adduced are relevant or convincing with respect to any proposed conclusion as a solution" (TLT, November 9, 1927).[67]

Dewey spends many pages detailing the failures of syllogistic logic, the rationalistic overemphasis on deduction, and, particularly, Mill's failed attempt at demonstrating induction as the sole operation capable of providing proofs. Dewey's claims regarding these are (with the exception of Aristotle) dependent on earlier claims made in the 1915–1916 lectures and *Reconstruction in Philosophy*. However, (at least) one interesting claim that moves Dewey beyond those texts is notable. In the context of his argument against Mill, Dewey admits that Mill is correct and induction *is* a sort of test. He calls it a "material test" (in contrast to the "formal test" of deduction) and turns to the example of chemistry.[68]

> A large part of chemistry is a knowledge of a physical test to be applied; you put on certain acids and you get certain results. In biology you put on certain chemicals and get a certain stain. That is the real inductive or material test—doing something experimental which gives a phenomena which can be depended upon as a part of the factual subject-matter, from which we are to make further inferences. These material tests represent the outcome in throwing the material into a form, where it can be most depended upon as that from which to reason. (TLT, December 12, 1927)

Indeed, both functions of inquiry are testing. The subject-matter is tested in induction, and the relationship between subject-matter and conclusion-as-consequence is tested in deduction. Testing is basic to inquiry in both of its distinctive functions. In this respect, Dewey does not vary much beyond his initial discussion of induction and deduction in *How We Think* (1910) and the 1915–1916 lectures, though he does strengthen and solidify his claims regarding the dual nature of these functions, their role in testing, and their identification with the material and formal phases of inquiry. What is novel in these lectures, and what differentiates these from his earlier statements in *How We Think*, is the assigning to induction the chief function of inference.

The Quest for Certainty (1929)

The Quest for Certainty represents Dewey's fullest published account of the role of logical forms in physical science prior to the 1938 *Logic*. Dewey had discussed Einstein in *Reconstruction in Philosophy* (1920), but the discussion was short; spread only over two pages. Dewey returned to the discussion of Einstein (and Arthur Eddington) in *Experience and Nature* (1925). However, Dewey did not return to the theme of the fallibility of the products of inquiry as regards leading debates in physics other than in his correspondence and lectures until 1929.[69] For the defense of the fallibility argument for the products of inquiry (as ideas, abstractions, conceptions, symbolic forms), as well as the functional role of propositions and conceptions in scientific inquiry, Dewey leans heavily on the history of science, especially the role of metaphysics in matter for Newton, and the changes wrought by the new physics of the late nineteenth and early twentieth centuries, particularly the Michelson-Morley experiment with light, and of course Einstein's theories of special and general relativity. Heisenberg returns as well, and Dewey reproduces some of the ideas he earlier had in his correspondence regarding judgments and the role of causality and temporality.[70] How all of this bears on his understanding of conceptions is the focus of this section.

Newton, Michelson-Morley, and Einstein

In *Experience and Nature*, Dewey discussed Newton's faulty reliance on sense-psychology in his articulation of matter. In *The Quest for Certainty*, Dewey echoes these earlier sentiments. Not only was Newton taken in by a faulty accounting of sense-perception, he was taken in by a faulty accounting of matter, as a false metaphysics of essential substances that served to infect his description of matter lay behind his further account of the laws of motion. This was a metaphysics of fixed substances (LW 4, 114) that existed in an empty and absolute space and time. For Newton, Matter (mass), as basic substance, was impervious to change (LW 4, 114). Changes in space-time were external changes, whereas substances themselves were static and unchanging. Motion itself must be absolute, because the substances themselves are impervious to change (LW 4, 115).[71] Time and space (and motion) turn out to be invariant as well (LW 4, 116). Dewey took the results of Michelson and Morley's experiments and used them to discredit the notion that matter was a metaphysical substance. Michelson and Morley had shown the relativity of mass as regards velocity. Mass was now shown to vary with velocity, and this put the lie to the intrinsic substantiveness of matter (LW 4, 102).[72] The important consideration (other than the relativity of space-time) for Dewey is not the particular physical formulae developed; rather, it is the importance Einstein in particular attached to the need for an experimental method to demonstrate the differences in the velocity of light.[73] The problem had to do with fields. In a specified field or range, if the simultaneity of two events could be ascertained, causality was demonstrable. But could the simultaneity of two events be present in two distinct fields? According to absolute space-time, in which space and time were invariants, the answer was yes. But the Michelson-Morley experiments suggested otherwise. The question of how to reconcile these distinctive findings was answered by Einstein, and the answer was experimentally (LW 4, 116).[74] The upshot was that "temporal relation of events was to be measured by means of the consequences of an operation which constitutes as its outcome a single field of observed phenomena" (LW 4, 116). There is no absolute time; all times are local. And this signified that physical time "designated a relation of events, not the inherent property of objects"—a claim Dewey had forcefully advanced since *Reconstruction* and *Experience and Nature*. By relativity of space, time, and motion, Einstein did away with the earlier view of these and matter (as mass) as inherent substances. This was not only a natural-scientific proof of the relational nature of science, but, for Dewey, a nail in the coffin of earlier rationalistic and empiricist metaphysics.

Heisenberg

The context for the introduction of Heisenberg is (once again) experimental method. The problem is Newton's claim that a body (in space) can be determined as to both position and velocity irrespective of positions and velocities of other bodies. Einstein, of course, had denied this implicitly in his rejection of the possibility of a general spatial-temporal field in which a universal observer reigned. Heisenberg demonstrated otherwise as well; the inability to glean a precise measurement of both position and velocity because of observer interaction necessitates reliance on probability to assign the second variable (LW 4, 162). The upshot for Dewey is "Since either position or velocity may be fixed at choice, leaving the element of indeterminacy on the other side, both of them are shown to be conceptual in nature. That is, they belong to our intellectual apparatus for *dealing with* antecedent existence, not to fixed properties of that existence" (LW 4, 162). On the basis of his discussion of Heisenberg, Dewey draws several conclusions in favor of an experimental, as opposed to a rationalistic, method. The first is "What is known is seen to be a product in which the act of observation plays a necessary role" (LW 4, 163). The second is "Knowing is seen to be a participant in what is finally known" (LW 4, 163). The final is "the metaphysics of existence as something fixed and therefore capable of literally exact mathematical description and prediction is undermined. Knowing is, for philosophical theory, a case of specially directed activity instead of something isolated from practice" (LW 4, 163).[75]

Conceptions in Physical Science

Physical science deals in space, time, and motion. This much Dewey makes clear in his articulation of physics. Space, time, and motion are in turn properties of relations; properties of inquiry into events (LW 4, 101). Dewey follows his discussion in *Experience and Nature* as regards the relationship between events and the qualities had, and the products of inquiry. The scientific conceptions of space, time, and motion are "the generalized system of these correlations of events" and are "doubly dependent upon operations of experimental art" (LW 1, 101).[76] But these conceptions are logical: they are the formal conditions of the validity of inference when placed in the context of a specific experimental design. In Einsteinian terms, they signify "*relations of events*," for they no longer contain inherent properties (LW 4, 117). They do the work of translating various inferences into one another, or to "make them available to one another" (LW 4, 117). The fully functional characterization of conceptions is at play here.

Dewey takes this functional characterization of conceptions into the context of mathematical conceptions. The question, of course, is whether a fully functional and operationalized understanding of conceptions breaks down in the face of mathematical objects. Dewey distinguishes the *operational performance* of conceptions with the *symbolic execution* of operations. We act or perform in terms of consequences; ends-in-view. This (rather crudely) characterizes operational performance of conceptions. But we also operate experimentally with symbols having their own consequences; their own ends-in-view. These particular consequences, symbolized, "do not therefore commit us to actual or existential consequences" (LW 4, 121). Historically, the formation of geometry by the Greeks is the best illustration of this. In doing geometry, we abstract from a concrete situation. In mathematics, many operations are performed symbolically, with further operations also of a symbolic nature. Yet it is rationalistic in the extreme to consider symbolic operations as a domain entirely separate and free from situations and events, for there is no abstraction in general (LW 4, 123). In fine, mathematical operations are *possible* operations: operations of what could be done in an actual, existential situation. "The fundamental mathematical conceptions of equivalence, serial order, sum and unitary parts, of correspondence and substitution, are all implicit in the operations that deal with such situations, although they become explicit and generalized only when operations are conducted symbolically in reference to one another" (LW 4, 124). The implicitness of these mathematical conceptions owes to their use in a specified inquiry. The conclusion is that there is no ontological distinction between the logical forms of existence and the forms of mathematics.

The further consequence is that symbolic operations (and the conceptions therein) are suggestive of further operations. Dewey locates three characteristics or traits of *technical* symbols. First, "they are selected with a view to designating unambiguously one mode of interaction and one only" (LW 4, 126). They are not free-floating operations, designed for universal use. They are localized and contained by the overall inquiry of which they are a part. Second, "They are linked up with symbols of other operations forming a system such that transition is possible with the utmost economy of energy from one to another" (LW 4, 126). They are not independent operations, as they serve further relations. Third, "the aim is that these transitions may occur as far as possible in *any* direction" (LW 4, 126). Their function is to emancipate consequences, and not to block the road of inquiry.[77] But they do something further. For mathematical ideas in particular do not test with respect to existence, but with respect to the "non-incompatibility" of further operations (LW 4, 128). This non-incompatibility is not coeval with consistency. Rather, it "indicates that all developments are welcome as long as they do not conflict with one another, or as long as restatement of an operation prevents actual conflict" (LW 4, 128).[78]

Thus, there are two kinds of (functional) operations: material and symbolic. Material operations undoubtedly involve both existential propositions and universal (if . . . then) conceptions. Symbolic operations involve symbol-systems as in mathematics and theoretical physics. But (and this is the upshot for Dewey), this must not lead us to conclude that there are two types of *logic*, one material and the other formal. Rather, though formal logic concerns symbolic operations exclusively, it is an "offshoot" of material thinking (LW 4, 129). Ideal or symbolic relations (those that these operations symbolize) are relations of *possibility*. However, certain conclusions follow from the hypothesis, and, as such, are (also) relationships of hypothetical necessity. "If one is to attain a specified result one must conform to the conditions which are means of securing this result; if one is to get the result with the maximum of efficiency, there are conditions having a necessary relationship to that intent" (LW 4, 131). Indeed, all general conceptions (which for Dewey include ideas, theories, and thought) are hypothetical. Thus, all general conceptions are *universal conceptions*, insofar as they operate to isolate specific consequences or ends-in-view. Scientific conceptions, then, are "a system of hypotheses, worked out under conditions of definite test, by means of which our intellectual and practical traffic with nature is rendered freer, more secure and more significant" (LW 4, 132).

Conclusion

It is fair to say that by 1925, Dewey's roles for habit, language, and culture in respect of inquiry were firmly established. But this is not yet the case for the relationship of science to social inquiry, and we are as yet far from a definitive establishment of a theory of logical forms. Whereas Dewey made a number of rhetorical and substantive gains in the period 1916–1924, in this period, Dewey's substantive gains outweigh the rhetorical. And whereas Dewey left key questions regarding the role of experience in inquiry unanswered in that period (especially with regard to various functional types of judgments and propositions), here he responds. From the standpoint of the 1938 *Logic*, Dewey's theory of logical forms and propositions begins to take shape only in this period. And while much work remains to be done on this front, the basic components of propositions, judgments, and operations (including scientific and mathematical operations such as abstracting) for a logical theory are in place, and the relations among these components are articulated, if not fully. It will do to summarize these gains as regards Dewey's logical theory in order to set the stage for the final period of Dewey's logical development.

Dewey's account of experience was only fully developed by 1925 and the publication of *Experience and Nature*. This development allowed Dewey to answer several questions regarding the role of experience in inquiry. First, and perhaps most notably, it allowed Dewey the wherewithal to functionally distinguish two kinds of experience first hinted at in *Reconstruction and Philosophy* (1920) as primary and secondary. These would become the gross and macroscopic and refined experiences distinguished in the second introduction to the book (1929). These distinctions in turn set the stage for further interventions as regards the relationship of experience to inquiry. In *Experience and Nature* and related works, Dewey develops his theory of generic traits. These traits are unique to the situation or event, which is the interaction (later, transaction) of organism and environment.[79] These traits are qualities, and qualities are existentially *temporal* (as stability and precariousness; continuity and discontinuity; rhythm and dysrhythm; indeed, temporality itself). But these qualities are not existentially *serial*; they become serial only in a secondary or refined experience; inquiry. Continuity exists both generically, as a trait, *and* as the serial and temporal ordering of events through their qualities or traits. We may say, then, that there is a *double continuity*, consisting of two traits or aspects. The first is an (existential) trait of gross and macroscopic or primary experience; the second the (logical) trait of a refined one. It is through this ordering that meanings accrue. For meanings (though not "things") are first immediate, and only through language and the relation to other meanings do they become refined and logical. Importantly, immediate meanings are qualitatively had, but they are not the end of the matter. For investigation into the event or situation that results in an immediate meaning changes subsequent immediate meanings; they will differ as to their qualities as a result of investigation. There is a loose circle of qualitative events and situations, the (immediate) meanings had, and mediate or refined meanings, themselves the products of inquiry. The latter serve to transform the former.[80] We will see Dewey's account of experience prominently displayed, especially in chapters 2 and 3 (the Existential Matrices of Inquiry) of the 1938

Logic, as well as in chapters 6 (The Pattern of Inquiry) and 8 (Immediate Knowledge: Understanding and Inference).

Dewey made gains in his accounting of the relationship of science and social inquiry in this period as well. Of course, Dewey's famous claim in *Experience and Nature* that science is properly the handmaiden of art is a tremendous declaration. But it should not be surprising, given Dewey's understanding of art. Art is qualitative and connotes the unsettlement and settlement of situations. Science is the means to the settlement of situations. The two operate in a nexus of means to consequence. Science leaves a deposit in terms of meanings, which art takes up and uses in fulfillment of (qualitative) situations. There is continuity between the serial, temporal ordering and relations of science and the qualitatively temporal traits of experience. The former serves the latter. This conclusion also finds its way into the 1938 *Logic*, especially in chapters 2 and 3. It will also find its way into *Art as Experience* (1934), where it is further refined. Dewey's distinction between pure and applied science in the pages of *The Public and Its Problems* is also valuable for the 1938 *Logic*. We are warned to not assimilate the methods of social science to the physical sciences, and we are reminded that the methods of social sciences bear more resemblance to commonsense inquiry than the methods of the physical sciences. Dewey will return to these pronouncements in chapters 4 (Common Sense and Scientific Inquiry) and 24 (Social Inquiry) in the 1938 *Logic*.

Dewey's greatest gains, however, are to be found in his elucidation of the forms and propositions in inquiry. This is thanks largely to his voluminous 1927–1928 Types of Logical Theory lectures. But it is also a theme elsewhere in his works during this period, including his correspondence. Dewey makes (at least) three notable advances in his logical theory: further and fuller distinctions between existential, universal, and abstract propositions and conceptions; elucidation of the role of universal and abstract conceptions in physical science (including the new physics); and the role of functions and operations (including induction, deduction, and the use of propositions) in judgments. As regards the relationships between existential, universal, and abstract propositions and conceptions, the first are factual/existential, the second and third hypothetical. Existential propositions are statements that operate in the context of generic judgments, having to do with classes and/or kinds. What are at stake for existential propositions are *qualities*. The proposition acts in an inference to link a particular quality (e.g., sweet) with other qualities (e.g., the visual, olfactory, tactile qualities of sugars). Thus, existential propositions deal with sensuate material in their use to make inferences across all cases of the kind. Universal conceptions are if . . . then claims; they are hypothetical necessities. To use the example of "sugar is sweet" (as Dewey never tires of) is to form the hypothesis that "if this is sugar, then it is sweet" (as well as a host of other qualities, which are inferred through use of existential propositions). This is not a new claim, for Dewey made a similar claim on behalf of practical judgments in "The Logic of Judgments of Practice" (1915) and beyond. But in this period the claim is extended to all universal conceptions. Note also that universal conceptions are not propositions; they are in fact judgments. They operate in tandem with generic judgments (a judgment involving classes and kinds) to make claims regarding the relationship of cases to kinds and kinds to cases. Abstraction is the activity of thinking consequences. It is ideal. And it is an operation, not a (logical) product. Of course, we can think of an abstraction as the product or outcome of thinking consequence. But Dewey wants to highlight not the outcome, but rather the activity. The languages of the activity determine the nature of the abstraction as scientific, as mathematical, as straightforwardly commonsense. Much scientific and all mathematical abstractions use symbol-systems that preclude existential grounding. The relationships of abstractions using symbol-systems are to other abstractions using symbol-systems. Yet abstractions, too, are claims of hypothetical necessity, for they too operate along a means-consequence continuum. No universal claim is exempt from this.

As all thinking is abstraction inasmuch as it sets for itself anticipated consequences that are ideal, not existential, all thinking is a claiming of hypothetical necessity. But not all operations within inquiry are of hypothetical necessity. Generic judgments, or judgments involving classes and kinds, operate with existential propositions that relate directly to phenomena or material. These are propositions that make no claims about the hypothetical necessity of this or that material.[81] Nevertheless, existential propositions, together with the generic judgments they serve, are necessary for the inquiry into situations and events that results in an evaluative response. We see this particularly as regards scientific inquiry where, strictly speaking, there are no true and false *propositions*; only true and false *judgments*.[82]

The drastic changes in physics gave Dewey the opportunity to enact his theory of propositions in the context of leading scientific debates about relativity and indeterminacy in classical mechanics. Of course, Dewey had both the faulty British sense-psychology and the rationalistic, substantive metaphysics that frequently accompanied this in mind when he marshalled the results of Einstein and Heisenberg to his advantage. But these changes also gave Dewey the opportunity to show how all claims in physical sciences must be hypothetical, including the claims of theoretical physics. This helped solidify his arguments for the nature of universal conceptions and the operation of abstraction; if leading theoretical physicists were on board with the fallible nature of claims, empirical support for Dewey's account was strengthened. It also encouraged Dewey to think of chance elements in the universe—a line of thinking Dewey broached in his correspondence but did not otherwise develop in this period, though it was a line to which he would recur in chapter 12 of the 1938 *Logic* (Judgment as Spatial-Temporal Determination: Narration-Description).

Finally, Dewey honed his account of induction and deduction, together with other operations in inquiry. These twin functions were firmly settled in the context of scientific inquiry—a context that was more or less assumed from the time of *Studies* (1903), but never fully articulated. From this point forward, Dewey would nest these in his account of scientific method, as in chapter 23 of the 1938 *Logic* (Scientific Method and Subject-Matter). By 1929, Dewey had developed two broad categories of operations; material and conceptual. In the former, Dewey placed existential and universal propositions. In the latter, he placed the operations of abstraction. This suggested that operations involving classes and kinds (whether directly or hypothetically) counted as material, whereas purely symbolic operations such as mathematics and theoretical physics were conceptual. Dewey maintains this broad categorization of operations in the 1938 *Logic*, especially in chapter 20 (Mathematical Discourse). Further, Dewey made inroads into the functional classification of judgments and propositions in this period. In addition to the formal operations of material and conceptual, Dewey had robust accounts of generic and universal judgments, existential propositions, abstractions, as well as judgments of practice and narration-description. He did not yet have the notion of judgment as requalification (chapter 10 of the 1938 *Logic*), though he did have the operations of affirmation and negation. Nor did he yet have a general theory of propositions (chapter 15 of the 1938 *Logic*). The nomenclature of existential propositions had not yet changed to generic propositions (chapter 14 of the 1938 *Logic*). Some of these accounts (e.g., generic propositions) would be developed in the period 1933–1937. Others would find their first appearance in the 1938 *Logic*.

Table 3. Dewey's Logical Theory circa 1925–1932: Important Conclusions

Themes	Conclusions	Location
Traits, Meanings, and the Indeterminacy of Situations	• Experience gross and macroscopic; refined • Fuller list of generic traits of existence • Existential temporality of events and situations • Continuity as a generic trait *and* as a logical trait • Immediate meanings change on reflection as a result of logical traits, inquiry • Chance elements in the universe	*EN* (1925) "Qualitative Thought" (1930) *Lectures* (1927–1928) *Correspondence*
The Matrices of Inquiry	• Art and science in a nexus of means-consequence	*EN* (1925)
Scientific and Social Inquiry	• Physical and social science differ as to their methods • No assimilation of physical science to social science	*PP* (1927)

Propositions and Inferences in Inquiry	• Judgments of Practice
	    Judgments of affirmation and negation
	    Directive judgments
	    Judgments of command and request
	    Judgments of desire
	    Judgments of inquiry or inquiring-into
	    Judgments of advice and council
	• Material and conceptual operations
	• Universal, existential, and abstract propositions
	• Existential propositions deal with classes and kinds
	• All universal conceptions are hypothetical
	• Generic and existential propositions not hypothetical
	• Generic judgments (judgments of kinds and classes)
	• Abstract thinking an ideal operation
	• Abstractions are hypothetical claims
	• Claims of theoretical physics are hypothetical
		Lectures (1927–1928)

Chapter 4

Dewey's Logical Development 1933–1937

If *Experience and Nature* and the 1927–1928 Types of Logical Theory lectures are the mainstays of Dewey's logical development in the period 1925–1932, then his correspondence, together with three essays written for the *Journal of Philosophy* in 1936 ("Characteristics and Characters: Kinds and Classes"; "What Are Universals?"; "General Propositions, Kinds, and Classes"), serve in this capacity in the years 1933–1937. The formative gains made in this period concern logical forms and propositions, inclusive of the role propositions play in regard to judgments; the existential and universal functions of propositions; propositional definitions and classifications; and the role of propositions and judgments in temporal determinations, including serial orderings and causal-explanatory sequences. By 1933, Dewey had articulated working definitions of several classes of judgments and propositions, but the exact relationship between universal, existential, and generic propositions remained an open issue. We find Dewey struggling toward an answer, first in his correspondence with friends and colleagues Sidney and Joseph Ratner and Sidney Hook as well as other interlocutors such as Arthur Bentley, and second, in his three articles for the *Journal of Philosophy*. By 1937, Dewey is able to provide an account of the operating definitions of both; definitions that are carried into his 1938 *Logic*, especially in The Continuum of Judgment: General Propositions (chapter 13), and Generic and Universal Propositions (chapter 14).

Another area that receives attention in this period is Dewey's ongoing commitment to continuity as the basic trait of inquiry. Continuity received a great deal of attention in *Experience and Nature* (1925) and essays leading up to and including "Qualitative Thought" (1930). That primary or gross and macroscopic experience and secondary or refined experience have continuities of their own (though what counts as temporal is unique to each), and that the business of refined experience is to provide for a serial ordering of events that are existential, immediate, and qualitative, is established in *Experience and Nature* and elsewhere. Likewise, causality, which is central to scientific method and the explanatory mechanism brought to bear on scientific subject matters, is treated in terms of its spatiotemporal and serial dimensions in texts such as *The Quest for Certainty* (1929). Dewey continues this development of continuity, particularly in *Art as Experience* (1934). The role of refined experience, or reflection upon experience involving immediate doing and undergoing, is returned to here, and redeveloped in terms of the generic traits of existence. What unfolds is a thoroughgoing parallel continuity between the immediacy of experience had and undergone, and the serial ordering of events by refined experience. These parallel continuities are unified as a double continuity in the latter ordering of events. And this is the theory of continuity involving serial ordering, narration-description, causal explanation, and their roles in situations that Dewey will bring to bear on various chapters of his 1938 *Logic*, including the Existential Matrices of Inquiry (chapters 2 and 3); Common Sense and Scientific Inquiry (chapter 4); Immediate Knowledge: Understanding and Inference (chapter 8); The Continuum of Judgment: General Propositions (chapter 13); and Scientific Laws: Causation and Sequences (chapter 22).

Dewey's gains, then, fall into three major camps. The first gain concerns continuity, and the first theme, "traits, meanings, and the indeterminacy of experiential situations." The second gain concerns logical forms and propositions and the fourth theme, "forms and propositions in logical inquiry." The third gain concerns causality, and the role of continuity and logical forms and propositions in causal-explanatory orderings of the subject matter of inquiry. I also touch upon areas of refinement in Dewey's overall account as regards the second and third themes, "the matrices of inquiry" and "scientific and social inquiry." As regards the second theme, Dewey's expanded yet simplified second edition of *How We Think* (1933) is helpful concerning the further articulation of the context in which inquiry takes place, while regarding the third theme, Dewey's *Art as Experience*, together with incidental essays regarding authority and the role of science therein, are helpful. These essays include "Authority and Social Change" (1935) and a review of Bertrand Russell's *Religion and Science* (1935). I also discuss further salient material as regards the fourth theme, especially Dewey's reviews of Peirce's *Collected Papers*, and the stand-alone paper, "Peirce's Theory of Quality" (1935). This material bears on Peirce and Dewey's causal theory of knowledge.

Finally, and as regards the pattern of inquiry, Dewey reconstructs the stages of inquiry he articulated at length in chapter 6 of the first edition of *How We Think* (1910) as "the complete act of thought." He offers a thoroughly revised version of this earlier articulation, with attention to the flexibility and self-corrective nature of inquiry; the stages of inquiry are now "phases" or "aspects" (e.g., LW 8, 200). Two changes in particular are worthy of discussion for the context of Dewey's logical development. The first is the role played by recursion—that phases of inquiry can be entered into and exited from with no loss to the overall pattern established with respect to inquiry—with the role played by previous inquiries in present observations of phenomena. The second is the meaning of the conclusion of an inquiry, which is cast in the second edition as an evaluative judgment of the inquiry's success or failure at settling an (qualitative) unsettled or indeterminate situation, itself composed of many otherwise separate situations. The futural nature of the conclusions of inquiry (as probabilities of habit for future inquiries) is also pointed up in Dewey's revisionary account.

Traits, Meanings, and the Indeterminacy of Experiential Situations

By 1930, Dewey had effectively developed a theory of naturalistic metaphysics with generic traits of existence as key ingredients. They are both first and last philosophy for Dewey; as regards the immediate qualities felt yet unarticulated, they are first; in terms of their subsequent investigation and naming as traits, they are logical products and therefore last. They are present at each and every beginning and ending. These traits are qualitative features of an experience that is itself had and undergone. The to-and-fro of passivity (undergoing) and activity (doing) is the basic form of the interaction—later transaction—of the human organism and her environment (LW 5, 247). The traits are features of this interaction. Dewey accounts for these features in various places in *Experience and Nature* and elsewhere. As I mentioned in chapter 3, in *Experience and Nature* there are more than thirty designated generic traits of existence, though not all of these are discussed at length.[1] Some of those that are include back-and-forth-ness, completeness, beginning and endings, continuity, together with "qualitative individuality and constant relations, contingency and need, movement and arrest" (LW 1, 308–9). To these, Dewey adds many others throughout the text. As well, experiences immediately had evinced their own continuity; their own temporality. This temporality is suggested both by the back-and-forth of the interaction between human organism and environment and the nature of the traits themselves, which are qualitatively had and often dialectically arranged.[2]

It is the business of refined experience to grasp these features, these traits of immediate experience. Dewey places great stock in the ability of refined experience to conduct a "serial history," a "consecutive history" of "events," with "events" connoting the qualitative features, especially the beginnings and endings, of an (immediate) experience (LW 1, 112). Continuity emerges as the greatest of the qualitative traits of inquiry; for serial ordering of events is not merely a product of inquiry; it is a *felt need* (LW 1, 197–98). In scientific method and in corresponding subject matters, causality is the dominant mode of serial ordering of events. The events, of course, are not merely observed; they are very often the controlled and directed effects of researchers. They are phenomena suffused with purpose. The events, in other words, are often *intended*. Indeed, they are very often predicted for (LW 1, 112). Now, the problem for Dewey is the supposed gap between the two functional kinds of experience: one "gross and macroscopic" and immediate, the other "refined" (LW 1, 15). How does Dewey get primary or immediate experience to its refined counterpart?

The answer can only be the activity of denoting. In denoting, the experiencer points to and picks out a qualitative feature of an event and connects that qualitative feature to a series of features through temporal-serial ordering (inquiry). There is a felt need of refined experience to isolate and exploit its very own trait of continuity. And the materials for this continuity can only be found in the qualitative features or traits of immediate experience, including the immediate objects of enjoyment (LW 1, 114–16). Thus, the felt need to serially order events (which are terminal affairs, having beginnings and endings) is equally the need to bring an indeterminate situation (because of its own trait of incompleteness) to completion. This need is, for inquiry, the existential counterpart to the closure of an (immediate) experience. Dewey does not say this in so many words in *Experience and Nature*.³ It is more fully fleshed out in his essay "Qualitative Thought" (1930) in his discussion of "situation" (e.g., LW 5, 254). And it is further refined in *How We Think*, second edition, and especially in *Art as Experience*, to which I now turn.

How We Think, Second Edition (1933)⁴

How We Think, second edition, is Dewey's attempt to provide a "restatement" of his earlier treatise on the role and scope of thinking for teachers (LW 8, 107).⁵ The middle section, containing the theory of thinking proper, is almost completely rewritten. Yet, and for this, the text is regrettably superficial. Dewey suggested he wanted to make the text less complicated to read than the first edition. In his estimation, he produced a work "considerably simplified in statement" (LW 8, 107). The result is a text that provides few new ideas in logical theory.⁶ What it does do, though, is refine and, in some cases, expand upon Dewey's thinking in the 1925–1932 period. In regard to our theme here, this is the question of immediate experience and meaning.

In line with the first edition (MW 6, 260), Dewey considers ideas as distinct from judgments. Judgments are settled and more or less complete. A judgment such as

> Umbrellas are to be carried when it is raining

is a settled affair, whereas an idea is suggestive (MW 6, 265; LW 8, 222). Ideas are "suggested as possibilities," and in their treatment as "suppositions," "a possibility," "it becomes an idea." Ideas, furthermore, have the following traits: "suggestion," "conjecture," "a guess," "hypothesis," "or a theory. That is to say, it is a possible, but as yet doubtful, mode of interpretation" (LW 8, 222). So, for example,

> If it is raining, then I will take my umbrella

is an idea that has been transformed into a hypothesis. The ongoing claim of Dewey's, that ideas and judgments are "logical instruments," with ideas serving in the capacity of suggestion, is at least as old as 1903; the fluidity of judgments, ideas, and hypotheses is foregrounded here. What distinguishes the three are the purposes to which they are put.

This carries forward Dewey's estimation of ideas in his earlier edition of *How We Think* and serves to make clear the ultimately functional basis for discrimination among these three operations.

The uniqueness of *How We Think*, second edition, as regards the role of ideas in meanings owes to Dewey's *Experience and Nature* and similar writings. Dewey begins to talk of the progress of intelligence as a rhythm in the second edition—a way of combining the continuity of inquiry with the continuity of events that is absent from the first edition. When we progress in knowledge, we do so in part "*using meanings that are directly grasped as instruments for getting hold of obscure and doubtful meanings*" (LW 8, 227). There is a rhythm, a "rhythm of direct understanding—technically called *ap*prehension—with indirect, mediated understanding—technically called *com*prehension" (LW 8, 228). Unfortunately, at this point Dewey avails himself of the account of habit provided in *Human Nature and Conduct* and elsewhere, and does not dwell on the generic trait of rhythm beyond this passage. The introduction of rhythm amounts to nothing as evidenced by the insistence that "vague wholes" of perception constitute the backdrop for further "definiteness" and "consistency" in forming meanings. The mystery of how the rhythm of refined experience meshes with the rhythm of immediate experience is left to the reader, though it is clear that Dewey thinks this is an important consideration. (Dewey, of course, addresses this elsewhere—for example, in *Art as Experience*.)

Art as Experience (1934)

More helpful to the issue of enmeshment of refined and immediate experience is *Art as Experience*. Here, Dewey expands on claims first made in *Experience and Nature* and "Qualitative Thought" concerning the role of refined experience as regards situations. While, in my opinion, Dewey doesn't solve the issue of their engagement once and for all, he comes closest here.[7] Dewey turns to the qualitative features of an experience in chapter 3: Having an Experience. The continuity of experience—of experiencing continuously—is stressed (LW 10, 42). An (individual) experience is distinguished in this continuity of experiencing and its features isolated. As with the discussion in *How We Think*, second edition (LW 8, 228), the feature of wholeness, of unity or completeness, is foregrounded in this individual experience (LW 10, 42–43). The consummatory nature of an experience is tied to its completion; its unity (LW 10, 42–43). *In* an experience, qualitative features "flow freely" (LW 10, 43). There are no "holes or mechanical junctions, and dead centres when we have an experience. There are pauses, places of rest, but they punctuate and define the quality of movement. They sum up what has been undergone and prevent its dissipation and idle evaporation" (LW 10, 43). Continuity within the experience is highlighted, and breaks, irruptions, periods of rest, are all said to coalesce to form this continuity. This continuity, as unity or whole, is "the single quality that pervades the entire experience in spite of the variation of its constituent parts" (LW 10, 44).[8]

The experience of thinking, as refined experience (e.g., LW 1, 15), is experience nonetheless. Thus, it has its constituent parts, as well as its whole, its unity, its continuity. It has, therefore, its own aesthetic quality (LW 10, 45). "In short, esthetic cannot be sharply marked off from intellectual experience since the latter must bear an esthetic stamp to be itself complete" (LW 10, 45). What seems to be the key qualitative trait common to both esthetic (consummatory) experience and refined or intellectual experience is continuity, manifest here as completeness, unity. This completeness *is* its continuity. A similar argument to this was articulated by Dewey in *Experience and Nature* (e.g., LW 1, 16; 269).[9] But here, the phenomenological stress on the felt need as "sensed" is even more evident. The felt need for closure (continuity; completeness, unity) is foregrounded (LW 10, 47–48). Dewey characterizes this felt need as emotion (LW 10, 48).

Continuity, completeness, and unity running together thus characterize all experiences, inclusive of intellectual and consummatory, and are characterized as a felt need, as a state, as emotion. To these, Dewey will add "our constant sense of things as belonging or not belonging, of relevancy, a sense which is immediate" (LW 10, 198). These traits, existential *and* intellectual, are felt. Dewey carries this account into his discussion of seriality, spatiality, and temporality in chapter 9: The Common Substance of the Arts. The context is the substance of the arts—the material and matter for the artist. For the artist, space and time are acutely felt and not merely perceived (LW 10, 210). In the direct (immediate) experience of the artist, movement is experienced as qualitative change (LW 10, 211).[10] "Movement in direct experience is alteration in the qualities of objects, and space as experienced is an aspect of this qualitative change. Up and down, back and front, to and fro, this side and that—or right and left—here and there, feel differently. The reason they do is that they are not static points in something itself static, but are objects in movement, qualitative changes of value" (LW 10, 211). Dewey is struggling to articulate the engagement of primary and secondary, immediate and refined experience here; there is a qualitative change in the objects immediately had (alteration), which is felt, though not (yet) cognized. As with space, so with time: up and down, back and forth, exploit the temporal dimension of this felt sensing. They are experienced as "actions and reaction," as "the very stuff out of which the objects and events we experience are made" (LW 10, 211). In immediate experiencing, time and space are first qualitative features.

Digging even deeper, Dewey finds that the qualitative features of time and space are "infinitely diversified" (LW 10, 212). We can't reduce the infinite diversification of forms to kinds or classes, but we can exemplify them according to "themes" (LW 10, 212). The themes for space are "Room, Extent, Position—Spatiousness, Spatiality, Spacing," and in terms of time, "transition, endurance and date" (LW 10, 212). This includes and incorporates "occupancy, filling," shrinking, rising and falling, position and extension (LW 10, 213). We first grasp these as immediate qualities of the experience and, in due measure, refine these in an experience that logically and objectively settles them. What we grasp of these is their relationships, as qualities, to each other. These relationships, Dewey says, are "reciprocal" (LW 10, 216–17). We may have now a rising, then a falling; or now a filling, then an emptying. As these qualitative features are never static (they are constantly changing), we are able to map their changes and locate spatio-temporally their rises and falls; their filling and emptying.[11] It is this qualitative to-and-fro, Dewey claims, that becomes the material for refined experience. But, and this is key to Dewey's argument through this section, they are first qualitative traits of an experience had and undergone. Spatiality and temporality are the "constant quality" (a constancy in dynamic tension) of the existence of things, as regards their behavior (LW 10, 214).

Here we have Dewey pressing his claim in *Experience and Nature* and elsewhere; there is a qualitative feature operative in immediate experiencing to which we may affix the label "temporal" (e.g., LW 1, 92) in contrast to the temporal series he discusses as a feature of logical investigation or inquiry. It manifests as a constituent part of the qualitative features of an experience; it is felt and is therefore properly emotional. It is a feature resulting from the to-and-fro of doing and undergoing; acting and reacting. It doubtless plays a role in the unity, completeness, and continuity of experiencing, not least through making this quality evident.

And of course, it is the trait that is alighted on in serial ordering—the business of refined experience.[12] Dewey tells us that *what* we pick up on *when* we examine this qualitative to-and-fro of temporality *is* this reciprocity in relationship. And this is a perceptual matter, involving the perceptual apparatus of the human organism. What Dewey doesn't tell us here (and in my opinion, never adequately tells us) is how refined experience converts qualitative features immediately had and felt into serial orderings of events that are then able to be construed as causal relations. *That* a conversion takes place is doubtless articulated. But precisely how it takes place requires a (further) metaphysical account of the nature of the (refined) traits of experience that Dewey, with his customary account of impulse, desire, habit-formation, and inquiry appealed to in such instances, is loath to provide.[13] I return to Dewey's understanding and use of the term "situation" in the final section of this chapter; the pattern of inquiry.

The Matrices of Inquiry: Habit, Language, Culture

By 1933, Dewey's account of habit was solid. It received its fullest expression to date in *Human Nature and Conduct* (1922) and remained more or less intact from that point forward. Dewey's account in *Human Nature and Conduct* was more or less adopted in subsequent texts such as *Experience and Nature* and *The Quest for Certainty*, and, in terms of the contribution of habit to logical theory, the years 1933–1937 did little. In contrast to logical theory, in these years Dewey's account of the habit of intelligence played a more important role in terms of education and particularly political theory. There is, however, one area in logical theory in which habit took on a novel direction—at least from the perspective of Dewey's earlier consideration as regards thinking. This area is the role of habit to freedom, and the text is *How We Think*, second edition. Beyond this, *How We Think*, second edition, is notable for its chapter on the role language plays in thought; a role involving both habit and culture, and presaging Dewey's later claims in chapters 3 and 13 of his 1938 *Logic*.

How We Think, Second Edition (1933)

In the first edition of *How We Think* (1910), Dewey aligns freedom with the systematic aims and methods of inquiry, and the need for passing from facts to meanings in a continuity built up through "the dynamic ties that hold things together" (MW 6, 285). The context is only marginally that of the individual inquirer. In the second edition of *How We Think*, the context shifts to the individual. None of this material is new; Dewey borrows heavily from his earlier accounts of habit in *Democracy and Education* (1916) and *Human Nature and Conduct*, and the vast majority of the claims made here are wholly reminiscent of claims made in these earlier works. However, Dewey places his account of habit and freedom squarely in the middle of a discussion regarding thinking and the individual, and this is (in contrast to the first edition) novel. The specific issue is that of character, and the tension is between discipline on the one hand and freedom on the other. Dewey equates freedom with "the independence of external tutelage," and with "spontaneity" and "naturalness" (LW 8, 183–84). Freedom to pursue activities of reflection regarding the impediments of external activities requires personal reflection (LW 8, 184). And this in turn requires habits of thought that have their origins in early childhood: these are positive habits, in that they emphasize the traits of "carefulness, thoroughness, and continuity" (LW 8, 186). This wouldn't be of much note if not for Dewey's insistence in chapter 2 of the 1938 *Logic* (The Existential Matrix of Inquiry: Biological) that freedom is a key ingredient in the formation of the inquirer and is part and parcel of the inquirer's "natural continuity," and inhibition of this continuity through overapplication of external tutelage is to be discouraged (LW 12, 38).

In chapter 16 of *How We Think*, second edition, titled Language and the Training of Thought, Dewey adopts what might be considered a carrier theory of language: language is neither coeval with thought itself, nor a mere outer dress, but rather the material symbolization of meaning (LW 8, 301–2). That thought is itself non-material, yet requires a material carrier in the guise of symbols, is Dewey's characterization of the relationship of thought to language here. "Without meaning, things are nothing but blind stimuli, brute things or chance sources of pleasure and pain; and since meanings are not themselves tangible things, they must be anchored by attachment to some physical existence. Existences that are especially set aside to fixate and convey meanings are *symbols*" (LW 8, 302). Symbols are "inventions;" they are not natural forms. A symbol is rather an "artificial tool and utensil" for "the purpose of conveying meaning" (LW 8, 302).

It is clear that Dewey's earlier account of language in *Experience and Nature* (LW 1, 144–47) together with G. H. Mead's work on symbol-formation influenced Dewey profoundly as regards his account of symbols. For gestures, sounds, and other "physical existences" are the material upon which these signs are constructed (LW 8, 302).[14] Symbols are "particular, physical, sensible existences" (LW 8, 306).[15] They are symbols only in consideration of what they represent; and what they represent are meanings (LW 8, 306). Meanings allow us to move from the material and physical to the intellectual plane (LW 8, 304); and as a result, we are able to do linguistic commerce with symbols far more expediently than with material objects. "Speech forms" are the greatest carriers of these meanings (LW 8, 305). Sentences and propositions, as complex signs, are groupings of meanings. They allow us to classify, to define, to organize; they allow for inferences (LW 8, 305). Of course, the danger of nominalism lurks here. For, if we forget that naming and meaning are functionally distinct activities, we will be led to claim that the name consists of all the necessary and sufficient conditions of the meaning carried on the sign-object, or symbol. Dewey notes this danger as regards the education of children; if we forget the functional distinction between naming and meanings, we will teach that meanings reside in the names of things instead of isolating the meanings from names in the overall project of inquiry by getting at the practical consequences or bearings of naming (LW 8, 308–9). We see Dewey return to this concern in the 1938 *Logic*, especially in chapter 3, The Existential Matrix of Inquiry: Cultural, in his discussion of the role of sign, symbol, and meaning (LW 12, 57–59) and again, in chapter 13, The Continuum of Judgement: General Propositions (LW 12, 261–62).

Science and Social Inquiry

Freedom and authority as regards the use of intelligence were important considerations for Dewey in these years, and ranged beyond issues of habit and character; several papers and sections of books were written that concerned freedom and the role of political authority therein.[16] At least three of these dealt with science as an authority in matters pertaining to individual and social freedom, and these represented an extension of Dewey's arguments regarding the method of intelligence first presented in *The Public and Its Problems* (1927). There, Dewey drew on the baleful distinction between pure and applied science as a call for a unified method of intelligence or public inquiry, which would be a central tool in overcoming social problems (LW 2, 342–45). Here, the focus shifts somewhat to the topic of authority, the loss of authority of the method of intelligence, and the rise in its place of the authority of technologies in the interest of private individuals and corporations alike.[17] These three selections include *Art as Experience*, "Authority and Social Change," and Dewey's review of Bertrand Russell's *Religion and Science*.

Art as Experience (1934)

In the struggle between "our historic heritage" and the "structure of physical nature that is now disclosed by science," science has the difficulty of not yet being "naturalized in experience" (LW 10, 340–41). "It will be a long time," Dewey says, "before it so sinks into the subsoil of mind as to become an integral part of corporate belief and attitude" (LW 10, 341). Until then, science will exercise a "more or less disintegrating impact upon beliefs, and by equally external practical application" (LW 10, 341). Though we now see "a liberation of the spirit" by science; for it has stimulated "curiosity" and "alertness of observation" (LW 10, 342), we cannot think that the most "troublesome" aspects of science as we now encounter them are harbingers of the future; we can only judge correctly when "the experimental attitude is thoroughly naturalized" (LW 10, 342).[18] Returning to the past wholesale is out of the question (LW 10, 343).

This description concerning the unfinished project of the acceptance of science as a naturalized attitude sets Dewey up for perhaps his most fulsome claims about the necessity of art and the freeing of labor under the guise of intelligent method (LW 10, 344–46). So with the naturalization of the attitude of science, so with the naturalization of the attitude of (modern) art: people require training to recognize the modern arts of civilization: machinery, railway cars, steel and copper, together with the other examples Dewey uses (LW 10, 344). This training includes perception; how and what to take as aesthetic.[19] "I mean that the habits of the eye as a medium of perception are being slowly altered in being accustomed to the shapes that are typical of industrial products and to the objects that belong to urban as distinct from rural life" (LW 10, 345). The "radical social alteration" (LW 10, 345), which Dewey recommends for the participation of the worker in her means of production, is a modification of the nature of her experience in the name of freedom of imagination and personal interest (LW 10, 346). We see this theme emerging in the pages of the 1938 *Logic*, especially chapter 24, Social Inquiry (LW 12, 483–84).[20]

Authority and Social Change (1936)[21]

Dewey carries forward the theme of freedom and the role played by the method of intelligence in his address to the Harvard Tercentenary Conference of Arts and Sciences of 1936. The authority in question is the authority of social forces, specifically institutional agencies such as churches and states attempting to limit the applications of science to new technologies and new means of production (LW 11, 134–35). The individualism that developed on the part of those struggling against these limitations emphasized personal gain as the supreme authority over social life, with the result that an economic form of concentrated power prevailed (LW 11, 136). Contemporary society is in thrall to this concentrated power, and Dewey thinks the best hope for extricating ourselves from this undesirable situation is intelligent method (LW 11, 141). Unlike the authority invested in laissez-faire individualism and the concentration of power resting in the hands of monopoly capitalists, science "has made its way by releasing, not by suppressing, the elements of variation, of invention and innovation, of novel creation in individuals" (LW 11, 142).

Dewey then returns to a theme developed at some length in *The Public and Its Problems*. Whereas science, too, relies on the "free initiative, invention and enterprise of individual inquirers, the authority of science issues from and is based upon collective activity, cooperatively organized" (LW 11, 142). The method used "is a public and open method which succeeds only as it tends to produce agreement, unity of belief among all who labored in the same field . . . The contribution the scientific inquirer makes is collectively tested and developed and, in the measure that it is cooperatively confirmed, becomes a part of the common fund of the intellectual commonwealth" (LW 11, 142). The freedom of the scientist is one "supported by collective, organic authority and in turns changes and is encouraged to change and develop, by its own operations, the authority upon which it depends" (LW 11, 143). Dewey of course calls for a broadening of the method of intelligence; a broadening of the method of cooperative intelligence as "a working model of the union of freedom and authority" (LW 11, 143). This broadening is to be found in various sections of the 1938 *Logic*, especially chapter 1 (LW 12, 28).

Religion, Science, and Philosophy: Review of Bertrand Russell's *Religion and Science* (1936)

Dewey keenly followed Russell's work through the 1920s and 1930s. While the debate over Dewey's *Essays in Experimental Logic* cooled in the years following World War I, Dewey didn't stop reading Russell, and he didn't stop noting Russell's reliance on a faulty sense-psychology.[22] Dewey also reviewed Russell's popular works. For example, Dewey wrote a lengthy review of Russell's *Religion and Science* for the *Southern Review* in 1936.[23] In Dewey's estimation, Russell characterized the debate over science and religion as one in which "opposing conceptions of the authority by which beliefs are to be formed and regulated" are at the heart of the conflict (LW 11, 454). As authority and closely allied issues were those Dewey himself was grappling with at the time, he brought out concerns regarding the conflict of authority in matters of religion and science and the role of freedom therein, in particular direct language.

The question is, given the need for authority as a constant one, can and does "scientific method provide the authority that earlier centuries sought in fixed dogmas"? (LW 11, 455).[24] Earlier seats of authority were external to individuals, and placed outside of and beyond the "inquiries of intelligence" (LW 11, 455). Russell argues that governmental institutions are replacing the older religious institutions as seats of authority and repeating their (earlier) errors.[25] Dewey also asks over the cause of this novel state of affairs, this new turn to political authoritarianism in which "faith in the method of free experimental inquiry" is being supplanted by "the recrudescence of dogmatic authorities, backed by physical force?" (LW 11, 456). Dewey offers us two alternatives with which to view this situation: either the method of intelligence is doomed because it cannot challenge human habits, impulses, desires, and appetites; or there are "special causes" for the contemporary decline in the authority of science (LW 11, 456).

Russell distinguishes between the attitudes and tempers that coalesce to form science and the various technical methods that are involved in the application of science to daily life. Dewey endorses these and (with Russell) claims that, while the various methods of science have had almost exponential gain, scientific attitudes and tempers have not. Getting into the habit of thinking experimentally has not yet made its mark on the public. The upshot has been to restrict science to gains in special fields ("industry and commerce") and to a relatively small group of working scientists (LW 11, 457–58). Science remains fundamentally a laboratory science and not a general method composed of the attitudes and tempers of curiosity, experimentation, judgment, and evaluation (LW 11, 458).[26] The control of science, as technical methods involved in the application of industry and commerce to daily life, is for Russell "the modern danger of chaos and anarchy," for it threatens to authorize the commission of economic and political changes in the guise of an old, dogmatic authority, and not that of the method of intelligence. Russell, of course, bemoaned this. Dewey agreed with much of Russell's characterization of the social and economic events leading to the control of science. Yet Dewey found Russell's reliance on an older, British sense-psychology for his theory of sense-perception to weaken and perhaps undo his claim for the sort of intellectual community needed to thwart this authority. For Russell's reliance on the essentially private nature of experience inhibits the very sharing of experiences necessary for a community of inquirers, and this leads to searches for external authorization of thought and force (LW 11, 462). With the method of intelligence as a matter of the community, techniques for dealing with human problems could be sufficiently developed from among what Dewey calls "cooperative voluntary responses" (LW 11, 463). But this can only happen when the community of inquirers as a whole takes charge of the authority. Chapter 24 of Dewey's 1938 *Logic* (LW 12, 483–84) again stresses this point.

Forms and Propositions in Logical Inquiry

While the themes of experience, the matrices of inquiry, and the role of science to common sense were more or less filled out by the early 1930s, the issues involved in articulating a theory of logical forms and their propositions, judgments, and conceptions remained to dog Dewey until 1938 and, for a number of his critics, long thereafter.[27] In the period from 1916 to 1932, Dewey did make significant gains in his definitions, descriptions, and operations of these; but from the perspective of the 1938 *Logic*, there was still much to do. As I discuss at the end of chapter 3, Dewey still hadn't worked out the precise relationship between existential (generic) propositions and universal conceptions. The three essays written in 1936 ("Characteristics and Characters: Kinds and Classes"; "What are Universals?"; "General Propositions, Kinds, and Classes") for the *Journal of Philosophy* are remarkable for doing just this. Dewey downplays the term "existential proposition" in these articles, reserving it for special uses, and considers the term "generic" as having the proper significance for his theory of kinds and classes. The downplaying of "existential proposition" is presaged in his correspondence, particularly with Sidney Hook, in the years 1934–1935.[28]

I begin with the correspondence. From 1934 we have Dewey's earliest outline of a project that leads forward to the 1938 *Logic*. While the 1938 *Logic* has its intellectual genesis as early as 1925, there isn't an extant tangible outline produced until 1934. In fact, though, much of what concerned Dewey in this correspondence was not filling in his outline (though this obviously remained important), but rather the relationship of generic propositions to universal conceptions. It is easy to conclude that Dewey's correspondence from 1934 to 1935 served in the capacity of grounding the three essays to come in the *Journal of Philosophy*. What will particularly interest us are the gains made in the logical forms from the time of the 1927–1928 Types of Logical Theory to these three essays; what is taken up and incorporated into these will further concern us as we move toward the 1938 *Logic*.

The three essays are themselves emblematic of Dewey's shift from the terminology of existential to generic propositions (with existential propositions a term reserved for certain special kinds of generic propositions), inclusive of a fuller definition of generic, together with its extensional and intensional properties. Yet this is not all Dewey accomplished during these eventful years. Dewey's theory of causality, hinted at as early as 1916 in his paper "The Pragmatism of Peirce," and amplified to effect in *Experience and Nature*, is more fully expanded on in the correspondence, as well as in his paper "Peirce's Theory of Meaning," and the two reviews of Peirce's *Collected Papers*. In light of chapters 12 and 24 of his 1938 *Logic*, I believe we can conclude that Dewey had most if not all of the pieces of the puzzle in place for his claim that the qualitative elements that are operative in events/situations are causal in the sense that Peirce understands causality; as a semiotic or sign relationship of hypothetical necessity (though not sufficiency) between what is actual (Second) and what is lawful (Third).[29] An examination of Dewey's account of narration/description, serial ordering, and role of scientific method in regard to the causal chain is of key importance to us as we reconstruct Dewey's accounting of causality leading up to the 1938 *Logic*.³⁰

I begin with a discussion of the role played by generic propositions and universals in the correspondence. Several items are important in this regard, most importantly Dewey's refinement of generic propositions. After this discussion, I turn to the three essays composed for *The Journal of Philosophy*, published in 1936. These more or less complete Dewey's account of generic propositions and add greatly to his ongoing account of universal conceptions. I discuss these developments in regard to Dewey's statements in chapters 13 and 14 of the 1938 *Logic*. Also important, however, is the developing theory of causality and its role in the leading physical science of the day. I turn to Dewey's theory of causality and examine Dewey's article on "Peirce's Theory of Quality" (1935) and the reviews of Peirce's Collected Papers, volume 5 and volumes 1 through 6, written in 1935 and 1937, respectively. I discuss this theory in regard to claims Dewey makes for causality in chapter 12 and chapter 23 of the 1938 *Logic*.

Finally, I discuss the pattern of inquiry that forms perhaps the most quoted chapter from the 1938 *Logic*: chapter 6. The second edition of *How We Think* plays a large role in the development of Dewey's account of the pattern of inquiry. I examine the role that this text plays as regards chapter 8 through a comparison of Dewey's first edition of *How We Think* with the conclusive statement regarding inquiry in the 1938 *Logic* (LW 12, 108). Along the way, I try to dispel some of the criticisms that have accumulated regarding Dewey's patterning of inquiry: criticisms that infect some of the best scholarship on Dewey's logical theory.

Generic Propositions and Universals

Two issues in particular vexed Dewey during and after writing the 1938 *Logic*; the first concerned the pattern of inquiry and, specifically, the role that the evaluative conclusion of inquiry (as a settlement of an unsettled or indeterminate situation) meant in terms of the settled understandings of truth and reality in the history of philosophy.³¹ (I discuss this in a further section.) The other was the role of propositions as regards universals. This second issue, as we shall see, preoccupied Dewey in his correspondence with Ratner and Hook. It also became a bone of contention for Dewey's critics in the immediate period of the 1938 *Logic* and afterward. There are also a number of otherwise sympathetic interpreters, most notably Ernest Nagel, who believed Dewey never adequately solved the question of the distinction of propositions and conceptions, especially for judgments of quantity (All-some).[32] We will see how far Dewey progressed in hopes of a solution during the years 1933–1937.

Dewey's Correspondence

Although Dewey announced his intention to write a new treatise on logical theory as early as 1925, the first fruits of an outline for such a treatise don't emerge until 1934.[33] At this time, Dewey claimed he was working steadily, and, with *Art as Experience* behind him, was free to pursue the logic (Dewey to Joseph Ratner, December 7, 1934, 07361). In a letter to Sidney Hook dated November 22, 1934, Dewey enclosed an outline of what would become the 1938 *Logic* (see Appendix 1).[34] I discuss relevant features of the outline through a comparison with the table of contents of his completed 1938 *Logic*.[35] As with the 1938 *Logic*, the matrices of inquiry—biological and cultural—are toward the beginning and form sections two and three of the introduction. Dewey titles the second working part of the proposed manuscript The Operation of Inquiry, beginning with a section on the pattern of inquiry (corresponding to chapter 6 of the 1938 *Logic*). Included within The Operation of Inquiry are sections on the structure of judgments (corresponding to chapter 7 of the 1938 *Logic*); what Dewey calls "appreciate and directive" forms of judgment (content to be found in chapter 9 of the 1938 *Logic* under the title Judgments of Practice: Evaluation); judgments of assertion-affirmation and of negation (corresponding to material in chapter 10 of the 1938 *Logic*); judgments of quantity (corresponding to chapter 11 of the 1938 *Logic*); judgments of narration and description, temporal and spatial (corresponding to chapter 12 of the 1938 *Logic*); and systematic judgments in the context of "common sense," including disjunctive and hypothetical judgments (spread throughout various chapters of the 1938 *Logic*, but especially chapter 9).

The third working part of the manuscript is titled Technique of Control—Scientific Judgment Inquiry, and includes sections on induction and deduction (corresponding to chapter 21 of the 1938 *Logic*); a section on the theory of forms (corresponding to chapters 13, 14, the entirety of part 3, and chapter 19 of the 1938 *Logic*); a section on propositions and terms (corresponding to chapter 18 of the 1938 *Logic*); a section on the relational propositions (Dewey has in parenthesis "mathematics [?])" (corresponding to chapters 16 and 20 of the 1938 *Logic*); and a section on the logic of social inquiry (corresponding to chapter 24 of the 1938 *Logic*). In the final working part of the outline, titled Logic and Philosophy, Dewey includes sections on logic and epistemology (corresponding to chapters 22 and 26 of the 1938 *Logic*) and idealistic and realistic logics (corresponding to chapter 26 of the 1938 *Logic*). Following this, Dewey suggests the realm of possibilities (Dewey has in parentheses "metaphysics of Essence-subsistence"), which likely corresponds to Dewey's discussion of possibilities and potentialities (chapter 20, 396–401); and a section for a general conclusion.

Several conclusions can be drawn regarding Dewey's outline. First, Dewey had many if not most of the topics for a novel treatise in logical theory already in mind by late 1934. And by tracing Dewey's logical development up to and including 1934, we know from his analysis of reflective thinking in *How We Think*, second edition, that Dewey had reasonably settled accounts of the following: the general pattern of inquiry and various functional kinds of judgments, including affirmation and negation, narration-description; quantity; appreciative-directive (evaluation);[36] an almost complete account of induction and deduction; a theory of the matrices (existential-biological and existential-cultural); and from his presentation of the 1927–1928 Types of Logical Theory lectures and *The Quest for Certainty*, a theory of abstract relations (mathematics). Of course, Dewey had long had an account of the relationship of logical theory to epistemology and metaphysics, built up from *Essays in Experimental Logic* through to *Experience and Nature* and *The Quest for Certainty*. By 1934, Dewey evidently felt the need to stress the relationships among propositions and judgments and propositions and universals. This led Dewey to stress a *theory* of forms—a theory ostensibly for the discrimination of logical forms and propositions according to function.[37] It is the relationships among propositions and propositions, and propositions and universals, that occupies us as we examine the rest of the correspondence from 1933 to 1937.

Dewey's correspondence with Joseph and Sydney Ratner and Sidney Hook was to bear fruit for the ongoing development of Dewey's account of propositions. Dewey's correspondence regarding Joseph Ratner's writings on physical science in particular gave him the opportunity to engage his own thinking on matters of propositions.[38] We find Dewey discussing the propositions common to objects of science in a letter dated January 18, 1935, to Ratner:

> I do not see how we can ever recover past things—say before man appeared—in their immediacy and yet it seems to me they must have such immediacy or there would have been no individualizations. This is, I imagine, what is back of my insistence upon the intermediate character of objects <u>as such</u>. They are not <u>un</u>real, because their subject-matter content consists of relations among things that actually exist. But they are never the whole of any actually existing thing . . . Does an atom, Or electron or photon <u>exist</u> except as a nodal point in a complex interaction? Yet a mathematical proposition in which these things figure <u>must</u> cut if [sic] off and out." (Dewey to Ratner, January 18, 1935, 06965)[39]

Statements as these point to Dewey's antinominalist bent as regards relations inhering between (scientific) objects: they are *real* (existential) relations that propositions map, but do not completely inhabit.[40] Propositions express by way of symbols these real relations, and these are in turn necessary for mathematical relations (Dewey to Ratner, January 18, 1935, 06965). But the "matter" of propositions does the work of indicating "the operations by which actual and transitive qpplication [sic] to determination of actual existence may be effected" (Dewey to Ratner, January 18, 1935, 06965). That is to say, it is matter and form together that do the indicating. Whereas symbols express the "real relations" that are in turn required for abstract and/or mathematical relations, the "matter" of the symbol—the matter of the proposition—points to the actual operations needed to be undertaken to create a change in the phenomenon. And this change in phenomenon is existential, not (merely) symbolic.[41] The upshot is Dewey's insistence on the inextricable matter-form relationship of the proposition and the role, particularly of the matter, as regards existence. I return to this topic in the discussion of situations in the section concerning the pattern of inquiry at the end of this chapter.

The issue of propositions in syllogistic form is also raised in Dewey's correspondence with Ratner. In the 1927–1928 Types of Logical Theory lectures, Dewey admonished Mill for taking major *and* minor premises as existential, rather than the major premise as general and the minor premise as existential (singular) (TLT, December 12, 1927). Even if the major premise of a syllogism was once an existential proposition (e.g., "This flower is red"), in a major premise of a syllogism, the form propositions take is "All-some." Furthermore, this form entails *hypothetical*, not categorical necessity. In commenting on Ratner's manuscript, Dewey raises a similar objection.[42] "Since the qualitative thing is enjoyed or suffered—while the object is the <u>material understood</u>, the former is individual, the latter general. The individual (uniquely qualitative) <u>becomes</u> particular when certain analyzed features are treated as clue, sign, evidence—but not yet fully defined—We are not content just to enjoy or suffer as is—The general generic become universal in formula (freed from <u>specific</u> reference & available for any reference, not yet specified)" (Dewey to Ratner, May 01, 1935, 06971). Let us see how this is the case. Suppose we recur to the example of Socrates:

> All men are mortal
> Socrates is a man
> Socrates is Mortal

Mill (and apparently Ratner) takes both the major and minor premises (All men are mortal; Socrates is a man) to be existential. An existential proposition is a proposition of activity; doing, suffering, undergoing, having, and making. For Dewey, Mill mischaracterizes the major premise, which is a conception—a general class or kind. Individuals (Socrates) are particulars, but set in a class, the particular is a species of a genus, and that genus is a kind or class that is general. Particulars must be raised to generals, and in so doing, become logical objects—the objects that Dewey characterizes as "universal in formula."[43] Particulars and generals are not fixed forms, existing outside of and apart from the syllogism in which they operate; they are functions of operating syllogistically. A particular will become a general insofar as it is raised to the operation of major premise ("All-some") in representing its kind or class.[44] Dewey will recur to this characterization of the syllogism in his criticism of Mill in chapter 16 of the 1938 *Logic*, esp. 322–26.

In the spring of 1935, Dewey sent at least six working chapters (chapters I–VI) of his manuscript on logic to Ratner for comment. Ratner responded positively (Ratner to Dewey, May 30, 1935, 06973). In the meantime, Dewey wrote to Ratner (June 1, 1935, 06974) with these revealing comments: "Propositions are timeless—subject & predicate are interchangeable i.e., there is <u>no</u> subject, strictly speaking . . . Propositions have implicatory relationships—judgments inferential—Only (in the degree) when propositions have a number-measure content are the implicatory relations (indirectly) controlled by inferential relations . . ."

(Dewey to Ratner, June 1, 1935, 06974). Let us take the example of the syllogism in examining the force of this claim. The major premise "All men are mortal" is a proposition with a number-measure content. Therefore, it is controlled by an inferential relation. It properly belongs to the universal conception, not the proposition. Whereas "Socrates is a man" is not (by itself) inferential; only when used in an inferential context (such as a syllogism) does it take on inferential attributes. And in the context of inference, its role is implicatory; that is, it implicates itself in the operations of inference. Dewey's "unwritten rule" that existential propositions refer to singulars (This is of X), whereas generic propositions refer across the kind (All of X are of this kind), and universal conceptions refer to the feature or characteristic held by the kind (All X's have feature or characteristic Y), articulated first (and very briefly) in the 1927–1928 Types of Logical Theory lectures, is returned to here.[45] Dewey will recur to this again, in the *Journal of Philosophy* articles of 1936 and in the 1938 *Logic* at chapter 14, Generic and Universal Propositions, 266–69, and elsewhere.[46]

This discussion with Ratner would continue in two letters dated June 6, 1935. In the first letter, Dewey mildly admonishes Ratner for his inconsistency in his use thus far of the terms connection and relation. Connection is a term Dewey proposes to use for "existential ties" and "relation" for "formal (meanings) & "reference" for the contextually indicated reference to an existential situation, direct in judg [sic]. Indirect in props [sic]" (Dewey to Ratner, June 6, 1935, 07023). And in a separate letter of the same date, Dewey tells Ratner that "Particulars are whatever within the situation are treated as <u>signs</u>—potential material, data—<u>reduced</u> from their inherent existential status to intellectual cues or clues," whereas "The plan, methods of substitution, the code & key, is the universal—The solution is the requalified universal" (Dewey to Ratner, June 6, 1935, 07402). If we think again of the syllogism, the singular (This is of X) incorporates the sense of connection, and singulars are those signs (along with the particular propositions—X is doing or behaving Y) that index the existential material, phenomenon, or datum. Whereas relation incorporates the sense of formal meanings and reference (universal), and covers the formal operation of the syllogism proper, with the conclusion of the syllogism the requalified universal. This understanding of connection and reference would find its fullest treatment in chapter 9 of the 1938 *Logic*, esp. 174–75.

Finally, in the letters of late 1935 to Ratner and Hook, Dewey clearly emphasized the characteristic of generic propositions as existential in the role of the minor premise in a syllogism (Dewey to Ratner, August 4, 1935, 06978). This characteristic is carried forward in a letter of August 23 to Hook (Dewey to Hook, August 23, 1935, 05772). Mill is, as usual, the backdrop to the discussion of propositions here. Dewey signals the distinction between universal propositions as referring to "the relation of classes to each other," while "existential distinctions" "demarcate individuals as instances of a kind" (Dewey to Hook, August 23, 1935, 05772). Finally, Dewey makes it clear that universals are rules or principles for the ordering of kinds. Dewey says,

> The symbolic statement of the principles of identity, contradiction, excluded middle, associa[t]ivity, commutavity, etc, are propositional functions. They conform to the analysis of the latter just made, in that they state conditions to be satisfied in reasoning if the latter is to be rigorous-productive. They do not set forth characters properties of any exist specie actual propositions either in itself themselves or in theirits [sic] implicatory relations. They state what these propositions should be if any propositional arrangement is to be rigorous-productive. (Dewey to Hook, August 23, 1935, 05772)

Each of these characteristics finds its way into Dewey's 1936 *Journal of Philosophy* articles, as we shall soon see.

By mid-1937, Dewey had more material available (including the material produced for the *Journal of Philosophy* articles) for his 1938 *Logic*. In a letter to Sidney Hook dated June 7, 1937, Dewey claimed he had material for his chapters 8 and 9 outline (chapters 13 and 14 in the published 1938 *Logic*). The content would consist of the following divisions:

1. particular Singual [sic] Demoncrative [sic] particular propositions, This is hard, red etc.

2. Singular propositions. This is one of a kind. This is iron, water, whatever (miscalled class membership in recent texts

3. Relations of kinds. Iron is a metal:-involving disjunctive divisions, which however Ill [sic] take up later in detail.

4. Exisstential hypotheticals—contingent. If he makse s [sic] such and such a move at chess, Ill [sic] make such-and such, etc.

5. Universal hypotheticals, if-then propositions where antecedent and consequent are taken to have a necessary relation to each other. Propositions of a relation of abstract characters, "category" definitions of a category (Dewey to Hook, June 7, 1937, 05796).

The first three divisions make sense, given Dewey's articulation of propositions thus far. The fourth is a surprise: for if-then propositions have been characterized thus far by Dewey as hypothetical and universal. Yet this is an *existential* hypothetical.[47] The only argument that can satisfy Dewey's criteria for this hypothetical must be: a singular of this kind (e.g., chess move X) demands a singular of a similar or the same kind (e.g., chess move Y), as opposed to a universal hypothetical, in which a total range of qualities of a kind (the totality or essence of the kind) demands the total range of another kind (the totality or essence of that kind) for the proposition to function. I believe Dewey's claims regarding the essential features of universals in the *Journal of Philosophy* articles will help us see the importance of this distinction, and it is to these we now turn.

The *Journal of Philosophy* articles

Contemporaneous with Dewey's correspondence to Joseph Ratner and Sidney Hook is the publication of the three *Journal of Philosophy* articles, beginning with "Characteristics and Characters: Kinds and Classes" in May 1936. In the same volume was Dewey's follow-up to "Characteristics and Characters" titled "What are Universals?" In the following issue of December 1936, Dewey published "General Propositions, Kinds, and Classes." These three articles are tremendously important for Dewey's late account of logical forms and propositions and, taken together, form the penultimate account of what would be finalized in the 1938 *Logic* as the (functional) logical distinction between generic propositions and universal conceptions. Indeed, they have been remarked upon as such.[48] With these articles, we see Dewey's logical distinction between particulars, singulars, generic, and universal solidify in preparation for the full accounting in the

1938 *Logic*, especially chapters 13 and 14, The Continuum of Judgment: General Propositions, and Generic and Universal Propositions.

By 1935 Dewey has a nascent though not as-yet fully self-conscious taxonomy of propositions, together with functional definitions. Much of this is begun in the 1927–1928 Types of Logical Theory lectures, though not articulated in detail. The self-conscious articulation begins in Dewey's correspondence of the mid-1930s and especially with the publication of the *Journal of Philosophy* articles in 1936. These articles constitute material that first emerged as drafts for Dewey's manuscript on logic.[49] At the time of writing the articles, Dewey's basic taxonomy of propositions and conceptions looked roughly like this:

Particular (existential) propositions as those resembling "X does activity or behavior Y"

Singular (existential) propositions as those resembling "This is of kind X"[50]

Generic propositions as those resembling "All W's are of kind X"

Universal conceptions as those resembling "All X's have Y's"

The supposition is that each of these plays a specific role in judgments. Propositions of particularity and singularity refer to the existential activity, quality, characteristic, feature or attribute, or to the suitability of a singular for consideration in a kind (e.g., "X has behavior Y"; "W is of kind X"). Generic propositions refer to the fit of all the representative singulars (These) in a kind. Thus, propositions of particularity, singularity, and generality refer to kinds. Universal conceptions, on the other hand, do not refer (directly) to kinds; they refer to the conclusion of a judgment (e.g., a syllogism) and are evaluative and consequent in their function. That is to say, they are universal in that they refer not to a, or even some specific kind, but as a rule for all specified kinds. The problem, as one readily sees, is the difficulty in discriminating between generic propositions and universal conceptions; for the context is what determines propositions of mere quantity, which are generic, and universal conceptions, which are inferential, evaluative, and abstract. In other words, in a syllogism in which the conclusion is "All X's have Y's," the operation (function) is inferential and the conclusion universal. Whereas as a single claim regarding the position of an object in relation to its kind, the function is not inferential and the claim generic. Dewey obviates some of this confusion with the claim (also present in the 1927–1928 Types of Logical Theory lectures) that universal conceptions are if-then conceptions, and can be placed in the logical form of hypotheticals, whereas generic propositions, owing to their strict relationship with the kind in question, cannot.[51] This is more fully articulated in the 1938 *Logic* than in Dewey's 1927–1928 lectures (e.g., LW 12, 303). Another way to pursue the point is to claim, with Dewey, that generic propositions, as they deal with kinds, concern the extensional characteristics of the concept; whereas universal conceptions, as they deal with inferential relationships in a judgment, concern the intensional characteristics of the concept. There is support for this reading in Dewey's correspondence (e.g., Dewey to Ratner, May 1, 1935, 06971).

The context of the article "Characteristics and Characters: Kinds and Classes" is the confusion in logical theory when terms such as "attribute" and "quality" are used interchangeably to refer *either* to existential matters *or* logical forms. Similarly, terms such as "when" are often run together with the hypothetical terms "if-then" (LW 11, 95). The problem is attributed chiefly to Mill and is discussed in passing in the 1927–1928 lectures (TLT, December 12, 1927). Distinguishing the uses of such terms requires delineating their contexts, and this in turn requires distinguishing the logical forms of universal propositions (Dewey will drop the term proposition, and talk only of the universal) from existential propositions. In existential propositions such as "blood is red," "red" is the characteristic or quality that allows us to distinguish the blood as blood (LW 11, 96). In contrast, in definitions of "blood" in which there is no invocation of a particular case of being blood, we have a proposition in which the features or characteristics are related (if blood, then red). We are meant to notice the difference between these two cases; the first makes reference to a particular case; the second makes reference to all cases.

The case of "All-some" is similarly problematic. Dewey gives us the example of "All men are mortal" (LW 11, 96). If it is to refer to "Every human being who has ever existed, now exists, or will exist in the future [and] has died or will die," it has existential import. On the other hand, "All men are mortal" can refer to the universal conception,

"*If* anything whatever is human, *then* that thing is mortal," and this clearly has no existential import; rather it is a universal attribution.[52] The upshot for universal conceptions is the relationship between "being" human and "being" mortal; in other words, the relationship between being and "being" (LW 11, 97). This is a function of definition: "For what it states is that what is *defined* as mortal is necessarily related to that which is *defined* as human" (LW 11, 97). A proposition in which what is defined is related to what else is defined is termed a universal proposition—a definition (LW 11, 97). Definitions are given in if-then form, and are non-existential (LW 11, 99).

It will do to give a better example than Dewey gives. Suppose we take the proposition "All squares have four 90 degree angles." This is an existential proposition, as it refers to (quantifiable) angles that can be isolated, pointed to, and measured. A universal might at first glance look similar to this existential proposition but, on further inspection, will show different characteristics. Take, for example, the universal, "Squares have quad-angularity." This is to be read as "the being of all squares is related to the being of their four angle-ness." The first proposition (All squares . . .) refers to the instance of existence; the second (Squares have . . .) refers to the essential feature(s) or characteristic(s) of something related to the essential feature(s) or characteristic(s) of something else. The role of "hypostatic abstraction" (e.g., LW 12, 462–63) looms large in the second example, for we are moving from existential qualities to qualities "of a different logical order"—the selection of a particular quality to be abstracted removes that quality entirely from its existential context (LW 11, 99).[53] Furthermore, the second proposition can be cashed out in a hypothetical or if-then claim.

We have two distinct logical forms: existential or generic propositions and universals. The first relates a particular case to a class or kind; the second relates an essential-because-abstract feature to another essential-because-abstract feature. The first claims things (what Dewey calls "characters") are such-and-such; the second claims a relationship between two or more essential features or "characters" (LW 11, 99). Dewey then turns to the problems inherent in defining. The foil is, once again, Mill. Take the case of whiteness. In Mill, Dewey claims, whiteness is arrived at inductively, and stands for all the similar features of particulars that are white. But this characterization fails because it neglects to distinguish between logical forms of existence and universality. For Dewey, whiteness is a definition; a definition of the conditions to be met for something to be white (LW 11, 99). If white can be validly affirmed (of any existence), then it will have the essential feature or characteristic common to all white things. Notice the change in logical form from a relation of quality or feature to kind to a relation between an essential feature and another essential feature. What these essential features are and do have their historical and psychological counterparts: this is certainly the case in physical science, where discoveries count as actual counterparts.[54] But they remain logical forms of a different order than their counterparts.

The upshot of this particular confusion in Mill and other thinkers (Dewey does not say who) is to miscategorize universal conceptions as existential ones, with the consequence of making scientifically derived concepts (Dewey uses the examples of weight and color, but we might add mass, force, work, energy, and innumerable other logical categories) into existences (LW 11, 101). When ordered syllogistically, Mill's characterizations evidence generic propositions in the role of the major premise, and the conclusions drawn have no proper universality because they do not start out with the requisite if-then universal conceptions. Syllogistically, if universals serve in the role of major premise, they must be of the if-then form; the existential or generic proposition then serves as the minor premise (Dewey maintains this as well in Dewey to Ratner, August 4, 1935, 06978 and in Dewey to Ratner, August 23, 1935, 05722). Unfortunately, logical theory generally has not done a good job of distinguishing generic, existential propositions from proper universals (if-then claims), and this has led to faulty characterization of universals. Dewey finds the problem rampant in biology (LW 11, 102) and urges that "class" be restricted to universals of the if-then type (LW 11, 103), whereas "kind" may stand for the inductively arrived at concept in generic propositions.[55]

Dewey follows on the argument made in "Characters and Characteristics" in his next essay, "What are Universals?" The occasion gave Dewey the opportunity to expand on his account of universals. Consider the content of the definition, triangle. Triangle, as it is understood for the operation of the universal in a judgment, is triangularity. Triangularity is a concept of intension; it is a concept that contains all of its features, attributes, and characteristics within, such that one characteristic is functionally identical with others under the concept.[56] Dewey gives us the example of "plane figure" (LW 11, 105). Triangles are plane figures, and triangles, as plane figures, are "modes of *being* plane" (LW 11, 105). Triangles are of the class "plane figures." The class "plane figures" cannot be further divided, for it is *intensional*, not *extensional*. The essential feature or characteristic (plane figure) is potentially infinitely applicable to existences because it is an abstract, universal concept. This cannot be said about the kind, plane figure, in a generic proposition. Here, the universality of the plane figure is only as strong as the specific instances (particulars) to which it is related by the copula.[57]

The nature of universals, Dewey says, is that of a rule—a rule of operations (LW 11, 107). The upshot is that universality is itself an operation—an operation to be performed that takes the form of an if-then claim, or an antecedent and consequent (LW 11, 107).[58] By themselves, these are not premises; rather they "guide the formation of all premises and conclusions" (LW 11, 108). In a BARBARA-style syllogism, for example, they operate on the major premise (All men are mortal) through recharacterizing the major premise as a hypothetical-universal claim (If all men are, they are mortal). Each term in the major premise is an essential feature (humanity; mortality). The major premise serves as the guide and orders the further premises. The minor premise (Socrates is a man) is an existential or generic proposition that refers to a particular and a kind. The major premise, as a universal, guides us in picking out the features or qualities of the thing of that kind (LW 11, 108). With universals, we are able to tell what qualities count as evidence and what do not (LW 11, 108).

When we form universals, we move generic propositions into a new context, and in so doing, we transform one logical form (generic) to another (universal). We fit the generic proposition (All men are mortal) with the capacity to be "a determinant of evidence" (LW 11, 109–10). The generic proposition counts for the kind, mortal, insofar as it includes and incorporates all those designated through the copula. It is an extensional concept, for it does not indicate any of the (other) features inclusive of the kind, mortal. Whereas, transformed into a universal form, it designates the humanity of all in relation to the mortality of all. It is now an intensional concept and, as such, is able to be a determinant of evidence of particular characteristics of the kind (characteristics of, e.g., humanity). Through transforming kinds into concepts that take the logical form of if-then, or antecedent-consequent, Dewey thinks we obviate the problem of how logical forms inhere ontologically in matter; for it turns out they don't.[59]

Finally, Dewey makes the strong claim that universals are ideals; ideals of operations to be performed (LW 11, 110). Two issues confront

Dewey here. First, the ideality of universals is easily assumed to mean there is no connection whatsoever between the universal and the particular (existential). This is not the case, for the universal has as its functional form the rule or principle by which existential kinds count as evidence in operations (judgments).[60] Second, it might seem that universals have no contingency; for, once established, they are free to operate as timeless and eternal verities. This is also not the case. Dewey emphasizes the nature of these as "*working* hypotheses," as amenable to change in light of the success or failure of the operations they prescribe (LW 11, 111).[61] An understanding of generic propositions as synonymous with logical kinds (Mill's understanding of logical forms) fails in this regard, because it takes the existential qualities or features found in all cases of a kind to be equivalent to the essence of that kind. This sets up a logical form that is question-begging, for it will always be the case that a quality or feature abstracted from a kind having a close extensional relation to that quality is a universal or near-universal. Only by transferring the operations of inference to universal logical forms is amenability to change assured.

Another issue drawn from Mill and featured in contemporary logical texts may be raised: how, given the establishment of the generic proposition as enfolding two formal functions (existential and universal), does universalizing the generic account for the formation of mythical and fantastic objects that have existential traits?[62] How, in other words, do we account for mythical conceptions such as centaurs and mermaids having "real" existential qualities?[63] And how do we account for the fact that in some universals (e.g., squareness, rectangularity), there seems to be a hierarchy in which one (rectangularity) is superior to, and enfolds the other (squareness), at least in terms of their extensive capabilities? These issues are the focus of Dewey's final paper for the *Journal of Philosophy* titled "General Propositions, Kinds, and Classes." Dewey's argument is of course to deny the functional meaning-synonymy between generic propositions and universals. Indeed, running them together is precisely the basis of the problem; for, with no purely logical basis on which to rely, the issue of extension proves that rectangularity enfolds squareness (LW 11, 125). But this *only* holds for particulars. It doesn't hold for the *definitions* of rectangularity and squareness, in which we are dealing with *intensional* attributes and characteristics, not *extensional* ones. The intensional features of a square are distinct from the intensional features of a rectangle, even if these are similar across both, and rectangularity, in its application, covers more cases.[64]

Toward a Theory of Causality

We have seen in examining Dewey's *Experience and Nature* (1925) and *Art as Experience* (1934) that causality is a complex affair, involving experience both immediate and refined, with immediate experience having its very own traits such as wholeness or totality, rhythm, beginning and ending, stability and precariousness—and indeed, temporality—and that these features of experiencing, while in no serial order or historical setting, nevertheless have with them a felt qualitative continuity (or dis-continuity) as the result of certain features coming (or not coming) together.[65] It is the business of refined or reflective experience to grasp these traits and settle them in a larger whole through ordering. This is a serial ordering and gives rise to both history and causality. The serial ordering of events and situations through the isolation of traits is a situating of situations; an ordering that gives rise to logical temporality through succession, simultaneity, and interactivity.[66] We may therefore say that *causality* is a matter of serial ordering of events and situations, and therefore properly belongs to refined experience, or reflection. And this is correct. Yet there is a quality(s) or trait(s) at work at the level of immediate experience that makes the causality at the refined level of experience possible. This is captured in the claim that it is traits of events and situations, and especially that of temporality, that form the subject matter of refined experience. Immediately felt traits are the proper subject matter of refined experience, as refined experience mediates between qualitatively immediate experiences (beginnings and endings). The problem is explaining how this takes place. I think the best (though incomplete) answer Dewey gives is the one found in the original (1925) introductory chapter to *Experience and Nature*, together with *Art as Experience*; in pointing out (indexing) and discriminating, refined experience (reflection) exploits the trait of temporality, and in so doing, relies on the continuity of its *content*—the temporality arising from the natural relations of qualitative traits of immediate experience—for its own continuity (e.g., LW 10, 214–17). In this way, temporality at the reflective level arises from temporality at the level of immediate experience. Thus, the *double continuity* that is inherent with any unified experience.

Is causality a term applicable to non-logical situations and events that seem to come across to us as objects, that is, as objects that seem to be immediately had? I don't mean objects that exist only in mythology (centaurs, fauns, gorgons, and the like), or objects of mere imagination, but rather objects of and in perception, containing tangible qualities in the guise of traits as their form and matter? To put the point more bluntly, can there be a causal theory of reality in which a real event or situation is necessary for a (real) object? The classical formulation is: "S can be said to have knowledge that Y if Y is causally connected 'in an appropriate way' with S's believing that Y." Peirce, of course, has such a causal argument, through his semiotic of Firstness, Secondness, and Thirdness. Does Dewey as well? To see, I want to examine Dewey's 1935 and 1937 Reviews of the *Collected Papers of Charles Saunders Peirce* and the stand-alone paper of 1935 titled "Peirce's Theory of Meaning" in light of his claims in *Experience and Nature* and *Art as Experience*.

Peirce's Theory of Quality (1935)

The impetus for this article was an earlier article published by Thomas Goudge in the *Journal of Philosophy* early in 1935.[67] While Dewey thought the paper was timely, he took the opportunity to point out numerous misconceptions, particularly as regards Peirce's theory of quality, or Firstness. What is important for this project is Dewey's understanding of the relationships between quality and object, and his estimation of Peirce's accomplishment in drawing this relationship out. Dewey cites a lengthy passage of Peirce's at CP 1, 424–25 in favor of his own reading (LW 11, 90).[68] In the passage, Peirce is referring to the role of quality as an idea in itself; as a monad. From the standpoint of law, habit, the object, the quality is more than mere potentiality; it is a necessary quality for these. Having and undergoing a quality is an experience in which the quality is "ineffable" (LW 11, 90). This quality would be akin to Peirce's First of a Second—the possibility of an actual event or situation involving the organism and environment. This is the *dynamis* of an *energia*, as Dewey is wont to put it (LW 11, 89); a potential of an actual. When it is "denotatively mentioned" or "described," on the other hand, there is "another experience having its own, so to say, totalizing unifying quality—and so on *ad infinitum*" (LW 11, 90). Only from the standpoint of denotative mentioning (which is akin to refined experience) is the potentiality of the quality noted (LW 11, 90).

Quality pervades all phenomena, whether immediately had or refined. In Peirce's terms, there is Firstness of Secondness in each Second and Firstness and Secondness of Thirdness in each Third: there is pervasive qualitative immediacy and actuality in every law, habit, and object. This is the occasion to remind readers that all existence is qualitative, and that even imaginaries (mythical creatures) have their qualities, though not their actualities (LW 11, 90–91).[69] For Peirce, in novel experiences, qualities from previous experiences play a role as Firsts (CP 1, 539). Because a novel experience is a Third, it contains its First and Second as signs. The First is the qualitative expression of a previous sign. Let us use the example of Icon, Index, and Symbol. The First of the new experience is the Icon, and is qualitatively had; felt. It presents the actual possibility for the Index. The Index of the new experience is the actual pointed-to; the denoted "this" and "that" (singular) of the First, and includes and incorporates the action/reaction of this new experience.[70] The Third is the mediator; the law or habit that interprets the First and Second and, in so doing, brings them together in a triadic whole. The object formed is first a qualitatively immediate sign-representation, then a dynamic (active-reactive *and* actual) object.[71]

It is clear to me that Dewey is reading Peirce as placing the actuality/actualization of things (Seconds) in the position of reality. And this is a position on which Peirce concurs.[72] The dynamic object (the actual object of the third phase or level in the trichotomy of signs) is the expressive object that transcends characterization; it remains what it is irrespective of interpretation by a Third.[73] Of course, this is a metaphysical claim, and Dewey remains shy of following Peirce through to his metaphysical conclusion, as a footnote makes clear (LW 11, 89, footnote). But the pervasive quality of the actual with regard to perceptual objects nevertheless stands. The actual, or dynamic object, does not dissolve in the experience of describing a previous experience; the change is in regard to the quality of that new experience. Whatever kernel of actuality is present as Second in relation to First and Third remains intact and beyond interpretation, whereas the qualitative features and dimensions (as Firsts) are novel in the novel experience.

We might want to cast Dewey's pronouncements on Peirce's theory of quality in Deweyan terms. Firstness, or qualitativeness (including the qualitative traits of existence first felt in perception) is the possibility of the actual. Dewey's Firstness is possibility in relation to Secondness, or the actual. Dewey says that Firstness gives generality to Secondness as potential (*dynamis*) provides generality to the actual (*energia*) (LW 11, 87). The particular traits of an event or situation change with each subsequent situation experienced; we experience these as an event with qualitative meaning—a qualitative event. Though the traits or qualities of this vary from experience to experience, what does not dissolve is the actual—Peirce's dynamic object, or Second. For the actual (dynamic) object is the object of signification of the encounter (Peirce might say "clash") of the human organism with its environment, first qualitatively felt and responded to; actualized. This actualized object cannot be taken back or transformed into something other. It is, in itself. The object as rule, as law, as habit, as mediator of First and Second, is the refined object; the logical object with its conceptual apparatus of extension and intension. But it relies causally on the qualitative features (First) of an immediate experience and the resultant actual object (Second) of that experience. And while it is true that in a serial ordering of events (a Third), objects change, they change in terms of their qualities or features, and do so from event to event. That is to say, there is a kernel to each triad, and that kernel is the actual, dynamic object of perception. This dynamic object of perception in Peirce is the actual event for perception in Dewey.[74]

Peirce's causal theory of reality, then, does not function because Thirdness or habit merely mediates First and Second in habit, law, or proposition. It mediates what is real; and what is real is the actual, itself a transaction. The real, or actual, is the fusion of qualities of feeling in an action/reaction. Dewey has a similar causal theory of reality, and along similar lines as Peirce. Of course, Dewey has two caveats; to begin with, matter is itself first qualitative, not quantitative. Matter (mass) as physicists define it is a logical product of inquiry, not that which stands outside of or beyond experience. Matter, in other words, is properly a Third for Dewey, as it is the mediate conclusion of action/reaction, and not action/reaction itself.[75] Second, Dewey limits causal explanatory operations to serial ordering, which is itself a concern for refined experience. This is the account of causality that Dewey makes evident in chapter 22 of the 1938 *Logic*. The causality I am talking of here is not *that* causality, but rather causality as regards the issue of what needs to be in place (what is hypothetically necessary though not sufficient) for logical objects that are the matters of serial ordering of events and situations. For qualities of an event or situation are not merely picked up and drafted for logical use as objects. They are had in an activity of perception, and what perceived is actual owing not only to the traits and qualities of the event or situation, but the physiological and cultural responses and reactions of the organism to these. (Hence, the importance of chapters 2 and 3 on the matrices of inquiry in the 1938 *Logic*.) This actual is further refined as a logical object in its placement and use in propositions of kinds and classes. But this does not detract from the fact that an actual—a real—is immediately available to us for refined experience. The qualities of this actual undergo change in the operation of inquiry, in activities of isolation, analysis, synthesis, and testing. This testing will, if it is successful, lead to a logical object—a causal object in the senses Dewey describes in chapter 22 of the 1938 *Logic*—as a product itself the resolution of a single continuous event—together with its own specific qualities and traits (LW 12, 444–45). But it will not deny the actual or real—formed of qualities of the transaction of person with her environment. For that, once had, is a qualitative whole in its actuality and cannot be taken back; and neither can its actuality (Peirce would say Secondness) be denied. This actuality is best understood in Dewey's notions of "event" and "situation." While the qualitative features of objects change during the transformation from immediate to refined, the actual—itself the result of the fusion of the human being (and her perceptual apparatus) with the environment—does not. The real or actual is, as it is with Peirce, the linchpin on which scientific-logical causality turns.

Reviews of the *Collected Papers of Charles Saunders Peirce* (1935 and 1937)

Dewey wrote two reviews of the *Collected Papers of Charles Saunders Peirce* for *The New Republic*; one in 1935 exclusively on volume 6 and one in 1937 on the entire set of six volumes. Dewey characterizes Peirce's account of Secondness in the second of the two reviews.[76] Peirce's account of science, continuity, and his "critical common-senseism" also receive attention here (LW 11, 480; 483). He softens somewhat his criticism of Peirce's "laboratory mind," noting that Peirce has no truck with the view that philosophy is to be based on the conclusions of science (LW 11, 481). Importantly, Dewey follows Peirce in articulating Secondness as "actuality," "in its most literal and brute sense" (LW 11, 482). It is "non-intellectual" and "non-rational" and "can only be experienced and then indicated to others (who undergo the same brute interactions)" (LW 11, 482). For Peirce, "Our sensations are not knowledge nor a source of knowledge; they just are" (LW 11, 482).[77] As regards Thirdness, Peirce is given credit for an account of "the open universe" before William James; this gives Peirce pride of place among pluralists (and against monists).

While not wanting to put too fine a point on it, I think it is time for a reexamination of Peirce's role in scholarship on Dewey's logical theory.

It is clear here and elsewhere that continuity—at least rhetorically—forms much of Dewey's admiration for Peirce (e.g., LW 11, 483). Continuity for Dewey in the context of his discussion on Peirce meant "continual growth in the direction of interrelations," and this included the scientific community whose role was evaluative as well as productive (LW 11, 483). For Dewey, Peirce's continuity included nature (LW 11, 423). The sense of this continuity as potentially infinite—a continuity with no limit—was of course more amenable to Dewey than a community of final consensus on this or that truth or reality. Peirce's earlier characterizations of truth and reality as that which is subject to the final arbiter of the scientific community in the long run gave way to an account of truth and reality having an ideal limit: a regulative ideal of truth and reality in which, *were* inquiry sustained long enough, truth and reality *would* emerge.[78] This is a species of "Probabilism" and is entirely consistent with "fallibilism" in Dewey's mind (LW 11, 483–84). It is a normative and moral, rather than a merely descriptive, conclusion (LW 11, 483). Dewey puts it this way: "The sole justification of science as a method of inquiry is that if it is persisted in, it is self-correcting and tends to approach ever closer to stable common agreement of beliefs and ideas. Because science is the method of learning, not a settled body of truths, it is the hope of mankind" (LW 11, 484).[79] As we will see with respect to the role of the future in the pattern of inquiry, probability plays a more important role than ever for Dewey's functional kind of evaluative judgment.

The Pattern of Inquiry: *How We Think*, Second Edition (1933)

Here, I discuss the changes in the second edition of *How We Think* by first turning to certain statements Dewey made about the pattern of inquiry in the first edition (1910). These serve to set the stage for the revisions that followed. Then I examine two issues; the flexibility of the stages (or "phases," as Dewey calls them in the second edition) of inquiry and what the conclusion of a settled situation in light of a theory of knowledge means. Both of these issues underwent great revision during the period 1910–1933, and it will do to see what the differences are and where they resurface in the 1938 *Logic*. In the first edition of *How We Think*, Dewey refers to the "complete act of thought" as consisting of "stages" or "steps" (MW 6, 236–37).[80] Though Dewey nowhere indicates that these are fixed and settled stages, he nevertheless does not indicate that they are recursive. Dewey's absence of a commitment to recursion, however, did land him in trouble with certain critics complaining of Dewey's penchant for a fixed stage theory of thinking in spite of his penchant for flexibility and fallibility.[81] In regard to the conclusion of a settled situation in light of a theory of knowledge, Dewey tells us the key component to the fifth stage of "the complete act of thought" is "some kind of experimental corroboration, or verification, of the conjectural idea . . . If we look and find present all the conditions demanded by the theory, and if we find the characteristic traits called for by rival alternatives to be lacking, the tendency to believe, to accept, is almost irresistible" (MW 6, 240). The emphasis here is on verification as "experimental corroboration" (MW 6, 240). Dewey continues: In a conclusion, "*conditions are deliberately arranged in accord with the requirements of an idea or hypothesis to see if the results theoretically indicated by the idea actually occur*" (MW 6, 240). The upshot is one of functional fit between idea (as hypothesis) and the actual occurrence of phenomena (fact). This fit is a practical one, inasmuch as it concerns the practical bearing of the idea on the establishment and/or presence of the phenomenon at hand. Whatever verification came to mean historically in classical pragmatism and logical positivism, this is Dewey's understanding of the term in 1910.[82]

Matters are different in Dewey's account of the pattern of inquiry in 1933. Not only is the overall pattern of inquiry not static, one phase may be expanded and others contracted. Each phase may be subdivided into further phases (e.g., LW 8, 206–7). Dewey emphasizes the back-and-forth and to-and-fro movements of the phases of inquiry in the second edition. Phases may be exited and entered depending on need and circumstance. Various hypotheses, for example, are entertained and re-entertained while the matter of a genuine problem is undergoing settlement. Testing of hypotheses may be halted and a return to the genuine problem undertaken. "Telescoping" of phases (phases that take place simultaneously) is often encountered (LW 8, 207). Phasing the pattern of inquiry is a functional characterization of the traits of reflective thinking in outline (LW 8, 207). The logical traits of inquiry—the functional patterns inquiry takes on when it operates—do not follow in lockstep order; rather they establish themselves in part according to the context (including the subject matter of the situation at hand) in which inquiry finds itself and operates. Dewey will refer to this in chapter 6 of the 1938 *Logic* in the discussion of the determinants of a (problematic) situation (LW 12, 112–15) and in the roles played by generic propositions and universals in chapter 14 (LW 12, 244–46). Reflective thinking or inquiry is a situation—a situation of situations—with its own traits, captured in outline in the description of the pattern of inquiry. But it is the pattern of these five (logical) traits, with their subdivision into further traits at each phase of inquiry, that constitutes reflective thinking (LW 8, 208).[83]

The issue of the conclusion of inquiry is one both of evaluative judging and the constitution of a situation. We have discussed at length the components of a situation. Situations arise in encounters of organism and world. They are determinate or indeterminate—open or closed, in the language of Dewey's 1938 *Logic*. Situations are marked by qualitative features. These features are generic; they are features common to all experiencing. In inquiring, we feel from the situation its rhythms, its back-and-forth, its to-and-fro, its stability or precariousness, and above all, its completeness (totality) or incompleteness. Situations of course arise in and from the encounter, and the encounter includes both physical and social conditions. But what we feel are traits or qualitative features of these conditions, and not (yet) the articulated conditions, which are properly products of inquiry.[84] The articulated conditions (including linguistic meanings) serve as habits, rules, principles, and logical forms by which we orient ourselves in the world of experiencing; but what is novel in any situation is the qualitative dimension—the traits of existence—to which we respond when we inquire.

Now this understanding of Dewey's is not novel for 1933. It was a feature of his 1916 *Essays in Experimental Logic*—at least in outline. And it can even be read into his first edition of *How We Think*, excepting the account of generic traits of existence as qualifying our experiencing. Verification is Dewey's term for the conclusion of inquiry in the first edition of *How We Think*, and it returns in the second edition, together with "experimental corroboration" (LW 8, 205). It is the agreement of the hypothesis (idea) with "*the results theoretically indicated*" (LW 8, 205). It is confirmation: confirmation "so strong as to induce a conclusion—at least, until contrary facts shall indicate the advisability of its revision" (LW 8, 205). The elements of fallibility and contingency run through Dewey's account of verification, now as in 1910. But notice that what we have here is *logical* and *experimental* confirmation; *logical* and *experimental* verification. Here, Dewey does not speak of an *existential* confirmation or verification. (The terms logical and experimental are, in any event, inapplicable to existential situations.) For the impetus for inquiry is an unsettled situation. And a settled situation is the proper closure to inquiry. There are logical traits that must line up (must be put in order) for a logical settling of inquiry to occur. But there are *existential* traits that must be in evidence for an *existential* settling of an unsettled situation. Chiefly, there must be the qualitative trait of completeness present. And neither confirmation nor verification are operative concepts with this as existential characteristics or features: while confirmation and verification connote the settling of an inquiry, they may only presuppose, not demonstrate, the *existential* settling of an unsettled situation. In fact, for a logical situation to be closed, there must be a simultaneous existential closure of the unsettled situation. And the only way for this to occur, I suggest, is the traits of existence run parallel to the traits of logical inquiry; the pattern of inquiry in outline must at least be consistent with the traits of existence (especially continuity and completeness) in a settled situation. Dewey does not say this in *How We Think*, second edition. But it is implied in chapter 9 of the 1938 *Logic* in the section on Judgments of Appreciation (LW 12, 176–78). My best guess in reading these pages is that the trait of continuity (in a settled situation) is felt and organized in inquiry (reflective thinking—itself a refined experience) as the trait of continuity (which is also present with the overall pattern of inquiry). There are, therefore, two continuities—one existential and one logical-temporal. The existential manifests as the felt sense of continuity running through an event or situation, itself in association with various other traits in relationship, such as rhythm and dysrhythmia, stability and precariousness, and beginning and ending—what Dewey in *Art as Experience* calls the reciprocity in relationship (LW 10, 216–17). The logical and temporal manifests as serial ordering, history, narration-description, and causal-serial explanation, expressed in the overall pattern of inquiry. Together, these combine in a *double continuity*, a *unity of continuities*, with each continuity remaining susceptible of inquiring-into. Further, I suggest the former is manifest in the latter. I believe this is as close as Dewey gets to an overall accounting of how the traits of inquiry line up with the traits of existence by the end of our period (1933–1937). By 1943, Dewey would consider the act of inquiry as an event unto itself. But in 1933, Dewey had not fully broached this characterization.[85]

Needless to say, we must understand the double-barreled nature of experience—as refined *and* as gross and macroscopic—together with the double nature of continuity—as existential *and* logical traits—if we are to understand Dewey's account of a situation. Situation is vital to Dewey's broadest definition of inquiry, both in *How We Think*, second edition, and the 1938 *Logic*. In *How We Think*, second edition, Dewey defines reflective thought as follows: "*The function of reflective thought is, therefore, to transform a situation in which there is experienced obscurity, doubt, conflict, disturbance of some sort, into a situation that is clear, coherent, settled, and harmonious*" (LW 8, 195). We can compare this definition to its more famous cousin: "*Inquiry is the controlled or directed transformation of an indeterminate situation into one that is so determinate in its constituent distinctions and relations as to convert the elements of the original situation into a unified whole*" (LW 12, 108).[86] Situation is the key term in both.

Careful readers of Dewey understand the double nature of situation; situation refers not only to the qualitatively had and undergone experience in and from which traits of existence emerge, but also the logical operations involved in and with these that result in settlement or completion. They understand that what is serially ordered for the purposes of historical or causal-explanatory discourse are situations. They understand that reconstruction of situations through settlement or completion results in new events, new situations, which are themselves serially ordered for causal-explanatory and/or historical purposes; that is, they understand that the "unified whole" of a settled situation is a new situation for further serial ordering.[87] All of this presupposes that an understanding of the role and function of the logical theory of inquiry depends upon a robust account of situation and its traits and features.

Conclusion

By 1932, Dewey had amassed a vast number of theoretical accomplishments that would resurface in the 1938 *Logic*. The basic articulation of accounts vital for the backdrop of logical theory, including sophisticated versions of experience, reflective thinking, form and subject matter, practical applications of logic, together with definitional terms such as "event," "situation," "traits," "continuity," "habit," "language," "culture," "pattern," "form," "proposition," "abstract," "induction," "deduction," and "judgment," was more or less complete by 1932. Further refinements of many of these terms would take place in the years between 1933 and 1937, but the basic sense of each of these was established. Much of this was in turn due to Dewey's 1927–1928 Types of Logical Theory lectures, which formed the basis for the overall pattern of the 1938 *Logic*. Further work on science and scientific method, chiefly established in Dewey's correspondence with Sidney Hook and Joseph Ratner, together with the historical accounting of physical science and its role in commonsense inquiries in *The Quest for Certainty*, solidified Dewey's account of serial ordering and causal explanation, and helped him to form an account of the relations between existential phenomena and universal and abstract conceptions. Perhaps most importantly, the distinctions between generic and universal (and abstract) began to take shape in earnest in these years. And though the fruits of this particular labor would not yet emerge in 1932, they would by 1938, largely owing to further attention in the following period.

With the important exceptions of the role of Peirce for Dewey's account of causality (and antinominalism), and the place of verification in evaluative judgments of inquiry, the distinctions among logical forms and propositions, and, of course, the development in writing of the 1938 *Logic*, these were years of refinement, not novelty. Of course, it is worth talking about these exceptions, for each is in its own way essential to the development of Dewey's 1938 *Logic*. By 1933, Dewey had functional definitions of existential, generic, and universal propositions. He had not yet distinguished generic propositions as those solely of class and not kind. He had not yet distinguished between generic propositions that have hypothetical functions and those that do not. He had not yet strongly downplayed the tendency to run existential propositions together with generic propositions. And he had not yet clearly distinguished existential propositions of contingency from those of definition (universals). All of this would take place in 1933–1937, first in his correspondence with Ratner and Hook and later with his three articles for the *Journal of Philosophy*. Coeval with the development of distinctive functional definitions of logical forms was the development of an ongoing outline, gradually filled in during these years. Though its actual genesis can be traced back as far as 1925, the outline was first established in Dewey's correspondence with Sidney Hook only in late 1934. Proposed chapters in late 1934 are, in comparison with the table of contents of the 1938 *Logic*, recognizable in terms of their ultimate position in the published version of 1938. The three articles written for the *Journal of Philosophy* serve as primary content for chapters 13 and 14 of the 1938 *Logic*.

Dewey's paper, "Peirce's Theory of Quality," together with his two reviews of the *Collected Papers*, helped to establish his account of causality as regards the debate between nominalism and realism. Dewey emerges as an antinominalist and realist as a result of his endorsement that actuals (Peirce's Seconds) are in a real relationship to qualities of an experience, on the one hand (Firsts of Seconds), and to logical objects (objects involved in generic propositions and universal conceptions, or Thirds) on the other. Though this was not a new claim (Dewey had made several such claims without the Peircean endorsement early in his scholarship, most notably in "The Postulate of Immediate Empiricism" [1905] MW 2, 164), the logical demonstration of the relationship between qualitative traits and serial ordering of events had to wait until Dewey's ongoing account of continuity between primary and secondary or gross and macroscopic and refined experience was sufficiently filled out. Dewey's endorsement also demonstrates his causal theory of reality; for reality demands an actual in relation to a logical object (concept). And an actual demands qualitative traits of existence that are immediately had and felt in a Peircean action/reaction. For this account, there must be a continuity between the traits of existence qualitatively had and felt, the actual with its meanings (relations), and the refined or logical object with its conceptual apparatus of intension, extension, and its functional significance (as symbol) for all inferences. *How We Think*, second edition, also proved very helpful in Dewey's ongoing refinement of the pattern of inquiry. In contrast with the first edition, Dewey's phases of inquiry are more flexible; the recursive nature of these is stressed, as is the prolongation of a single phase, should that be required. The telescoping of phases of inquiry is also an important characteristic that is new to the second edition. *How We Think*, second edition, also proved helpful in articulating Dewey's account of verification in the years leading up to the 1938 *Logic*; an account that differs from those of the logical empiricists insofar as it has a far greater role for theory than the predominant early twentieth-century understanding of verification as empirical observation.

Looked at from a distance, it is evident that Dewey did far more than merely refine his logical forms and propositions in this span of time. While generic propositions and universals occupied much of Dewey's time and attention during these four years, it must be remarked that he was filling in the details of a much broader theory of continuity in its logical aspect. To see Dewey's logical theory as a theory of (logical) continuity would be entirely accurate, and in keeping with Dewey's remark on the central importance of continuity (and Peirce) for the 1938 *Logic* (LW 12, 3). With the biological and social bases of inquiry being established in chapters 2 and 3, as well as in chapter 8 of the 1938 *Logic*, the bulk of the rest of the text is given over to establishing logical continuity among events through historical, narrative-descriptive, serial, and causal-explanatory orderings. But this continuity depends upon an existential continuity that is first felt; a qualitative continuity that is articulated more fully in *Experience and Nature*, "Qualitative Thought," and *Art as Experience* in discussions of events and situations, immediacy in and of perception, and the relationship between the immediate and the mediate, than it is in the 1938 *Logic*. The advantage of taking these and other texts into consideration as regards the development of Dewey's logical theory is the revelation of the importance of continuity as the central trait of inquiry for logic, both in form (logical theory) and content (subject matter); a trait that (again) Dewey thought was of enough fundamental importance to single out for especial mention in the preface of his *Logic: The Theory of Inquiry* (LW 12, 3). What remains is to set out Dewey's 1938 *Logic* in the context of his theory of continuity. This would be a project in which Dewey's logical theory is made self-conscious by way of reflection on the various contents and operations that construct and maintain its essential trait of continuity across the existential and logical domains of experience.

Table 4. Dewey's Logical Theory circa 1933–1937: Important Conclusions

Themes	Conclusions	Location
Traits, Meanings, and the Indeterminacy of Situations	• Reals (actuals) in relationship to qualities and to logical objects • Double Continuity; continuity between qualitative traits and traits of logical objects • Temporality specific to primary *and* secondary experiences, yet linked together in a double continuity • Causal theory of reality with actuals distinct from logical objects	*AE* (1934) "Peirce's Theory of Meaning" (1936) "Peirce's Theory of Quality" (1936)
The Matrices of Inquiry	• Role of freedom in inquiry • Symbols as physical existences	*HWT* second edition (1933)
Scientific and Social Inquiry	• The need for acceptance of science as a naturalized attitude	*AE* (1934)
Propositions and Inferences in Inquiry	• Separation of generic and existential propositions • Generic propositions as solely of class or kind • Generic propositions of two kinds; those that have hypothetical functions and those that do not • Existential propositions as singulars ("This"; "That") • Existential propositions as either contingent (might be) or definitional (is) • Only logical objects as involved in propositions (from "This" or "That" to inference to an object) • Recursivity, telescoping nature of pattern of inquiry	*Journal of Philosophy* papers (1936) *Correspondence* *HWT* second edition (1933)

Appendix 1

Dewey's Outline of *Logic: The Theory of Inquiry*, November 22, 1934

Dear Sidney,

I have followed your suggestion and made out an outline. As you also suggested it will be modifed doubtless.

If you have any suggestions about topics that dont seem to be covered by the outline I shall be glad to have them at your leisure. AS well as suggestions about proper order.

I have rewritten I and Iv, and am just starting on V. AS you see from outline I am now inclined to believe that these [*pencil del.*] ₐfirst 4ₐ [*in pencil w. caret*] chapters go together as Introductory.

Sincerely yours, | John Dewey ||

Part I Introduction

I   The issue

II   Existential   Matrix- Bilogical

III   "" "" Cultural

IV   Common Sense World

Part II The Operation of Inquiry

1   The Common Pattern

2   The instruments of Inquiry- Ideas and [double pencil underline] Understanding.

3   The Conclusion "" "" :- Judgments, Its structure.

$4   Forms of Judgment - Appreciative and Directive

5   "" "" Assertion- Affirmation and Negation.

6   "" "" Quantitative-

7   "" "" Narration and Description- Temporal and Spatial- of past and future; of observation with intercalations ^as to observable field.^ [in pencil]

8   Syatematic Judgments- on Common Sense level- disjunctionve and hypothetical

Part III Technique of Control-Scientific Judgment Inquiry

1. Inference and Proof- summary and preparatory.

2   Induction and Deduction. (Including sense-sdata (?))

3   Formal and Material - theory of forms

4   Propositions   and terms- relation to judgment; to communication and language- syntax

5   Relational   Propositions   - mathematics (?)

6. Logic of social inquiry - relations of ^(to)^ [in pencil] 'natural' science and ^action-^ of ^(to)^ [in pencil w. caret] a return to material   existential   beliefs

Part IV PLogic and Philosophy

1. Logic and Epistemology

2. Idealistic and Realistic Logics.

3. Realm of Possibilities- metaphysics of Essence, subsistence

4. General Conclusions:- Return to Common Sense.

Notes

Introduction

1. John Dewey, "Is Logic a Dualistic Science?," *Open Court* III (January 1890).

2. John Dewey, *Studies in Logical Theory* (Chicago: University of Chicago Press, 1903).

3. James applauded Dewey's efforts in numerous places, including his correspondence and the lectures that would become *Pragmatism*. For his part, Peirce chided Dewey for producing a "Natural History" of logical development, rather than a theory of forms. "Thereupon, I remark that the 'thought' of which you speak cannot be the 'thought' of normative logic. For it is one of the characteristics of all normative science that it does not concern itself in the least with [what] actually takes place in the universe, barring always its assumption that what is before the mind always has those characteristics that are found there and which Phänomenlogie [sic] is assumed to have made out" (Peirce to Dewey, June 9, 1904, 00930).

4. John Dewey, *How We Think* (New York: Henry, Holt & Co., 1910); John Dewey, *Essays in Experimental Logic* (Chicago: University of Chicago Press, 1916).

5. See James Scott Johnston, *John Dewey's Earlier Logical Theory* (Albany, NY: State University of New York Press, 2014), especially chapters 1–2.

6. John Dewey, "From Absolutism to Experimentalism," in G. P. Adams and W. P. Montague, *Contemporary American Philosophy: Personal Statements*, vol. II (New York: The Macmillan Co., 1930), 12–27; James Garrison, "The 'Permanent Deposit' of Hegel in John Dewey's Philosophy," *Educational Theory* 56, no. 1 (2006): 1–37.

7. Dewey, *How We Think*, MW 6, 246.

8. This is also the case as regards Dewey's naturalistic metaphysics. The to-and-fro of traits, very often opposed or in dialectical tension, give rise to a further quality or qualities that inquiry investigates. See Raymond Boisvert, *Dewey's*

Metaphysics (New York: Fordham Press, 1988), 111–12. See, more recently, Paul Chemlin, "John Dewey's Theoretical Framework from 1903–1916: Prefigurations of a Naturalistic Metaphysics," *The Pluralist* 12, no. 2 (2017): 62–63.

9. John Dewey, *Experience and Nature*, 2nd ed. (Chicago: Open Court Publishing, 1929).

10. John Dewey, "The Logic of Judgments of Practice," *Journal of Philosophy, Psychology, and Scientific Methods* 12, no. 19 (1915): 505–23.

11. John Dewey, *Art as Experience* (New York: Minton, Balch, and Co., 1934).

12. Johnston, *John Dewey's Earlier Logical Theory*, 224.

Chapter 1

1. Johnston, *John Dewey's Earlier Logical Theory*.

2. Dewey was also responding to various critics and supporters of his logical theory and associated works. Chief among these were the Critical Realists, the so-called Six Realists, and Bertrand Russell. I discuss these in part 2.

3. I refer the reader to my earlier volume, *Dewey's Earlier Logical Theory*, esp. 162–64, for more discussion of this.

4. John Dewey, "The Existence of the World as a Logical Problem," *Philosophical Review* 24, 1915, 357–70.

5. The so-called Critical Realists were a disparate group of thinkers of the first and second decades of the twentieth century who reacted against Idealism and were suspicious of new-found schools of thought such as Pragmatism. The group included Arthur Lovejoy, E. B. McGilvary, and the Six Realists. The Six Realists in turn, comprised R. B. Perry, E. B. Holt, W. P. Montague, Walter Pitkin, E. G. Spaulding, and W. T. Martin. For more on the Critical Realists, see my *John Dewey's Earlier Logical Theory*, 33–36, as well as Robert Westbrook, *John Dewey and American Democracy* (Ithaca: Cornell University Press, 1991), 120–24.

6. E. B. Holt, *The New Realism* (New York: MacMillan, 1912); Westbrook, *John Dewey and American Democracy*, 120–24.

7. John Dewey, "Rejoinder to Dr. Spaulding," *Journal of Philosophy, Psychology and Scientific Methods* 8 (1911): 77–79. A debate between Dewey and Spaulding, representative of the Six Realists, played out in the pages of this and other journals, beginning in 1910 with Dewey's paper "The Short-Cut to Realism Examined." John Dewey, "The Short-Cut to Realism Examined," *Journal of Philosophy, Psychology, and Scientific Methods* 7, no. 15 (1910): 553–57. The "six" followed with "The Program and Platform of the Six Realists." E. B. Holt et al., "The Program and First Platform of Six Realists," *Journal of Philosophy, Psychology and Scientific Methods* 7 (1910): 393–401. Spaulding wrote a separate

article, titled "Realism: A Reply to Professor Dewey and an Exposition." E. B. Spaulding, "Realism: A Reply to Professor Dewey and an Exposition," *Journal of Philosophy, Psychology and Scientific Methods* 8 (1911): 63–77. The latter is the paper to which Dewey is responding.

8. Daniel Levine, "Randolph Bourne, John Dewey, and the Legacy of Liberalism," *The Antioch Review* 29, no. 2 (Summer 1969): 534–44, 539. Though the Bourne-Dewey debate was contextualized in the matter of the entrance of the United States into the First World War, one of Bourne's chief criticisms of pragmatism was its positivism as regards the role science was to play in social affairs. Dewey responds to Bourne indirectly in his *Public and Its Problems* (1927).

9. Bertrand Russell, "Professor Dewey's Essays in Experimental Logic," *Dewey and His Critics: Essays from the Journal of Philosophy*, ed. Sidney Morgenbesser (New York: Journal of Philosophy, Inc., 1977), 248–49.

10. Westbrook, *John Dewey and American Democracy*, 118–19, 168; George Dykhuizen, *The Life and Mind of John Dewey* (Carbondale: Southern Illinois University Press, 1973), 137. During this period, he was also professor of pedagogy at Teachers College.

11. For example, Westbrook, *John Dewey and American Democracy*, 118–19; Alan Ryan, *John Dewey and the High Tide of American Liberalism* (New York: W.W. Norton), 1995, 164; Thomas Dalton, *Becoming John Dewey: Dilemmas of a Philosopher and Naturalist* (Bloomington: Indiana University Press, 2002), 9; Boisvert, *Dewey's Metaphysics*, 127; Ralph Sleeper, *The Necessity of Pragmatism: John Dewey's Conception of Philosophy* (Urbana: University of Illinois Press, 1986), 7. Of these, Sleeper's account is the best, particularly as it discusses the role Woodbridge played in the lead-up to Dewey's writing *Experience and Nature* (1925).

12. This by no means excludes the influence of Hegel and Hegel's "method" on Dewey's logical theory, as I make clear in *John Dewey's Earlier Logical Theory*. Sleeper is right in saying that a common philosophical thread, from Aristotle to Hegel, also runs through Dewey. I have said that, at least for Dewey's earlier logical theory, Hegel had the most influence. Dewey would increasingly turn to others to fill out the logical program begun in earnest in 1903. But the realist roots were already in place by the time of *Studies*.

13. Though Woodbridge seems to have had his greatest effect on Dewey's writing of *Experience and Nature*, and the changes made for the second introduction. These proceeded Dewey's "discovery" of Aristotle by approximately ten years.

14. Johnston, *John Dewey's Earlier Logical Theory*, 38–41. There, I discuss the limitations of the turn to Aristotle in light of Dewey's Hegelianism for Dewey's earlier logical theory.

15. John Dewey, Types of Logical Theory (1915 and 1916), in *The Lectures of John Dewey*, vol. 1, ed. Donald Koch (Carbondale: Southern Illinois University Press, 2012). Cited as TLT in text. These class lectures were taken down by Walter B. Veazie, a student in Dewey's course. Dewey discusses Aristotle as well

in *Democracy and Education*, though his treatment there is generally restricted to matters of education and the virtues.

16. Dewey recommended the following bibliography to his students:

Bibliography on Aristotle's Logic "Barthélemy St. Hilaire's translation of Aristotle's Logic and his commentary. Wallace, Outlines of the Philosophy of Aristotle. Condensed with Greek references. Chap. 3 on logic. Read carefully. Aristotle's Organon . . . In Bohn's library in translation. Windelband's account of Aristotle's logic. Article in Encyclopaedia Britannica on Aristotle by Adamson. Adamson's Development of Greek Philosophy, p. 170f. on logic. Gomperz, Greek Thinkers, vol. 4, chaps. 4 and 5. (Logic prior to his account of metaphysics and physics.) Benn, Greek Philosophers, 2 vols. Vol. I, 375f."

Though later parts of the manuscript have dates, significant sections do not. The section on Aristotle, which covers more than sixty pages of typed, double-spaced text, is unfortunately undated.

17. Boisvert, *Dewey's Metaphysics*, 126–27.

18. Larry Hickman, *John Dewey's Pragmatic Technology* (Bloomington: Indiana University Press, 1990), 94–96.

19. William James, *Principles of Psychology*, vol. 2 (New York: Dover Press, 1918), 654–55.

20. John Dewey, *Outlines of a Critical Theory on Ethics* (Ann Arbor: The Inland Press, 1891).

21. John Dewey, *Lectures on Ethics, 1900–1901*, ed. D. Koch (Carbondale: Southern Illinois University Press, 1991), 38.

22. Dewey did not waver in his estimation of Mill and Locke. As late as 1942, we find essentially the same criticisms of the sense-psychology common to both. See John Dewey, *Unmodern and Modern Philosophy*, ed. Phillip Dean (Carbondale: Southern Illinois University Press, 2012), esp. 106.

23. Dewey evidently has his students reading J. S. Mill, *Studies in Logic, Ratiocinative and Inductive: Being a Connected View of the Principles of Evidence and the Methods of Scientific Investigations*. People's Edition (London: Longmans, Green, and Co., 1889), together with William Whewell's *The Philosophy of the Inductive Sciences, Founded upon Their History*, 2 vols. (London: J.W. Parker, 1840). The discussion regarding Mill and Whewell hearkens to the supplemental article in *Studies* on the two.

24. Indeed, empiricistic logics generally are chastised for trafficking in sense-psychology. This includes a number of notable logicians of the nineteenth and early twentieth centuries, including Leonard Hobhouse, *The Theory of Knowledge: A Contribution to Some Problems of Logic and Metaphysics* (New York: Macmillan & Co., 1895); William Stanley Jevons, *The Principles of Science: A Treatise of Logic and Scientific Meth*od (London: Macmillan & Co., 1887); William Ernest Johnson, *Logic: Parts 1–3* (Cambridge: Cambridge University Press, 1921–1924); Bertrand Russell, *Our Knowledge of the External World as a Field for Scientific Method in*

Philosophy (Chicago and London: Open Court Publishing, Inc., 1914); John Venn, *The Principles of Empirical or Inductive Logic* (London and New York: Macmillan & Co., 1889). Hobhouse is symptomatic of this reliance on sense-psychology: in his *Theory of Knowledge*, the first two chapters are given over to a discussion of "apprehension," in which extension, size, shape, and position are said to be immediately apprehended (Hobhouse, 1896). These thinkers and the criticisms of them recur in the 1927–1928 Types of Logical Theory.

25. By far the best of these is Thomas Burke, *Dewey's New Logic: A Reply to Russell* (Chicago: Chicago University Press, 1994). On metaphilosophy, and from the side of Russell scholarship, see Jane Duran, "Russell on Pragmatism," *Russell: The Journal of the Bertrand Russell Archives* 14 (Summer 1994): 31–37.

26. See my *John Dewey's Earlier Logical Theory*, 36–38 for a brief history of the debate up to and including 1917.

27. Bertrand Russell, Dewey's New Logic, in *The Philosophy of John Dewey*, ed. P. Schilpp and L. E. Hahn (La Salle: Open Court, 1989), 135–56; Bertrand Russell, *History of Western Philosophy* (London: George Allen & Unwin, 1979).

28. John Dewey, "China and the West," *Dial* 74 (1923): 193–96.

29. Sleeper, *The Necessity of Pragmatism*, esp. 57–50; 201–5 is central in this reestablishment of Peirce's role in Dewey's logical theory.

30. See my *John Dewey's Earlier Logical Theory*, esp. 22–25. The differences between Peirce and Dewey are well captured in the correspondence between the two. See especially Peirce to Dewey, June 9, 1904, 00930.

31. John Dewey, "The Pragmatism of Peirce," *Journal of Philosophy, Psychology, and Scientific Methods* 13 (1916): 709–15.

32. To my mind, this is the very first account of Peirce's pragmatic method that insists upon its being a theory of meaning, and not of truth.

33. Peirce himself seems to aver to this in his own correspondence with Dewey as regards the publication of *Studies* in 1903. See Peirce to Dewey, June 4, 1904, 00930.

34. See for example, Dalton, *Becoming John Dewey*, 116–18.

35. Also responsible was Klyce's bullying and hectoring of Dewey's various positions on philosophy of science, logic, and the theory of knowledge. Klyce attributed Dewey's shortcomings to character flaws. Dewey finally became exasperated at Klyce's constant refusal to understand his position.

36. John Dewey, *Reconstruction in Philosophy* (New York: Henry, Holt & Co., 1920); John Dewey, *Human Nature and Conduct: An Introduction to Social Psychology* (New York, Henry, Holt & Co., 1922).

37. Dewey frequently complained of his lack of knowledge of advanced mathematics to his interlocutors. See, for example, Dewey to Bentley, September 23, 1935, in *John Dewey and Arthur Bentley: A Philosophical Correspondence*, ed. S. Ratner, Jules Altman, and J. E. Wheeler (New Brunswick, NJ: Rutgers University Press, 1964), 44.

38. John Dewey, Types of Logical Theory, 1927–1928, in *The Lectures of John Dewey* vol. 2, ed. Donald Koch (Carbondale: Southern Illinois University Press, 2012). Cited as TLT in text. These notes were taken down longhand by a student in Dewey's last logic class, Marion E. Dwight, and typed by a secretary. Ernest Nagel apparently had Dwight present these notes to Dewey. Additionally, she produced a topical outline of the course, which ran some twenty pages, and is appended to the *Lectures*.

39. The 1927–1928 Types of Logical Theory are structured thematically, rather than in terms of historical figures. Aristotle's contribution to logical theory is thus spread out over some 440 pages of the manuscript. Likewise, with discussions of Mill and Peirce. The importance of these logic lectures on Dewey's subsequent intellectual development toward the 1938 *Logic* cannot be overestimated. Dewey himself remarked that his lectures on logic were the mainspring of his intellectual ideas on logical theory (Dewey to Hook, 1 September 1938, 06032).

40. Notable texts Dewey drew on in consideration of empirical logics for the 1927–1928 lectures beyond Mill include Hobhouse, *The Theory of Knowledge*; Jevons, *The Principles of Science*; Johnson, *Logic: Parts 1–3*; Russell, *Our Knowledge of the External World as a Field for Scientific Method in Philosophy*; Bertrand Russell, *Logical Atomism* (New York: Macmillan & Co., 1924); Bertrand Russell, *The Analysis of Matter* (New York: Harcourt, Brace & Co., 1927); Venn, *The Principles of Empirical or Inductive Logic*. Dewey recommends Mill and Venn as exemplars of empiricistic logic to his students at the first lecture, October 27, 1927.

41. John Dewey, The Development of American Pragmatism, in *Studies in the History of Ideas*, ed. the Department of Philosophy (Columbia University, New York: Columbia University Press, 1925), 2: 353–77.

42. There is correspondence demonstrating Dewey's knowledge of Einstein by 1920. See Dewey to Klyce, May 8, 1920, 04621).

43. The correspondence to Ratner and Hook in particular suggests that Dewey had a firsthand knowledge of Einstein, Bohr, and Heisenberg. We also have a good indication of the texts he was working with, thanks to the meticulous scholarship conducted by Jo Ann Boydston for the SIU edition of Dewey's works. As by example, for the period 1925 to 1932, we may note Dewey's footnotes to *The Quest for Certainty*, in which the following texts are mentioned: Frederick Barry, *The Scientific Habit of Thought* (New York: Columbia University Press, 1927); Percy William Bridgman, *The Logic of Modern Physics* (New York: MacMillan and Co., 1927); Arthur Stanley Eddington, *The Nature of the Physical World* (New York, Macmillan and Co., 1928); Albert Einstein, *Relativity: The Special and General Theory*, trans. R. W. Lawson (New York: Henry Holt and Co., 1920); Pierre-Simon Laplace, *A Philosophical Essay on Probabilities*, trans. F. W. Truscott and F. L. Emory (New York: John Wiley and Sons, 1902); J. C. Maxwell, *The Scientific Papers of James Clerk Maxwell*, vol. 2, ed. W. D. Niven

(Cambridge: Cambridge University Press, 1890); Isaac Newton, *The Mathematical Principles of Natural Philosophy*, vol. 2, trans. A. Motte (London: Benjamin Mosse, 1729); Isaac Newton, *Optiks, or, A Treatise of the Reflections, Refractions, Inflections and Colours of Light*, 3rd ed. (London: William and John Innys, 1721); Edmund Noble, *Purposive Evolution: The Link Between Science and Religion* (New York: Henry Holt and Co., 1926).

44. Robert Dewey, *The Philosophy of John Dewey: A Critical Exposition of his Method, Metaphysics, and Theory of Knowledge* (Dordrecht: Springer, 1977), 123. Alison Kadlec, *Dewey's Critical Pragmatism* (Lexington, KY: Lexington Books, 2007), 26. Hans Siegfried, Dewey's Logical Forms, in *Dewey's Logical Theory: New Studies and Interpretations*, ed. F. Thomas Burke, D. Micah Hester, and R. B. Talisse (Nashville: Vanderbilt University Press), 180–201, 197.

45. John Dewey, "The Postulate of Immediate Empiricism," *The Journal of Philosophy, Psychology, and Scientific Methods* 2, no. 15 (1905). In MW 3, 164.

46. Richard Feynman, Robert Leighton, and Matthew Sands, *The Feynman Lectures on Physics*, vol. 1 (New York: Basic, Books, 2006), 15–3; 15–9.

47. Dewey, *The Philosophy of John Dewey*, 126; Kadlec, *Dewey's Critical Pragmatism*, 26. Siegfried, Dewey's Logical Forms, 197. It was Einstein (1905) who first theorized the particular nature of light (photons).

48. The actual probability of finding a particle in a predefined region is represented as an integral.

49. Operators in physics are representations of physical variables in equations. Specifically, they are mathematical rules that move one vector to another.

50. Richard Feynman, Robert Leighton, and Matthew Sands, *The Feynman Lectures on Physics*, vol. 3 (New York: Basic, Books, 2006), 1–11.

51. Werner Heisenberg, *Physics and Philosophy* (London, Penguin Books, 2000), 93. This of course brings Heisenberg in line with Peirce, who argued for the same.

52. We do need to remember that Einstein and Heisenberg carried on a fractious correspondence, symptomatic of a larger rift developing in the physics community after 1925 in regards the "research programme" of quantum theory. As is well-known, Einstein refused to participate in Bohr's "anarchism," in which inconsistency was thought a trait of nature. Planck took Einstein's side, and Bohr, Heisenberg's. See Imre Lakatos, "Falsification and the Methodology of Scientific Research Programmes," in *Criticism and the Growth of Knowledge*, ed. I. Lakatos and A. Musgrave (Cambridge: Cambridge University Press, 1970), 91–196, 144–45.

53. Dewey had already claimed as much in *Experience and Nature*. See esp. LW 1, 92.

54. Alan Ryan, *John Dewey and the High Tide of American Liberalism*, 166–67; Franz Boas, *The Mind of Primitive Man* (New York: Macmillan & Co., 1911); Franz Boas, "The Methods of Ethnology" [1920], in *Race, Language, and*

Culture (Chicago: University of Chicago Press, 1940), 281–89. The influence extends to Boas's students, including Ruth Benedict.

55. Dewey had, of course, averred that all (practical) judgments were hypothetical in "The Logic of Judgments of Practice" (1915). But this claim did not seem to extend universally. Here, it does.

56. John Dewey, *The Quest for Certainty: A Study of the Relation of Knowledge and Action* (New York: Minton, Balch & Co., 1929).

57. John Dewey, *The Public and Its Problems: An Essay in Political Inquiry* (New York: Henry, Holt & Co., 1927).

58. John Dewey, "Characteristics and Characters: Kinds and Classes," *Journal of Philosophy* 33 (1936): 253–61; John Dewey, "What Are Universals?" *Journal of Philosophy* 33 (1936): 281–88; John Dewey, "General Propositions, Kinds, and Classes," *Journal of Philosophy* 33 (1936): 673–80. Dewey first tried material for these out in a presentation to the members of the Philosophy Club, an informal gathering of philosophers in New York City. To judge by Dewey's reaction, the presentation was not an unqualified success (Dewey to Hook, March 16, 1935, 05766).

59. I have included as an appendix, the outline of 1934 dated November 22, that Dewey shared with Sidney Hook.

60. John Dewey, *How We Think: A Restatement of the Relation of Reflective Thinking to the Educative Process* (Boston: D.C. Heath and Co., 1933).

61. Charles A. Madison, Oral History Interview, November 8, 1967, 5, in Kathleen Paolos, Textual Commentary.

62. The class Dewey refers to is undoubtedly the 1927–1928 class attending his Types of Logical Theory lectures at Columbia University.

63. John Dewey, "The Founder of Pragmatism," *Collected Papers of Charles Saunders Peirce*, vol. 5: *Pragmatism and Pragmaticism*, ed. Charles Hartshorne and Paul Weiss (Cambridge, MA: Harvard University Press, 1934), *New Republic* 81 (January 30, 1935): 338–339; John Dewey, *Collected Papers of Charles Saunders Peirce*, 6 vols., ed. Charles Hartshorne and Paul Weiss (Cambridge, MA: Harvard University Press, 1934), *New Republic* 89 (February 3, 1937): CP 1, 415–16.

64. John Dewey, "Peirce's Theory of Quality," *Journal of Philosophy* 32 (1935), 701–8.

65. Arthur Bentley was introduced to Dewey by way of Ernest Nagel, who suggested the two correspond. In the interim, Dewey read Bentley's *Linguistic Analysis of Mathematics* and *Behavior, Knowledge, and Fact*.

66. Arthur Bentley, *Linguistic Analysis of Mathematics* (Bloomington, IN: Principia Press, 1932).

67. Oliver Reiser, *Philosophy and the Concepts of Modern Science* (New York: Macmillan and Co., 1935).

68. L. Susan Stebbing, *A Modern Introduction to Logic* (New York: Thomas Y. Crowell Co., 1930).

Chapter 2

1. I discuss the entire volume at length in chapter 6 of *John Dewey's Earlier Logical Theory*. The following discussion is a summary.

2. John Dewey, *Theory of Valuation* (Chicago: University of Chicago Press, 1939).

3. Note Dewey is not claiming that biology and sociology are foundational, or are sources for logical theory. The analogy applies to understanding the history and development of logical theory, and is not an elucidation of its sources. Much mischief has been made of Dewey's so-called biological and naturalist arguments for the sources of the method of inquiry. See, for example, the Marxist-inspired writings of Maurice Cornforth, *In Defense of Philosophy: Against Positivism and Pragmatism* (New York: Lawrence and Wishart, 1950); Harry Wells, *Pragmatism: Philosophy of Imperialism* (New York: International Publishers, 1954), and Paul Crosser, *The Nihilism of John Dewey* (New York: The Philosophical Library, 1955). Russell, too, can be understood as making the claim that pragmatism draws on accounts of biological development. See Russell, *A History of Western Philosophy*, 823–25.

4. These themes are developed at some length in my *John Dewey's Earlier Logical Theory*, chapter 7. The first theme concerns logical theory as regards Dewey's evolving theory of experience and incorporates his understanding of continuity; the second theme concerns logical theory as regards Dewey's naturalistic theory of habit; the third theme concerns logical theory as regards the similarities and differences between so-called scientific and commonsense inquiries; and the final theme concerns Dewey's increasing awareness of the importance of propositions (and their role in judging) for logic and the theory of knowledge. A fuller discussion of what constitutes each of these can be found in the introduction.

5. The paper is reply to Daniel Sommer Robinson's "An Alleged New Discovery in Logic," *Journal of Philosophy, Psychology, and Scientific Methods*, 14 (1917): 225–37.

6. Johnston, *John Dewey's Earlier Logical Theory*, 199.

7. The quotation is drawn from a footnote Dewey attached to a passage in the introduction. In the footnote, Dewey thanks Scudder Klyce, an interlocutor of his with whom he had begun to correspond in 1913. Dewey is referring in the footnote to Klyce's manuscript, *The Universe*. Dewey's point is that terms such as experience and situation have no existential referent to point to beyond themselves, for they are the continuum in which all referents exist. Thus the difficulty with the terms. Taken seriously, experience and situation become something almost Peircean—indicated (as an indexical or Second), but not grasped as an object. Continuity plays a large role behind the scenes here. But the development of a theory of continuity to go along with experience and situation will have to wait until Dewey rediscovers Peirce, beginning in 1916 and

continuing into the early 1930s. See Scudder Klyce, *The Universe* (Winchester, MA, 1921); Dalton, *Becoming John Dewey*, 116–19.

8. Johnston, *John Dewey's Earlier Logical Theory*, 164.

9. Chemlin, "John Dewey's Theoretical Framework from 1903–1916: Prefigurations of a Naturalistic Metaphysics," 70–71 reminds us that Dewey did have a vague understanding of usage of generic traits at the time of *Essays*, and that these included "continuity."

10. This is a problem Raymond Boisvert picks up on as residue from *Essays*: the distinction between object and event (*Res*) in Dewey *is* made there, but not sufficiently to ward off objections that objects are idealist in essentials. See Raymond Boisvert, *Dewey's Metaphysics*, 89.

11. John Dewey to Scudder Klyce, April 14, 1916, 03552.

12. I discuss this essay fully in section 4 of this chapter.

13. See Donald Koch, introduction to *The Lectures of John Dewey*, vol. 1. 2012. As in chapter 1, I label these TLT, or Types of Logical Theory.

14. Ironically enough, Dewey thought James himself could be read as endorsing an absolutizing experience, and Dewey charges him with this in "The Concept of the Neutral in Recent Epistemology," *Journal of Philosophy, Psychology, and Scientific Methods* 14 (1917): 161–63, MW 10, 50–51. The article was published approximately a year after the lecture was written. I thank Jim Garrison for pointing out this reference to me.

15. In *Experience and Nature*, Dewey will distinguish between "gross and macroscopic" and "refined" experience; the former according with immediate havings and doings, the latter with reflection or inquiry. See LW 1, 15–17.

16. Dewey described Klyce this way: "In some ways he is the prize freak of the world but fundamentally simple I think, even if more or less mad" (Dewey to Albert Barnes, December 29, 1920, 04115).

17. Klyce to Dewey, July 24, 1916, 03554. "[N]either the past nor the future has any real existence; everything is now, or more strictly has no time aspect at all, time being an arbitrary logical form." Klyce's criticisms of Dewey's logical theory are less than transparent, as he often weaves psychological insights into his criticisms and praise. But the point about past and future having no existence is clear enough.

18. Doing so seems to be the main point Klyce raises against so-called "agnosticism—" "patient, blind endurance of the chain" of cause and effect (Klyce to Dewey, July 24, 1916, 03554).

19. Klyce seems to think he has solved the problem of infinite regress—a problem he thinks Dewey cannot solve owing to his remaining dualism. For Klyce, time is "zero time": present time. All infinite regress therefore must be zero time. Infinite regress is instant, immediate knowledge and is "solved" by grasping this fact. This is roughly Klyce's understanding of the Buddhist conception of Nirvana. One must note that Dewey did respond to Klyce, though not directly,

in his essay published in 1922 titled "Realism without Monism or Dualism." John Dewey, "Realism without Monism or Dualism," *Journal of Philosophy* 19 (1922): 309–17 (MW 13, 40–60). The paper is a direct response to Arthur Lovejoy's "Pragmatism vs. the Pragmatist," in *Essays in Critical Realism*, ed. Durant Drake (London: Macmillan and Co., 1920), 35–81 (MW 13, 443–81).

20. Dewey says in an ink postscript to the April 23 letter, "I ought to say I have never (since I got over my childhood theology) been personally interested in monism—I am content just to take it for granted & let it go."

21. Letters aren't extant to show Dewey's responses to Klyce. The next letter we have from Dewey is dated March 3, 1917, and it concerns a letter sent presumably the 19th of February.

22. I therefore disagree with David Hildebrand's claim that novel attributes of "experience" and "situation" are found in *Democracy and Education*. I don't see anything new in the way of these than is found, for example, in the introduction to *Essays in Experimental Logic*. Novel attributes of *temporal continuity*, however, and particularly as regards habit and reflection, are to be found. While both experience and situation remain of signal importance, their importance does not hang on their having features not found in contemporary (1916) works. "Situation" undergoes its greatest transformation in *Experience and Nature* (1925) and especially "Qualitative Thought" (1930). See Hildebrand, "The Importance of Experience and Situations in *Democracy and Education*," *Educational Theory* 66, nos. 1–2 (2016): 73–88, 75.

23. Though Dewey does echo claims made in the introduction to *Essays in Experimental Logic* and his 1915–1916 Types of Logical Theory—to wit, the claims that thinking is itself a sort of experience. These claims will be amplified in Dewey's later *Reconstruction in Philosophy* (1920) before undergoing a drastic reconstruction and amplification in *Experience and Nature* (1925).

24. By this, I mean that each person has a unique set of operations of inference at any particular phase or stage of development; operations vary from person to person and no two people have exactly the same set.

25. In a letter dated December 5, 1920, Dewey writes to Albert Barnes and discusses his recently published *Reconstruction in Philosophy* (Dewey to Barnes, December 5, 1920, 04113). He says, "Speaking of the book, I have criticized at more length the influence of routine and mechanical ⇐ **habit** ⇒ and imitation in this book than anything Ive [sic] written before. I had this done before getting your recent letters, but Iin [sic] view of your letters Ive [sic] gone over one or two spots and made the criticisms still stronger. The order of discus-||sion is the same ofas [sic] that of my Calif lectures two or three ₐand a half₍ years ago bnamely [sic], ⇐ **Habit** ⇒, Impulse, Intelligence—the place of each in conduct.[5] You may seem something from the order of my topics the conflict with Mc Dougall's point of view, many of the things he attributes to instinct I think are due to faixation [sic] of ⇐ **habits** ⇒ under social influ-

ences. In other words, while he is more interested in accounting for society in terms of human psychology Im [sic] more interested in accounting for human psychology in terms of social institutions and customs. Ive [sic] coame [sic] to the same conclusion tha [sic] some years ago that all psychology as distinct from physiology is social not individual." The "Mc Dougall" to whom Dewey is referring is William McDougall, author of the hugely influential *An Introduction to Social Psychology*, first published in 1908. William McDougall, *An Introduction to Social Psychology* (London: Methuen & Co., 1908).

26. Russell, "Professor Dewey's 'Essays in Experimental Logic,'" 231–52.

27. There, Dewey championed knowledge as playing an intermediary role in experience, having its own distinctive intellectual quality, and suggests that its position vis à vis experience is as a distinct stage. Dewey does not refute himself in *Reconstruction*: he adds to the qualities and characteristics knowledge exhibits.

28. Dewey is speaking directly of biology here, and to the application of the evolutionary method to the biological sciences.

29. This paper was first published in the *Journal of Philosophy, Psychology, and Scientific Methods* 13 (1916): 709–15. Dewey published an encyclopedia entry for Peirce's term Tychism in James Mark Baldwin's *Dictionary of Philosophy and Psychology* in 1902. See MW 2, 259.

30. Dewey is among the first—and perhaps the first—to articulate clearly Peirce's use of the term "pragmatism" as a theory, not of truth of propositions, but meaning (MW 10, 72; 76). See further, John Shook, *Dewey's Empirical Theory of Knowledge and Reality* (Nashville, TN: Vanderbilt University Press, 2000), 211–12.

31. This is not dissimilar to the classical formulation of a causal theory of knowledge, though it does not apply to knowledge *simpliciter* here, rather meaning. The classical formulation is: "S can be said to have knowledge that Y if Y is causally connected 'in an appropriate way' with S's believing that Y." Alvin Goldman, "A Causal Theory of Knowing," *The Journal of Philosophy* 64, no. 12 (1967): 357–72. I have more to say about Peirce on the causal theory of reality in the discussion of forms and propositions in logical theory in chapter 4.

32. That is to say, our conception of the real must align with the real for the habit (including the practical bearings or consequences and the activity of engaging with the real) to be as real as the real. Peirce of course cashes this out in terms of First, Second, and Third, with each of these irreducible to the others. Dewey does not develop Peirce's metaphysics here. He is content to note a continuity or connection between the real and the object that thinking or reflection forms. This is in contrast to certain interpretations of Dewey—interpretations that suggest Dewey sacrifices "the particular" to "the act," whereas Peirce keeps them apart. See James Feibleman, "The Influence of Peirce on Dewey's Logic," *Education* 66, no. 1 (1945): 18–24; 19, and James Feibleman, *An Introduction to Peirce's Philosophy Interpreted as a System* (Boston: MIT Press, 1970), 474–75. If I

am correct about reading Dewey, he does not (at least in this essay) suggest any such sacrifice. Instead, he seems to endorse Peirce's realism. I have to investigate Feibleman's claim later in the book, as it bears significantly on Dewey's account of continuity in the 1938 *Logic*.

33. It is enough to note, I think, Dewey's acceptance of Peirce's account of the method of inquiry. At one place in the essay, he claims that Peirce is more of a pragmatist than James (MW 10, 76) and claims Peirce provides a way out of "the egocentric predicament"—a predicament Dewey's realist critics charged him with for supposedly being too idealistic in his theory of knowledge (MW 10, 78). The specific allusion is to R. B. Perry, "The Ego-Centric Predicament," *Journal of Philosophy* 7 (1910): 5–14.

34. Habits are, in short, habits of body/mind. This serves to foreshadow Dewey's account of the body/mind in chapter 7 of *Experience and Nature*.

35. Dewey's account of satisfaction is not to be thought of as a straightforward Utilitarian-hedonic accounting of love of pleasures; "Satisfaction is had wherever the agent is effective and recognizes his own effectiveness . . . If a person is to feel his effectiveness he must get the approval of others." John Dewey, *Lectures on Ethics 1900–1901*, ed. D. Koch (Carbondale: Southern Illinois University Press, 1991), 31. Dewey further claims, "The underlying idea on the logical side is that satisfaction is ultimately identical with an integrated experience, a harmonious experience in the sense that the various elements involved come to a whole" (Dewey, *Lectures on Ethics*, 31).

36. We will want to compare this with Dewey's account of felt meaning and experience in regard to the good, especially as he outlines it in the *Lectures on Ethics*; "The good must be an ideal . . . and not a natural or given fact. Because the idea of it grows out of the failure of our experience to satisfy us, and then our projecting out ourselves beyond anything we have actually got and formulating this conception of what experience must be transformed into if it is to be satisfactory" (Dewey, *Lectures on Ethics*, 25). The ideal of the good here is not grasped immediately; what is grasped immediately is the (felt) failure of the experience. It is in the linking of the failure of that experience to the ideal that constitutes the object of striving for the good. Dewey's accounting is different in 1922 than in 1900. But notice that the key ingredients to a definition of the good circa 1922 are *already in place* in 1900: experience, satisfaction, ideal, and conception. What will remain for Dewey is to develop an account of deliberation that leads to the unification of the felt meaning of the good with the ideal.

37. Dewey, *Lectures on Ethics*, 25–26.

38. Dewey, *Lectures on Ethics*, 62–63.

39. Russell, "Professor Dewey's Essays in Experimental Logic," 246. Russell would charge Dewey with adopting a "common-sense view of causation . . ." which blinded him to the fact that "we must know particular causal laws . . ." and not merely discover them in a process of inquiry.

40. This sentiment I owe to my correspondence with Jim Garrison, who first suggested the qualification.

41. Perceptive readers will note the similarity in language between this claim and the further claim in *Logic: The Theory of Inquiry*, that scientific knowledge (*not* truth) is warranted assertability. See LW 12, 108.

42. This is similar to the instance of the "double movement" that Dewey discusses in *How We Think* and the introduction to *Essays*. In the former, reflection moves back and forth between the "given partial and confused data" to a "suggested comprehensive (or inclusive) entire situation; and back from this suggested whole . . . to the particular facts, so as to connect these with one another and with additional facts to which the suggestion has directed attention" (MW 6, 242).

43. Dewey will recur to some of these claims in his discussion of water and H_2O in *The Quest for Certainty*. See Dewey, *The Quest for Certainty*, esp. 126–27.

44. C. S. Peirce, "What Pragmatism Is," in *The Essential Peirce*, vol. 2, ed. The Peirce Edition Project (Bloomington: Indiana University Press, 1998), 343.

45. This article was first published in John Dewey, "Science, Belief and the Public," *New Republic* 38 (1924): 143–45. It was later reprinted in John Dewey, *Characters and Events*, ed. Joseph Ratner (New York: Henry Holt and Co., 1929), 459–64.

46. The reference is doubtless to Walter Lippmann, *Public Opinion* (New York: Harcourt, Brace and Co., 2004).

47. The implication of "tenacity" is doubtless a nod to Peirce. See C. S. Peirce, "The Fixation of Belief," in *The Essential Peirce*, vol. 1, ed. C. Kloessel and N. Hauser (Bloomington: Indiana University Press, 1992), 116–17.

48. See for example, "The Program and Platform of Six Realists" (MW 6, 472–82). See also Russell, "Professor Dewey's Essays in Experimental Logic," 242. See also Duran, "Russell on Pragmatism," who characterizes the entire debate as a category mistake. "To employ Rortian terminology, Russell believes in mirrors, and Dewey does not. But belief in mirrors is not necessarily reprehensible; one would like to know to what use the mirrors will be put. Russell criticizes the pragmatists' position on truth not only because he thinks it does violence to the English language, but because the attempt to employ a notion of truth that does not rest on some sort of correspondence must be insincere—it must rest, at bottom, on some other, unarticulated notion of truth. (Dewey, as we know, metaphilosophically criticizes the notion that a concept of truth can be arrived at by employing any of the standard a priori lines of categorization.) What one is immediately tempted to say here is that a certain sort of category mistake is being made—Russell and Dewey are not talking about the same phenomena, as it were" (32).

49. Russell defines "molecular propositions" as those that "contain other propositions which you may call their atoms, and by molecular propositions I

mean propositions have words such as "or," "if," "and," and so forth" (Russell, *The Philosophy of Logical Atomism*, 36–37). Molecular propositions have within them "atomic facts," which we can submit to quantification. Dewey also discusses Russell's molecular propositions in his letter to Scudder Klyce, dated April 23, 1915, 03517. That Dewey seems to have been actively working on Russell's understanding of propositions at the time seems evident; at this time, he was also writing the introduction to *Essays*.

50. For a similar claim, see MW 10, 343. Propositions set apart from inquiry face the problem of getting back into inquiry. This problem is avoided, Dewey thinks, if it is recognized that propositions are products of inquiry.

51. Dewey also mentions formal logic and mathematical methods in conjunction with inferences. He chides formal logic for ignoring the situation from which it arises. He draws the analogy of mathematical relations to relations with color and sourness (TLT, May 10, 1915). Dewey's analogy is not successful, but his point is clear: in making mathematical relations something apart from existential relations, we transform them into different logical kinds.

52. This is covered more fully in the introduction to *Essays*, esp. MW 10, 342–44.

53. I discuss these more fully in terms of Dewey's final consideration of propositions in chapter 4.

54. In *Essays*, Dewey likens propositions to "proposals," and uses the metaphor of a baseball game to press his suggestion that propositions be treated as proposals to engage in further judgment (propositions). The pitcher proposes to the batter, who proposes to the fielders, all of whom make their own judgments. See MW 10, 356. I am indebted to Larry Hickman for this example in Dewey.

55. Boisvert, *Dewey's Metaphysics*, 126–27.

56. Dewey, TLT May 3, 1915, "The difference and the of permanence and change had become one of the most important philosophical questions of the Greeks. A metaphysical and existential proposition which applies to mind itself for the Greeks. There is 'knowledge' and 'coming to know.' Learning is in the realm of movement, of change. 'Knowing' or science is in the realm of the eternal. It isn't eternally true that a fly is on the wall at a certain spot eternally, but scientifically recorded, that fact is an eternal truth. Learning on the other hand is in the realm of becoming. Problem of learning and knowledge: If all is learning then there is no knowledge; if there is knowledge then there is no learning. (Popular form of this paradox concerning knowing and not knowing a thing—if you don't know, how can you be sure when you get there; if you do know, you can't learn it as you already know it.)" This is doubtless the attempt to graft onto Aristotle's logic Dewey's terminology.

57. Sleeper, *The Necessity of Pragmatism*, 96. Dewey acknowledges Aristotle's influence in the introduction to *Essays* (MW 10, 360). Dewey also discusses Aristotle's method in "The Subject-Matter of Metaphysical Inquiry" (MW 8,

3–13). This essay was first published in the *Journal of Philosophy, Psychology and Scientific Methods* 12, no. 13 (1915): 337–45.

58. Dewey goes on to say, "A proposition regarding the conditions of the existence of a thing is just one particular type of proposition about it—one form which knowledge may take. The logical import of it is that it is a kind of proposition which occupies a position of control with reference to other kinds of knowledge. Our logical control of proposition of this kind (red is becoming to wear, etc.) is peculiarly bound up with the conditions of the existence of a thing. Statement, red is a certain number of vibrations same as statement that a geranium is red, but if latter type is doubted then the recourse is . . . made to that of the former type. The interest has been so great in modern science in those propositions which give control that there has been a tendency to regard propositions of subject matter as defining the real object and giving us a certain norm to which other propositions ought to conform. They are regarded as approximations of the standard subject matter. In that way inductive science has had a bad influence on logic, forcing it into this epistemological direction" (TLT, May 10, 1915).

59. Dewey seems to suggest existential propositions have their genesis *as* existential propositions in Hume. For example, "Do premises and conclusion bear any physical relationship to each other? Kant doesn't raise this question, but takes it as axiomatic that logical relations are different. Hume of course and his followers have asserted the existential character of logical propositions. "Association of ideas is an existential conception." In this view, logic is simply a name for a certain type of interaction of existent reals. The older logic held to the metaphysical reality of species and genera—the very nature of tree was involved. The natures of species and genera exclude each other. Even negative judgment is ontologically valid" (TLT, April 10, 1916). But, as we shall see, by the time of the writing of *The Quest for Certainty* (1929), it is doubtful that Dewey thought Hume could have supplied such understandings of existential propositions. See LW 4, esp. 154.

60. Dewey has less to say about universal propositions as such. (By contrast, he has a great deal to say about universals, but this is not our topic.) One curious relationship Dewey highlights on the topic of universal conceptions is Locke; Locke, it seems, came close to an accounting of these. Dewey says of Locke, "There is one condition under which there might be universal propositions concerning substance—if we know the constitution of the thing we call gold. (The distinction between real and nominal essences) . . . Universality exists only . . . in propositions which are implied by others or imply others. (Empirically at a given time propositions are taken out of the system.)" (TLT, March 31, 1915).

61. "According to Aristotle the inductive processes antecedent to complete knowing are included within this scheme of objective correspondence. Moore, Russell, Spaulding and Perry [all Critical or New Realists] regard the prelimi-

nary psychological processes which lead up to the universal as psychological and subjective alone. No point-to-point correspondence in the existential world—but the term or proposition itself has this correspondence. In Aristotle these comings to be of knowledge or genesis of knowledge have objective counterparts just as science itself has. (Essences and species of things have their counterparts as well as contingent potentialities of things.) The psychological processes correspond to changes in the things. More thoroughgoing realism than the modern point of view" (TLT, May 3, 1915). Compare this with Dewey's statements in the introduction to *Essays*, 360.

62. This presumably applies to Hegel and Hegelian idealists. Dewey says, "Hegelian type of logic—that judgment isn't knowledge at all but imperfect and passes over into universal necessity [the judgment of necessity] . . . Then you get the unfolding of the essence of the universal [as syllogism]. Is logic related to induction in science or is it purely psychological? Has the practice or art of knowing anything to do with the sense in which logic is knowing?" But for Hegel, the answer is clear; it is logical. See G. W. F. Hegel, *Science of Logic*, translated by A. V. Miller (New York: Humanities Press, 1969), especially 689–92. See Garrison, "The 'Permanent Deposit' of Hegel in John Dewey's Philosophy"; James Good and James Garrison, "Dewey, Hegel and Causation," *Journal of Speculative Philosophy* 24, no. 2 (2010): 101–20.

63. Dewey TLT, March 31, 1915. "The general proposition [arrived at through induction] might be itself an inference and yet it might be a principle which it is necessary to accept in order to give validity to any particular inference. It is an hypothesis. The corroboration does not lie in the cases leading up to it, but in the successful working in subsequent cases. Mill begs the question—if it is necessary to all proof it can't be proved by definition from inductions which don't assume it; hence it can't be proved by definition from inductions which don't assume it hence it can't be proved by induction at all but is arrived at by induction and is confirmed by scientific induction and corroboration."

64. It should go without saying that this is a corroboration of the hypothetico-deductive method common to Peirce.

65. Dewey attributes this to Mill's involvement with British psychology in the first half of the nineteenth century. "This which is true in Mill gets mixed up with his false British psychology of the nature of experience itself" (TLT, March 31, 1915).

66. Bertrand Russell, *Our Knowledge of the External World as a Field for Scientific Method in Philosophy* (Chicago: Open Court Publishing Co., 1914).

67. These are in addition to the propositions of "narration" and "description."

68. The copula bears a striking similarity to Hegel's understanding of the role of the copula in judgments. See Hegel, *Science of Logic*, 653.

69. Constructing a table of existential propositional forms for a generative grammar, as Burke has attempted, cannot be done ideally. For there will be as

many propositional forms as articulated existential qualities. Any taxonomy or table will underdetermine the quantity of forms, as these remain unarticulated until an existential situation emerges. See F. Thomas Burke, "Prospects for Mathematizing Dewey's Logical Theory," in *Dewey's Logical Theory: New Studies and Interpretations*, ed. F. T. Burke, D. M. Hester, and R. B. Talisse (Nashville: Vanderbilt University Press, 2002), 121–60, 151–52.

70. I discuss this at some length in *John Dewey's Earlier Logical Inquiry*, 167–68.

71. Dewey doubtless has in mind his use of "*Res*" in the introduction to the *Essays* of 1916 when he thinks of things as inclusive of their traits. See MW 10, 323.

72. The context here is Robinson Crusoe's first notice of footprints in the sand.

73. See as well Dewey's discussion of logical objects in the introduction to *Essays*, MW 10, 343–44.

74. Robinson, "An Alleged New Discovery in Logic," MW 10, 415–30. Durant Drake, who also writes on Dewey for the *Journal of Philosophy, Psychology, and Scientific Methods*, approaches Dewey as a fellow realist whose harshness on idealism seems to Drake to be overstated. See Drake, "What Kind of Realism?" *Philosophy, Psychology, and Scientific Methods* 9 (1912): 149–54, in MW 10, 431–38.

75. This claim, as we see in the next chapter, factors greatly in the discussion Dewey will have with his students in the context of the 1927–1928 Types of Logical Theory given at Columbia.

76. This is a claim that Dewey made at least as early as *Studies*. See MW 3, 307–8.

77. Dewey made a similar claim in *How We Think* (MW 6, 285–86) in regard to "individualized meanings." But here it is much clearer and more forceful. There is no room for ambiguity. Dewey is sometimes accused of being vague on the distinction between propositions and judgments; here he is very clear about the issue.

78. Another exception might be Dewey's short essay "An Analysis of Reflective Thought." John Dewey, "An Analysis of Reflective Thought," *Journal of Philosophy, Psychology, and Scientific Methods* XV (1922): 673–81 (MW 13, 61–71).

79. The other is Logical Method and Law, belonging to the year 1924. I discuss this next.

80. It is noteworthy to compare what Dewey has to say here regarding Locke with his claims regarding Locke in the 1915–1916 Types of Logical Theory, esp. the lecture of May 10, 1915.

81. One aspect of the Peircean account of truth that Dewey's own account in *Reconstruction* does not contain is that of truth as a regulative ideal. This would serve to distinguish Dewey from Peirce until the 1930s: we will have to wait until 1933 to begin to see this. While clearly objective in its demand that truth accord

with the objective conditions that resolve an inquiry, Dewey's understanding of objectivity does not (yet) seem to require, or support, a regulative ideal of truth as the condition that would obtain should a final consensus of the scientific community occur. See Peirce, "How to Make Our Ideas Clear," esp. 139.

82. "Logical Method and the Law," *Cornell Review* 10 (December 1924). In MW 15, 65–78.

83. Mark Mendell, in "Dewey and the Logical of Legal Reasoning," claims Dewey has the evolutionary theory "as a kind of model for logical theory." But whereas the evolutionary theory claims no intelligent or reflective factor involved in species determinations, the sort of theory Dewey has in mind does. For the "kind of natural selection" Dewey has in mind in the development of logical theory concerns reflection and selection of the best working methods, which is already a matter of intelligence. See Mark Mendell, "Dewey and the Logic of Legal Reasoning," *Transactions of the Charles S. Peirce Society* 30, no. 3 (1994): 575–635, 589.

84. The context in which Dewey challenges the syllogistic approach to law concerns the writings of Oliver Wendell Holmes, a sympathetic legal scholar and pragmatist.

85. In a letter to Scudder Klyce (August 21, 1922, 04644), Dewey, responding to Klyce's criticisms regarding *Human Nature and Conduct*, discusses the application of logical methods to the law. In so doing, he makes this revealing statement regarding the kind, universals. He says, "What I ntried [sic] to bring out with the class was the point of logic, that all . . . **universals** . . . are purely hypothetical, not . . . **existential** . . . , that || rules of law are methods of adjusting particular conflicts with a view to ˄social˄ consequences, and change therefore as new forces and conditions operate to produce new consequences, so that old rules if adhered will have an intent quite different from, even opposite to, that for which they were first selected and framed. Also legal conventions to assume not only fixed relations but also fixed particulars or facts and a separation of law and fact from each other. So I tried to show them that there are no more fixed or absolutistic facts than there are laws, and that the separation of the two is a working division of labor only. This of course is all keeping within the sphere of infinite plurality which is the only one that concerns the lawyer as such—or anybody else in a practical-intellectual matter. That is, it is not law as relationship in general, but as a relation of particular facts, a quantitative statement of their mutual variations with such exactness as the fcase [sic] permits."

Chapter 3

1. However, continuity is not exhausted in *Experience and Nature* or related articles. For, while the accounting of existential continuity is (almost)

fully developed, the parallel accounting of temporal-successive continuity remains to be completed. This, of course, is more a matter for the discussion of forms and propositions in inquiry, because these are the key ingredients in a temporal-successive accounting. And I do so in the fourth section of this chapter.

2. Thomas Alexander, "Dewey's Denotative-Empirical Method: A Thread Through the Labyrinth," *Journal of Speculative Philosophy* 18, no. 3 (2004), 248–56, 253.

3. Note these are not the "logical objects" Dewey discusses in contrast to Russell's sense-qualities. These objects are qualitative and immediately had. To take these objects as final or logical is to commit what Dewey calls "the philosophic fallacy" (LW 1, 116). In "Qualitative Thought," Dewey will characterize these immediate objects as an element in the complex whole, or "situation" (LW 5, 246). The rather vague use of "object" and "thing" in *Experience and Nature* gives way in "Qualitative Thought" (1930) to "event" and "situation," and henceforth is Dewey's preferred terminology for what we experience when we experience.

4. In the 1927–1928 Types of Logical Theory lectures Dewey says of situations, "'Situation' is a somewhat vague term but it signifies at least something which is a whole, which is relatively individualized and complete in itself, and which being a whole of experience is marked off with its own quality, its own pervasive nature, from other situations and has a certain internal complexity within itself. This character may be indicated by saying that this gives us a very different conception of logic from a thing which makes certain general ideas or particular things the important thing" (TLT, December 14, 1927). I suspect that the impetus for Dewey's move from the vague "object" and "thing" in *Experience and Nature* to "situation" was first broached in the lectures, as well as in the responses Dewey made to various interlocutors at and around the same time (e.g., Santayana, Hall).

5. These are not the only generic traits of existence. In *Art as Experience*, Dewey will add "our constant sense of things as belonging or not belonging, of relevancy, a sense which is immediate" (LW 10, 198).

6. Craig Cunningham, "Dewey's Metaphysics and the Self," *Studies in Philosophy and Education* 13 (1994): 343–60, 348; Roland Garrett, "Dewey's Struggle with the Ineffable," *Transactions of the Charles S. Peirce Society* 9, no. 2 (1973): 95–109. Dewey struggles with his nomenclature of "traits" and "qualities."

7. Alexander, "Dewey's Denotative-Empirical Method: A Thread Through the Labyrinth," 254.

8. I thank Jim Garrison for alerting me to these passages.

9. The context here is Dewey's discussion of consciousness, as social mind, in the service of the aesthetic.

10. Raymond Boisvert, "Dewey's Metaphysics: Ground-map of the Proto-typically Real," in *Reading Dewey: Interpretations of a Postmodern Generations*, ed. L. Hickman (Bloomington: Indiana University Press, 1995), 157. Boisvert has it

exactly right, here: the traits of existence, by themselves, don't do anything for the further improvement of experiences. It is the business of inquiry to facilitate this improvement.

11. We should consider language in Dewey's estimation to include G. H. Mead's gestures, as Dewey agrees with Mead that these are the building-blocks of speech. In moving from gesture to word, "it gains meaning" (LW 1, 145). See G. H. Mead, "Social Consciousness and the Consciousness of Meaning," *Psychological Bulletin* 7 (1910): 397–405. See also LW 1, 170–71.

12. The entire discussion is Peircean. In my opinion, this is no accident. Dewey is using Peirce's scientific metaphors from "The fixation of Belief" and "How to Make Our Ideas Clear" as his basis for his account of immediate meanings. These emerge as (in Peirce's later language) First of Thirds, or the qualitative and feeling aspect of habit or thought.

13. As I discuss further on, C. Everett Hall's essay seems to make this mistake.

14. Again, I think Boisvert has it quite right in his "Dewey's Metaphysics." If the generic traits of existence are the basis for mapping, they are only the basis insofar as a mapping can occur. And this mapping is a one of communication, discourse, and ultimately, (scientific) inquiry. This, I think, is the upshot of the second introduction (1929) to the volume.

15. Again, this is an antinominalistic stance; there must be real change involved with real events to allow me to characterize events as changing.

16. See Gerald Mozur, "Dewey on Time and Individuality," *Transactions of the Charles S. Peirce Society* 27, no. 3 (1991): 321–40, 327 for a helpful discussion of the distinction between temporal quality and temporal ordering. Mozur links temporal qualities to prior temporal orderings, so that the two operate as part of a loose circle. Temporal orderings refer back to temporal qualities as links in the overall continuity that is temporal succession.

17. The occasions for rewriting were manifold; certainly, George Santayana's scathing review of the volume, to which Dewey responded in 1927, contributed. Beyond this, Dewey's sympathetic colleagues, notably M. C. Otto and Joseph Ratner (whom Dewey mentions directly in the preface to the second edition) are chiefly responsible for the rewriting. See George Santayana, "Dewey's Naturalistic Metaphysics," in LW 3, 367–84, first published in *The Journal of Philosophy* 22, no. 25 (1925): 673–88. See also Dewey's response: John Dewey, "Half-hearted Naturalism," LW 3, 73–81, first published in *The Journal of Philosophy* 24, no. 3 (1927): 57–64.

18. The difference between the two introductions is not benign; in the second introduction, Dewey is saying the denotative method is a matter of refined experience, whereas in the first introduction, Dewey stresses the pointing-to, or indexical feature of the denotative method. The first introduction puts the denotative method on the side of qualitativeness—immediacy. The second

introduction puts the denotative method on the side of refinement; reflection or inquiry. To put the issue in Peircean terms, the first introduction makes the denotative method a matter of Secondness, and the second introduction makes the denotative method a matter of Thirdness.

19. Despite Dewey's overall positive conclusion regarding Peirce, he claims Peirce "was not at all a systematic thinker" (LW 2, 3). This claim doesn't hold up in the (later) scholarship on Peirce. As well for Dewey, Peirce was the laboratory thinker who generalized his findings to the world (e.g., CP 1, 411; 412).

20. In this latter article, Peirce of course is attempting to distinguish his Pragmaticism from James's Pragmatism. See Peirce, "What Pragmatism Is."

21. Dewey continues with his thesis of 1916 that Peirce gives us a theory of meaning in place of a theory of truth. See LW 2, 4. See also James Gouinlock, "Introduction," LW 2, xii–xiv.

22. Gouinlock considers these differences to be "minor" (Gouinlock, "Introduction," in LW 2, xiv).

23. First published as Everett W. Hall, "Some Meanings of Meaning in Dewey's Experience and Nature," *Journal of Philosophy* 25 (1928): 169–81. Republished as Everett W. Hall, "Some Meanings of Meaning in Dewey's Experience and Nature, LW 3, 401–14.

24. First published as John Dewey, "Meaning and Existence," *Journal of Philosophy* 25 (1928): 345–53.

25. Stephen Toulmin, who introduces the volume in the Collected Works edition, claims that it performs estimably in regards the first project, but shabbily in the second. See Toulmin, "Introduction," in LW 4, xxi).

26. Dewey also describes these objects as having a "two-fold character" (LW 4, 189).

27. We will notice that, unlike Peirce, Dewey places analysis prior to hypothesis formation and deduction. This seems to suggest Dewey is operating with a different model of inquiry than Peirce's hypothesis (abduction), deduction, and induction. But I would argue that Peirce has analysis built into the formation of hypothesis. Peirce tells us that an abduction is

> "The surprising fact, C, is observed
> But if A were true, C would be a matter of course
> Hence, there is reason to suspect that A is true" (Peirce, CP 5, 185).

This of course, requires analysis: analysis of C (whatever immediate object C happens to be).

28. First published as John Dewey, "Qualitative Thought," in *Symposium* 1 (1930): 5–32.

29. John Stuhr, 'Dewey's Notion of a Qualitative Experience," *Transactions of the Charles S. Peirce Society* 15, no. 1 (1979): 79; and Sandra B. Rosenthal,

"John Dewey: Scientific Method and Lived Immediacy," *Transactions of the Charles S. Peirce Society* 17, no. 4 (1981): 367 (footnote) come close to making this mistake. Rosenthal in particular, claims that "qualitative immediacy," a generic trait of existence, operates in "two different manners, each of which fits, in its own way, within the model of scientific certainty." She draws on Dewey's 1935 article "Peirce's Theory of Quality" (of which more is said in the next chapter), and in so doing, ascribes qualitative immediacy to "felt color." But this is mistaken. "Color" is not felt; what is felt is the qualitative immediacy that is in turn a trait of color, itself a reflected entity. "Color" requires the intervention of inquiry. "Things" do not have their qualitative immediacy stamped on them; rather, situations and events have this.

30. Cunningham, "Dewey's Metaphysics and the Self," 348.

31. John Dewey, "Conduct and Experience," in *Psychologies of 1930*, ed. Carl Murchison (Worcester, MA: Clark University Press, 1930), 409–22.

32. Dewey specifically mentions Max Meyer, *Psychology of the Other-one*, 2nd ed. (New York: Columbia University Press, 1922). Mead goes unmentioned. However, the argument on the genetic development of language from gestures owes in particular to Mead's 1910 "Social Consciousness and the Consciousness of Meaning."

33. Chief among these was Edward Tylor, *Primitive Culture*, 3rd ed., vol. 1 (London: John Murray, 1891); Franz Boas, *The Mind of Primitive Man* (New York: Macmillan Co, 1911); Alexander Goldenweiser, *Early Civilization* (New York: F.S. Crofts and Co, 1922); Bronislaw Malinowski, "The Problem of Meaning in Primitive Languages," in *The Meaning of Meaning*, by C. K. Ogden and I. A. Richards (New York: Harcourt, Brace, and Co, 1923); and Bronislaw Malinowksi, "Culture," in *Encyclopedia of the Social Science*, vol. 4, ed. E. R. Seligman and A. Johnson (New York: Macmillan Co, 1931). In the context of *Experience and Nature*, Dewey quotes approvingly the following (Hegelian) claim from Goldenweiser: "'A reconstructive synthesis re-establishes the synthetic unity necessarily lost in the process of analytic dismemberment'" (Goldenweiser, in LW 1, 42). See also Phillip Jackson, *John Dewey and the Philosopher's Task* (New York: Teachers College Press, 2001), 52–54.

34. See Dewey's unfinished 1949 introduction to *Experience and Nature*, esp. 331. See also Phillip Jackson's helpful discussion of this chapter in Jackson, *John Dewey and the Philosopher's Task*, esp. chapter 3.

35. John Dewey, "The Reflex-Arc Concept in Psychology," *Psychological Review* III, (July 1896): 357–70.

36. The comparison of Dewey's interaction of art and science with Hegel's categories of immediacy and particularity should be obvious. The "deposit" may be analogous to Mozur's "temporal qualities"; Mozur, "Dewey on Time and Individuality," 327. See also Alexander, *John Dewey's Theory of Art, Experience, and Nature*, 114.

37. Dewey does not mention who he has in mind here, though J. S. Mill comes in for especial criticism as one who proffered in the absolute logic, *malgré lui* (LW 2, 357).

38. See the discussion on pure and applied science by Gail Kennedy, "Dewey's Logic and Theory of Knowledge," in *Guide to the Works of John Dewey*, ed. J. Boydston (Carbondale: Southern Illinois University Press, 1972), 61–97, 86–87.

39. Dewey did not assign a text for the course, nor did he give references to texts in the course. Instead, he recommended certain texts for his students to read. Chief among these were the empirical logics of Mill and Venn; the pragmatic logic of F. C. S. Schiller and "Chance, Love, and Logic" by Peirce; his own *Essays in Experimental Logic*; the logical works of Bradley, Bonsaquet, Sigwart, and Lotze; Hegel's lesser logic from the *Encyclopedia of the Philosophical Sciences in Outline*, and various articles and encyclopedia entries from Russell, Hobhouse, Broad, and others (TLT, introduction). The last nineteen pages of the lectures are given over to Dwight's organization of the leading topics and a summary of definitions of various terms and concepts Dewey uses throughout.

40. John Dewey, *Philosophy and Civilization* (New York: Minton, Balch, and Co. 1931), 318–30. It may surprise readers of *Experience and Nature* and *Art as Experience* to learn that Dewey here advocates a neutral view of science. Technology, on the other hand, is not neutral, for it is bound up with amelioration of suffering and social problems. The distinction drawn seems to be between science as method and technology as social consequences. Hickman's exposition of the application of technology in the epilogue of *Dewey's Pragmatic Technology* does an estimable job of what is at stake. Larry Hickman, *John Dewey's Pragmatic Technology* (Bloomington, IN: Indiana University Press, 1990), 196–205.

41. Dewey continues, "The beginning of wisdom is, I repeat, the realization that science itself is an instrument which is indifferent to the external uses to which it is put . . . We are forced to consider the relation of human ideas and ideals to the social consequences which are produced by science as an instrument" (LW 6, 55). Of course, this does not diminish what Dewey has to say about the responsible use of technology, as he makes clear in *The Public and Its Problems*, "Science and Society," and elsewhere. See also Hickman, *John Dewey's Pragmatic Technology*, 202–3, for a discussion of the responsible use of technology.

42. For Klyce, this was largely disastrous, as physics (or so he thought) was moving inexorably away from realism toward a relativism that he could not countenance. Oddly enough, Einstein and Bohr were symptomatic of this move (e.g., Klyce to Dewey, July 11, 1927, 04800), though Einstein sided with the classical physicists against Bohr (and Heisenberg). His increasingly angry letters to Dewey, whom he accused of siding with the relativists as well as intentionally misreading him, demonstrated his alienation from mainstream thinking. The communication between the two ended abruptly in 1928, shortly after Klyce

published *Dewey's Suppressed Psychology*. It is fair to say that Klyce never grasped Dewey's fundamental anti-nominalism and realism.

43. Dewey seems to be quoting directly from Heisenberg's 1925 paper. Unfortunately, the correspondence gives us no hard evidence of this, but his use of quotation marks around certain phrases suggests this is the case.

44. To make this even more interesting, in a letter to Samuel Barnett, Dewey claims that probability "expresses the gap between the formula (universal) & the actual existence and occurrence (individual, as that is defined thru distribution oin [sic] a large no. of cases-" (Dewey to Barnett, January 2, 1931, 08081). Dewey also makes clear in this letter his rejection of the very notion of "immediate knowledge," and the probabilistic nature of scientific knowledge. By the time of *Essays* (1916), Dewey was close to considering all universal conceptions to be hypothetical (if-then) judgments. Probability therefore concerns the gap between the existential judgment involving existences and the hypothetical (universal) judgment involving claims about the necessity and completeness of existences.

45. It is clear that Dewey read both Bohr and Heisenberg's contributions as of a piece with the indeterminacy thesis. Indeed, this was the prevailing understanding of quantum physics at the time. By 1929, the "rationalistic and classical" physicists had begun to square off against the "relativistic and anarchic" quantum theorists, and Dewey easily sided with the latter. However, Dewey was not sufficiently read in the physics literature to see the yawning gap between Planck, who sided with the rationalists, and Heisenberg, who sided with the anarchists. Lakatos, "Falsification and the Methodology of Scientific Research Programmes," 144.

46. Mozur, "Dewey on Time and Individuality," 327. Dewey likely received textual support for this claim from Frederick Barry, *The Scientific Habit of Thought: An Informal Discussion of the Source and Character of Dependable Knowledge* (New York: Columbia University Press, 1927), whom he was reading at the time. Dewey mentions Barry (and Percy Bridgman) in a letter to Sidney Hook (Dewey to Hook, January 4, 1929, 05719). We find Dewey grappling with the findings of quantum physics in terms of the individual-in-relation. Of course, this was for Dewey a genetic-existential relationship. "Of course my general aim is to show from [t]he subjectmatter [sic] of physics as well as from the side of thought as method that science deals with objects in their instrumental relationships., not their inner nature intrinsic qualities, and then treat 'experience'—a word Im [sic] avoiding however—as direct realization of their qualities. If I knew enough I think I could show that the space-time events of modern physics involve genuine history, which involves tendencies toward 'ends'—that is limiting termini, and thus describe individuals., while || physical knowledge abstracts from individuals as such. I wish I knew enough physics to really get hold of Heisenbergs [sic] indetermination principle; I suppose you know the proof that veloecity [sic] and position cannot both be determined ˏof the same observed objectˏ [*in ink w.*

caret] and the consequent reinterpretation of Planck's quantum equation constant as indicating the limits of indeterminateness in prediction of any observation.ed [sic] event—I f[e]el sure that this means the scientific unit is a true individual but I dont [sic] know enough to make it clear. Also that the matter-energy problem is essentially the problem of the individual, as discrete [sic], and relations, [*ink comma*] interactions, as continuity. In other words, the social problem in petto." The problem of the individual-in-relation was a metaphysical one (involving the generic traits of existence) *and* a logical one (involving logical traits of serial-temporal ordering. Indeed, alongside continuity, it may be *the most important problem* for Dewey's philosophy considered as a whole.

47. Percy Bridgman was a physicist teaching at Harvard University whom Dewey drew upon in writing *The Quest for Certainty*. Bridgman is cited directly at LW 4, 89. Bridgman shows up first in Dewey's correspondence with Klyce (e.g., John Dewey to Scudder Klyce, July 9, 1927, 04699). Bridgman wrote Dewey on November 6, 1929, to congratulate him on the publication of *The Quest for Certainty*. Bridgman, however, took exception to Dewey's account of operationalism, which, in Bridgman's mind, had more to do with how things really were and less to do with what probability and statistics nets us. At the end of the letter, Bridgman states, "The only sense in which Nature can be said to be intelligible in the light of Heisenberg's principle and with my meaning of the words is a || statistical sense; if there are many cracks of sound we can predict or control their average behavior with some exactitude. It seems to me that the implications of this go beyond anything treated in your book; perhaps some day you will write another book dealing also with this" (Bridgman to Dewey, November 6, 1929, 06347). Dewey's correspondence with Hook shows that he was well aware of the statistical significance of reality, and endorsed this.

48. The entire discussion is framed by Dewey's account of the seminar on logical theory given in 1927–1928 at Columbia University. The account of reality Dewey presents is a consensus definition based on a report given by a student (Gruen) at the last class.

49. The reference for the abstract account is to J. B. S. Haldane's *Possible Worlds*, which was published in 1927, and perhaps to the essay "Some Enemies of Science." See J. B. S. Haldane, *Possible Worlds* (Edinburgh: Edinburgh University Press, 1927).

50. In the Kantian schema, the disjunctive judgment is the third of three judgments in the twelve judgments that make up the table of judgments. (See Kant, *The Critique of Pure Reason*, A 74.) Dewey is not the first to suggest upending these. Hegel, in the *Science of Logic*, made hypothetical judgments and disjunctive judgments (particular judgments and individual judgments) dependent on categorical judgments (general or absolute judgments), but each of these in turn dependent on the others for their use in syllogistic logic. The syllogism of induction follows the schema, not of Allness (I-P-U) but Individuality (U-I-P).

See Hegel, *Science of Logic*, 689. F. H. Bradley, following Hegel, also upended the ordering of the judgments. See F. H. Bradley, *Principles of Logic*, vol. 1, 53–54.

51. Dewey does provide extended treatments of Aristotle and Mill, both of whom are treated extensively in the 1915–1916 Lectures. Much of the discussion is repetitive.

52. Dewey would strike a consistent note in the 1938 *Logic*; Causality is a matter of and for inquiry, and not an ontological relationship between situations and their immediate qualities (LW 12, 455).

53. Dewey recurs to the water example in the lectures as well. The context is a question regarding the abstract nature of water. The response is couched in terms of what best describes the overall behavior of phenomena in question.

54. This is despite Dewey's (casual) use of the term in *Essays* (1916).

55. Aristotle perhaps did not see this, but certainly by the nineteenth century others, notably Hegel and Bradley, had. Thus, Dewey follows Hegel and Bradley, who both consider the first figure of the syllogism (BARBARA) as a universal affirmation. Not only this, they consider the movements of the syllogism to be sets of propositions that are themselves wholes, but are to take their places in further wholes. See Hegel, *Science of Logic*, 667. Bradley, *Principles of Logic*, vol. 2, 227–31.

56. Sleeper, *The Necessity of Pragmatism*, 86.

57. Russell, "Professor Dewey's Essays in Experimental Logic," 245. Dewey will turn the tables on Russell by agreeing with him in regard to the barrenness of the syllogistic form: neither the syllogism nor its premises say anything about substances, which is an existential-situational matter. The syllogism, then, can only operate as a set of logical operations in thought, not in existence, and so has intellectual, but not existential purport. See TLT, December 19, 1928.

58. Abstractions as operations are hinted at in *Studies* and *Essays*. But they are often cast as conceptions improving relations between thoughts. Here, the explicit linkage with conceptions is downplayed or removed.

59. Put this way, abstraction shares characteristics with the "suggestion" and "deliberative rehearsal" of Dewey's two editions of *How We Think* (1910; and esp. 1933). I discuss "deliberative rehearsal" at length in the following chapter.

60. Dewey follows Bertrand Russell, *Introduction to Mathematical Philosophy*, on this point. Note this is a concession to Russell from his critique in *Essays*. There, Dewey criticized Russell's faulty sense-psychology, rooted in classical empiricism. Here, Dewey avoids that discussion and points up Russell's insistence on the removal of logical operations from (metaphysical) claims about substances, including our perception of them.

61. In making this claim, Dewey gestures the students toward John Theodore Merz, *History of European Thought in the 19th Century*, 4th ed. (Edinburgh: William Blackwood and Sons, 1932).

62. "The whole subject of the subject, predicate and copula is a myth and the real subject is always an existence outside of the active judging" (Bradley, *Principles of Logic*, vol. 1, 133). For Hegel, "actuality" (*Wirklichkeit*), as "concrete existence" (*Existenz*; *das Konkrete*) is a categorization that precedes syllogistic operations. This categorization is the "true appearance" that plays its role in syllogistic operations as real. Hegel, *Science of Logic*, 512.

63. The particular principles of mathematics (for example, Euclid's axioms) are opening premises, not operations. They are tautological when attempts at a proof are made and imply and invoke no substance behind or beneath them. Dewey follows Hegel, Gauss, Riemann, Peirce, Bradley, Russell, and others in making this point. Here we have the beginnings of Thomas Burke's (correct) claim that "A universal term, as part of a symbol system, is an abstraction representing an ability (a possible way of acting or a mode of being)." F. Thomas Burke, "Prospects for Mathematizing Dewey's Logical Theory," 139.

64. John Dewey, "The Present Position of Logical Theory," *The Monist* 2, no. 1 (1891): 1–17.

65. In the lead-up to the 1938 *Logic*, Dewey aligns scientific induction with descriptive generalizations in terms of probability interpreted as a frequency distribution. Dewey Papers, *Logic*, II, 102, Box 52, File 17, Special Collections Research Center, Morris Library, Southern Illinois University, 2. Here, Dewey follows Peirce, CP 5, 179, who assigns a "probametric" [sic] measure to the agreement of theory with fact.

66. Dwight recurs to the metaphors of discovery and testing. It is difficult to say whether these are Dewey's because she says "Perhaps the best way of making clear what Dewey means is to put it this way . . ." Discovery is the novel in which we obtain something new as regards the primary subject-matter. Testing is the validation of the consequences (TLT, October 31, 1927). But in the same lecture, it seems Dewey does talk of these metaphors as phases of inference.

67. While it may seem astounding for Dewey to consider induction as the inferential function par excellence, and deduction as the testing of conclusions-as-consequences, there is plenty of historical precedent for this. Hegel, too, thought the "syllogism of induction" a higher because more reflected syllogistic operation than the bare "syllogism of existence," and furthermore, a necessary premise (together with the "syllogism of Allness") for any syllogism of something's necessity to be operative (Hegel, *Science of Logic*, 686–704).

68. Dewey maintained the testing function of induction in *How We Think* (MW 6, 243), but did not recur to this until the 1927–1928 Lectures. The upshot is to bring him close to Peirce, who conceives (along with Mill) of induction as a test *and* an inference. See Peirce, "Induction, Deduction, Hypothesis," 197. It is significant to note that in Peirce's loose circle of deduction, induction, and hypothesis, it is hypothesis that carries the speculative weight of inference on its shoulders.

69. Of course, Dewey does discuss the falsity of the reliance on British sense-psychology Newton uses in his *Principia Mathematica* and elsewhere, in *Experience and Nature*. See esp. LW 1, 143–44.

70. As I have discussed with respect to the correspondence, Dewey was reading Bridgman, Eddington, and Barry prior to writing *The Quest for Certainty*.

71. "There must be some evenly flowing external change—in reality no change at all—in reference to which they have fixed positions of before and after and of simultaneity. Since velocity and acceleration of observed motions would be disjointed from absolute position and date if they were relative to an observer-to the disruption of the whole physical scheme—motion must also be absolute" (LW 4, 115).

72. It also demonstrated, for Dewey, that all mathematical symbolization of physical events was relational, not qualitative or intrinsic. They were, in other words, matters of inquiry, not existence. We come back to this point in the final section on *The Quest for Certainty*.

73. Curiously though, Dewey does not mention the work of H. A. Lorentz in bridging the gap between Maxwell's equations and Newton's mechanics, nor the use Einstein made of these in his own theories of relativity. For it was through the Lorentz Transforms Einstein was able to conclude that mass was not conserved, though momentum was.

74. Dewey quotes from Albert Einstein, *Relativity: The Special and General Theory* (New York, 1920), 26. "We require a definition of simultaneity such that this definition supplies us with a *method* by which in particular cases the physicist can decide by experiment whether or not two events occur simultaneously." Italics Dewey's.

75. Dewey does not develop the claim about space and time suggested in his correspondence to Hook. Nevertheless, there is nothing in the pages of *The Quest for Certainty* to suggest that he abandons the notion of quanta as phenomenal artifacts. His insistence for this is congruent with his claim that qualitative events are not spatial-temporal for physical science. Nevertheless, Dewey, *The Philosophy of John Dewey*, 126; Kadlec, *Dewey's Critical Pragmatism*, 26; and Siegfried, *Dewey's Logical Forms*, 197, are all correct about Dewey's use of Heisenberg to buttress his experimental method in the pages of *The Quest for Certainty*.

76. In his discussion, Dewey recurs to the language of the 1929 introduction to *Experience and Nature*—experience as "gross" (LW 1, 15).

77. Dewey once again recurs to the example of water and H_2O, first presented in *Democracy and Education*, and the sugar and sweetness example in *Experience and Nature* and elsewhere.

78. Dewey gives the example of natural selection, "which is a principle of elimination but not one controlling positive development" (LW 4, 128).

79. The term "transaction" is famously defined and used in Dewey's 1946 paper with Arthur Bentley, titled, "Transactions as Known and Named," *Journal*

of Philosophy XLIII (1946): 533–51, republished in John Dewey and Arthur Bentley, *Knowing and the Known* (Boston: Beacon Press, 1949) (LW 16, 113–43).

80. Sandra Rosenthal gets this exactly right in "Scientific Method and Lived Immediacy," 362. "True to the model of the relation between the more concrete and the more abstract, qualitative immediacy conditions all the constituents of a given experience, but in turn the constituents of a given experience enrich the felt qualitative immediacy with the meaningfulness of the transactional context within which it emerges."

81. We see other sorts of statements operative in scientific contexts, and these involve manipulation of either phenomena themselves, or technologies that measure phenomena. "Put the substance in your mouth" is a statement that is necessary for the establishment of the conclusion that "sugar is sweet," but it doesn't carry the weight of hypothetical necessity on its back.

82. This problem doesn't get solved until 1938, with Dewey's distinction between the if . . . then statement or proposition, and the (evaluative) judgment in which it takes place, and of which it is a part. This was one of Ernest Nagel's great concerns regarding Dewey's theory of propositions—whether all propositions were relational in form, and if so, how does Dewey respond? The answer, it seems, is to be found in Dewey's distinction between the act of asserting an if . . . then claim and doing the evaluative work that ushers in a conclusion. The assertion is propositional; the evaluation is judgmental. See Patrick Suppes, "Nagel's Lectures on Dewey's Logic," in *Philosophy, Science, and Method, Essays in Honor of Ernest Nagel*, ed. S. Morgenbesser, P. Suppes, and M. White (New York: St. Martin's Press, 1969), 13. See also LW 12, 263, for the definitive response.

Chapter 4

1. Cunningham, "Dewey's Metaphysics and the Self," 348.

2. Of course, this is a claim Dewey made at least as early as the introduction to *Essays*. In *Essays*, the context is the immediacy of "things." "Things" turn out to have a dialectical quality, a to-and-fro that, in conjunction with the trait of uniqueness, characterizes the immediacy of objects immediately had (MW 10, 323). This earlier characterization of what would become a full account of Dewey's naturalistic metaphysics in *Experience and Nature* and "Qualitative Thought" stressed the completeness, the uniqueness, and the dialectics of traits in interaction.

3. Though he comes closest at LW 1, 371–72. Several have attempted to flesh this out. Among those who have worked on Dewey's theory of continuity to join the two functional kinds of experience are Thomas Alexander, *John Dewey's Theory of Art, Experience, and Nature*; Thomas Alexander, "The Aesthetics of Reality: The Development of Dewey's Ecological Theory of Experience," *Dewey's*

Logical Theory: New Studies and Interpretations, ed. F. Thomas Burke, D. Micah Hester, and R. B. Talisse (Nashville, TN: Vanderbilt University Press, 2002), 20; John Stuhr, "Dewey's Reconstruction of Metaphysics," *Transactions of the Charles S. Peirce Society* 28, no. 2 (1992): 161–76.

    4. John Dewey, *How We Think: A Restatement of the Relation of Reflective Thinking to the Educative Process*, 2nd ed. (New York: D.C. Heath and Co, 1933).

    5. For an examination of the middle section of *How We Think* (1910), the reader is referred to Johnston, *John Dewey's Earlier Logical Inquiry*, chapter 5, 150–57.

    6. The chapter on the "Analysis of Reflective Thinking," which corresponds to the chapter in the first edition titled "The Complete Act of Thought," is completely rewritten. The new version stresses the recursive nature of inquiry far better than the earlier: the phases or steps of inquiry don't follow in a set order (LW 8, 206). I discuss recursion and its role in the pattern of inquiry further in this chapter.

    7. Certain thinkers (e.g., Alexander) think Dewey has solved the issue. See, for example, Alexander, *John Dewey's Theory of Art, Experience, and Nature*, 113. Here, I attempt to show what Dewey did accomplish, and what remains for him to deal with in the 1938 *Logic*.

    8. Note this continuity is *not* coeval with the continuity built up in inquiry and equivalent to the causal-temporal linkage of events and situations in a pattern of inquiry. This continuity is immediate; it is had, felt, and is a pervasive quality of experience (LW 10, 198) that is undefined unless and until it, too, is subject to inquiry. This is one aspect or phase of a *double continuity*; a continuity that, conjoined with the continuity in inquiry, emerges as unity.

    9. The trait of continuity is associated with, though distinguished from, traits of rhythm and unity or wholeness in *Experience and Nature*. To say, for example, that there is a trait of continuity immediately felt in having an experience is to say that there is a trait of rhythm and unity in that experience. Though Dewey himself doesn't claim this congruency, it seems to follow from the claim for continuity.

    10. See Thomas Alexander, *John Dewey's Theory of Art, Experience, and Nature*, 95. See also Phillip Jackson, *John Dewey and the Lessons of Art* (Chicago: University of Chicago Press, 1998), esp. 122–24.

    11. I am specifically thinking of Dewey's mapping metaphors as discussed in *Experience and Nature* (LW 1, 124–25; 308–9). Maps do more than describe; they transform what is observed. I am also thinking of Raymond Boisvert's helpful commentary regarding Dewey's mapping of the traits of existence in "Dewey's Metaphysics: Ground-Map of the Prototypically Real," 155.

    12. Thomas Dalton, *Becoming John Dewey*, 282–83 chides interpreters of Dewey's logical theory for not taking seriously enough the dialectical quality, rooted in our biology and (natural) ontology of kinds, that is found in such

domains as affirmative and negative judgments. No doubt qualities do diverge in immediate experience; but the quality of divergence itself is importantly taken up in a reciprocity in relationship. This is the logical trait of continuity that pervades our judging. This is the important consideration for continuity in respect of logical inquiry, and it is a consideration I think Dalton misses.

13. Of course, and as I discuss when I come to Dewey's essay "Peirce's Theory of Quality," an answer can be given. Very briefly, it would bring Dewey close in line with Peirce on quality and the role of the (human) organism in acting and reacting on felt qualities. In other words, it would stress the role of Secondness in Dewey, and how Secondness manifests as ontologically real, with its qualitative components (traits) as First and the action-reaction of the human organism (the to-and-fro of doing and undergoing), gelled into a qualitatively integral real with meaning (This and That) as Second, and not merely the (haphazard) product of adaptive learning. For example, temporality would therefore feature as a qualitative trait (First) that plays a necessary role in the action-reaction of the human organism (Second) in the encounter of organism and world. This relationship of sign-to-sign is a causal one; the linkage between the existential, temporal quality (in this case) and the event or situation of experience had and undergone as "gross" and "macroscopic" (Second) is inextricable. From there, we go on to forming existential propositions in inquiry (Thirds) by isolated these traits as qualities (Firsts) in the two-and-fro of an experience of doings and undergoings (Second). Dewey comes closest to this, I think, in his characterization of denotation as pointing-to (LW 1, 371–72); indexing. This is the semiotic of Seconds in Peirce that begins for the inquirer the investigation into an experience.

14. See also G. H. Mead, "Social Consciousness and the Consciousness of Meaning."

15. This serves to distinguish Dewey's theory of language from that of linguistic idealism, most notably Robert Brandom's semantic pragmatism. For Brandom, there is no material basis for symbols, as he considers such a basis an aspect of the myth of the given. To speak of material is not to speak of matter, objects, or things; rather, commitments. See, for example, Robert Brandom, *Articulating Reasons: An Introduction to Inferentialism* (Cambridge: Harvard University Press, 2000), 34–35; Robert Brandom, *Perspectives on Pragmatism: Classic, Recent, and Contemporary* (Cambridge, MA: Harvard University Press, 2011), 51.

16. *How We Think*, 2nd ed. (LW 8, 182–86); *Art as Experience* (LW 10, 284–86); *Liberalism and Social Action* (LW 11, 46–48); "Authority and Social Change" (LW 11, 130–45); "Freedom" (LW 11, 247–55); and "Religion, Science, and Philosophy: Review of Bertrand Russell's *Religion and Science*" (LW 11, 454–63). Beyond these are numerous articles and presentations concerning the role of external authority on educational matters, specifically external authority, teaching, and the schools.

17. At this time, Dewey was reading (at least) two manuscripts with science and freedom as their subject matter: Julian Huxley, *Scientific Research and Social Needs* (London: Watts and Co., 1934), and Walter Lippmann, *The Method of Freedom* (New York: Macmillan Co, 1934).

18. Needless to say, a thorough naturalization of the experimental attitude would yield an attitude free from transcendentalisms and supernaturalisms; an attitude relying thoroughly on a genetic-historical (and fallible) accounting of methods and techniques in inquiry. This doesn't, however, discount the role in such a description of the naturalistic metaphysics Dewey offers in texts as *Experience and Nature* and *Art as Experience*. Indeed, for the full genetic-historical (and fallible) accounting, it demands them.

19. This goes along with the need for "the whole creature" to participate in the production of an (aesthetic) object (LW 10, 33). This "production" is inhibited "[w]herever conditions are such as to prevent the act of production from being and experience in which the whole creature is alive and in which he possesses his living through enjoyment" (LW 10, 33). Hickman, *Dewey's Pragmatic Technology*, discusses the various uses of the term production in *Experience and Nature* and *Art as Experience*.

20. It should be noted that this "social factor," discussed at length in the 1938 *Logic*, LW 12, 483–84, Dewey attributes to Peirce, and to the article that Peirce pens for James Mark Baldwin's *Dictionary of Philosophy and Psychology*. See Charles S. Peirce, Logic, *Dictionary of Philosophy and Psychology*, ed. James Mark Baldwin (New York, Macmillan and Co., 1905), 647–703.

21. John Dewey, "Authority and Social Change," *School and Society* 44 (October 10, 1936): 457–66.

22. We see this particularly in the 1927–1928 Types of Logical Theory lectures, the discussion in chapter 3 to which the reader is referred.

23. John Dewey, "Religion, Science, and Philosophy: Review of Bertrand Russell's Religion and Science, *Southern Review* 2 (Summer 1936): 53–62; Bertrand Russell, *Religion and Science* (New York: Henry Holt and Co., 1935).

24. Dewey was reading Oliver Reiser, *Philosophy and the Concepts of Modern Science* at this time; this was a text dealing with these same issues.

25. Russell draws on Andrew Dickson White, *A History of Warfare of Science with Theology in Christendom*, 2 vols. (New York: D. Appleton and Co., 1896) and William Edward Hartpole Lecky, *History of the Rise and Influence of the Spirit of Rationalism in Europe*, 2 vols. (London: Longman, Roberts and Green, 1865).

26. This was also, and characteristically, the charge against Peirce's conception of the community of scientific inquirers; they were chiefly laboratory scientists. See Dewey, LW 2, 3. One might say Dewey wanted to take the laboratory conception of Peirce and transfer it to the general public.

27. I am, of course, thinking of criticisms of Dewey's logical theory by Bertrand Russell and Hans Reichenbach (profiled in the *Library of Living*

Philosophers), together with Dewey's exasperated response to them in his rejoinder. John Dewey, "Experience, Knowledge, and Value: A Rejoinder," in *The Philosophy of John Dewey*, ed. P. Schilpp and L. E. Hahn (La Salle: Open Court, 1989), 515–608. Dewey's earlier commentators on the 1938 *Logic* don't discuss these particular critics and their issues, but later ones (Ralph Sleeper, Thomas Burke) do. Sleeper discusses a number of these critics in *The Necessity of Pragmatism*, especially in chapter 6 and the subsequent Critical Biography. Burke, of course, discusses them in *Dewey's New Logic*, and they form much of the backdrop to his own rendering of Dewey's logic. Many of Dewey's major biographers discuss these. Thomas Dalton, *Becoming John Dewey: Dilemmas of a Philosopher and Naturalist*; George Dykhuizen, *The Life and Mind of John Dewey*; Robert Westbrook, *John Dewey and American Democracy*; Alan Ryan, *John Dewey and the High Tide of American Liberalism*; Melvin Rogers, The *Undiscovered Dewey: Religion, Morality, and the Ethos of Democracy* (New York: Columbia University Press, 2009), all contain discussions of Dewey's retorts to his logical critics.

28. As we shall see, the term existential is gradually dropped in place of the more specific terms particular and singular. Dewey discusses existential propositions as particular and singular in his correspondence with Sidney Hook in 1935 (e.g., Dewey to Hook, June 05, 1935, 07402) and again in chapter 14 of the 1938 *Logic*, at 298–300, where existential propositions are referred to under the rubric of "contingent conditional propositions" and "matter of fact or contingent disjunctive propositions." Dewey also considers propositions ordered in sets to be existential (compare with the 1938 *Logic*, LW 12, 311–12). I discuss "contingent conditional propositions" (as Dewey calls them in 1938) further, in light of the distinctions Dewey draws between generic "All-some" propositions and universals.

29. For Peirce, the sign (as Second) is real in the most robust sense of the term, that is, in its effect on the Third (interpretant, law, habit, mind) (C. S. Peirce, "The Categories Defended," 177). I believe Dewey will characterize the reality formed of qualities in existential propositions as having a similar robustness, and that these qualities, refined in the experience of thinking, result in existentially real objects with meaning. I follow Ralph Sleeper in this regard. See Sleeper, *The Necessity of Pragmatism*, esp. 167. However, I disagree with Sleeper's conclusion that Dewey somehow thought Peirce's theory of continuity (synechism) was a "guarantee of eventual objectivity" and because of this, was duly reconstructed by Dewey (Sleeper, *The Necessity of Pragmatism*, 167). Some of Sleeper's characterizations of Peirce are simply wrong. To say Peirce "constructed his metaphysical schemes in terms of destiny, confident that everything would come out right in the end, that truth is what we are fated to come up with if we can just get our meanings clear" (Sleeper, *The Necessity of Pragmatism*, 126) only makes sense if one stops reading Peirce at 1878. For a view more conciliatory to mine on the theory of continuity, see Vincent Colapietro, "Experimental Logic:

Normative Theory or Natural History," in *Dewey's Logical Theory: New Studies and Interpretations*, ed. F. T. Burke, D. M. Hester, and R. B. Talisse (Nashville: Vanderbilt University Press, 2002), 43–71, esp. 50–51.

30. There is no recourse to "analytic" necessity in Dewey's logic. All necessity is a conclusion dependent upon the operations performed. Dewey makes this clear in a number of places, especially the 1938 *Logic* (LW 12, 327–28).

31. This, of course, would become the subject matter of chapter 26—The Logic of Inquiry and Philosophies of Knowledge.

32. This is a problem for Dewey's interlocutors, then and now. Ernest Nagel is probably the one who has said the most about Dewey's supposed failure to distinguish properly between generic propositions and universal conceptions in the 1938 *Logic*. Others have included Morton White, H. S. Thayer, and Lowell Nissen. Thayer follows White (who follows Quine) in his criticism of Dewey's so-called "analytic-synthetic" distinction between universals (analytic propositions) and generic (synthetic propositions); Morton White, *The Origins of John Dewey's Instrumentalism* (New York: Columbia University Press, 1943), 42; Thayer, *The Logic of Pragmatism*, 98; 216. Ralph Sleeper has gone some way in responding to these criticisms, as has Thomas Burke. I discuss the issue of the differences between the propositions in more detail when I discuss the *Journal of Philosophy* articles. For more on these criticisms, see Morton White, *The Origins of John Dewey's Instrumentalism*; Ernest Nagel, *Sovereign Reason and Other Studies in the Philosophy of Science* (Glencoe, IL: The Free Press, 1954); Patrick Suppes, "Nagel's Lectures on Dewey's Logic," esp. 12–13; Ernest Nagel, Introduction, LW 12, esp. xvi–xvii; H. S. Thayer, *The Logic of Pragmatism*, esp. 85–161; Lowell Nissen, *John Dewey's Theory of Inquiry and Truth* (Mouton and Co., 1966), esp. 61–67. For defenses of Dewey, see Ralph Sleeper, *The Necessity of Pragmatism*, 145–55; Thomas Burke, *Dewey's New Logic*, 176–214. Regarding Quine, see the discussion begun by John Shook, Dewey, and Quine on the Logic of What There Is, *Dewey's Logical Theory: New Studies and Interpretations* (Nashville, TN: Vanderbilt University Press, 2002), 93–120.

33. The letter is dated December 4, 1925, and sent to Albert Barnes (Dewey to Barnes, December 4, 1925, 04215). Here, Dewey specifically indicates he is working on a new treatise, which will be an "introduction to logical theory." See also the discussion of Dewey's 1927–1928 Types of Logical Theory in the previous chapter.

34. The letter indicates that Sidney Hook asked specifically for an outline. This strongly suggests Dewey was having an earnest conversation with Hook regarding the writing of the *Logic*. However, I can find nothing in the correspondence prior to the letter of November 22, 1934, containing an outline, nor a suggestion of an outline; as the letter makes clear, this is the first outline Dewey wrote. The textual apparatus appended to *The Collected Works* edition of *Logic: The Theory of Inquiry*, by Kathleen Paolos, based in part on the recollections of

Ernest Nagel, makes it seem otherwise. See Kathleen Paolos, Textual Commentary (LW 12, 533–49, 534).

35. The correspondences I claim here are rough; obviously, material that would categorically fit within the 1934 sections of Dewey outlines is found here and there in the 1938 *Logic*. What follows is therefore an approximation of the content of the outline on the basis of what Dewey actually did write in the 1938 *Logic*.

36. I discuss the pattern of inquiry as Dewey presents it in *How We Think*, 2nd ed., in an upcoming section.

37. As Dewey remarks in a footnote in the 1938 *Logic* (LW 12, 372), the basic theory of forms is in place by the time of *Art as Experience*. That theory, consisting of an account of "continuity, cumulation [sic], conservation, tension and anticipation," are the formal conditions of logical form as well as aesthetic form (LW 10, 143). Many thanks to Jim Garrison for pointing this passage out.

38. Dewey and Ratner were both reading Oliver Reiser, *Philosophy and the Concepts of Modern Science*, at the time much of this correspondence took place (1935). Reiser argued for a unified account of science and social science, with a natural law pattern as their shared basis. Reiser was one who took seriously the role played by method in social science, and argued for what would be later termed a post-positivist account of concepts in science.

39. Here, we have a good example of the importance for physical science of *individuation*; denoting, as Dewey puts it in the first introduction to *Experience and Nature* (LW 1, 372), is "pointing-to," and pointing-to turns out to be central in distinguishing the real, though as yet incomplete. As live creatures, we don't have a choice about pointing-to; it is part and parcel of our nature. But, for that, it is crucial in what follows: operations that do elicit real (logical) objects that consist in real relations of conceptions and their propositions.

40. We can compare what Dewey says here with his account of mapping in *Experience and Nature*, at LW 1, 125.

41. This is, of course, the point that Hans Reichenbach consistently missed in criticizing Dewey for having what amounted to an idealistic theory of relations in his article for the Library of Living Philosophers volume. It is also the point on which Dewey rested in his defense in the rejoinder. Hans Reichenbach, Dewey's Theory of Science, *The Philosophy of John Dewey*, ed. P. A. Schilpp and L. E. Hahn (La Salle, IL: Open Court, 1989), 157–92; Dewey, "Experience, Nature, and Value: A Rejoinder" (LW 13), 20.

42. Apparently, Ratner sent Dewey a copy of a manuscript on logic he was working on at the time. I cannot find among Dewey's collected papers any such copy.

43. Dewey also claims in the letter to Ratner that "the general generic—is the common sense common noun—the kind is essentially extensive (recurrence)—the universal is a formula—intension" (Dewey to Ratner, May 01, 1935, 06971).

Extension, then, applies *to the kind*; *intension* to the *universal*. We see how this plays out in terms of Dewey's account of classes and kinds in his papers to the *Journal of Philosophy*.

44. Again, the *locus classicus* of this is Hegel's *Science of Logic*, wherein major and minor premises, together with the individuals that are formed through their combination, become their opposites for one another. See Hegel, *Science of Logic*, 667; 689.

45. As we said as regards the functional distinctions Dewey makes beginning in the 1927–1928 Types of Logical Theory lectures, this is the true beginning of what will become Dewey's "taxonomy" (Burke, *Dewey's New Logic*, 172) of propositions and conceptions. As we will discuss, singular (This has X) and particular (That is doing X activity) propositions, as well as propositions ordered in sets, will take the place of existential propositions in the 1938 *Logic*. No one lays this taxonomy out as well as Burke, *Dewey's New Logic*, 176–90. See also Ralph Sleeper's (earlier) accounting of propositions, particularly the distinction between particular and singular, in Sleeper, *The Necessity of Pragmatism*, 146–47.

46. This should remind us how important the context is for Dewey as regards the role of propositions; singular propositions (This is of Kind, A) are not inferential in that they do no inferential work *by themselves*. Put them in a syllogism, however (as a minor premise), and they become part of an inference involving propositions and conceptions, which result in an evaluative judgment. This helps to distinguish conceptions as conclusions of evaluative judgments (which are hypothetical-universal) from mere propositions of quantity (All-Some assertions) distinguished from their use as a major premise in a syllogism.

47. I believe Larry Hickman was the first to notice the two functions of universals for the 1938 *Logic*, in his explication of universals as those that have either quasi-experimental import or no experimental import whatsoever. Larry Hickman, "Dewey's Theory of Inquiry," in *Reading Dewey: Interpretations for a Postmodern Generation*, ed. Larry Hickman (Bloomington, IN: Indiana University Press, 1995), 166–86; 183.

48. Curiously, Hans Siegfried makes no mention of these very important articles for Dewey's overall contribution to the theory of forms in the 1938 *Logic* in his otherwise well-written Dewey's Logical Forms (Hans Siegfried, "Dewey's Logical Forms," 2002). However, Thomas Burke does in his Qualities, Universals, Kinds, and the New Riddle of Induction (Thomas Burke, "Qualities, Universals, Kinds, and the New Riddle of Induction," in *Dewey's Logical Theory: New Studies and Interpretations*, ed. F. Thomas Burke, D. Micah Hester, and Robert B. Talisse (Nashville: Vanderbilt University Press, 2002), 225–36.

49. Kathleen Paolos, Textual Commentary (LW 12), 548.

50. It is important to remember that particular and singular propositions are formed in inquiry; they do not first appear to us as immediate, or as fixed and final forms then used in formal operations of inference (judgments); they are

the products of judgments and, specifically, the *evaluative* products of judgments. They operate as propositions in inquiries as yet settled. See LW 12, 467–69.

51. And this is of course dependent on their position (and role) in a syllogism. In a syllogism, a particular instance of X can never be a general unless and until it operates as a general (e.g., "All X's are Y's"). The relation between singular and kind remains generic unless and until it is used in an inference. Operations and inferences, and not fixed and final forms, dictate the position and role of particulars and generals in a syllogism.

52. Dewey indicates that it is part of a syllogism that requires a further, particular (minor) premise that designates the existence of (a) human (LW 11, 96). Particular attention to the context in which these propositions are used, Dewey thinks, will obviate the concern of distinguishing them. Nagel gets hung up on this and similar examples, for he seems not to see the logical distinction between the generic All-some and the universal All-some. See Nagel, Introduction (LW 12, xvii).

53. Dewey says, "But that which is universal cannot be logically grounded [inferentially derived] in what is existential, although psychologically and historically the latter may be a circumstantial occasion of its formation" (LW 11, 99). While it remains the case that the abstraction from a particular has its basis in psychological operations and can historically be accounted for, as an abstraction it is of a different logical form than an existential quality.

54. Dewey gives us the counterparts of whiteness in the findings of physical optics (LW 11, 99–100).

55. Dewey's claim is especially salient for the argument he makes in the 1938 *Logic* regarding existential propositions concerning contingency (LW 12, 298–300). Dewey will also refer to propositions involved in sets as existential, as is evidenced in a letter to Sidney Hook (Dewey to Hook, February 3, 1938, 06011) and again in the 1938 *Logic* (LW 12, 311–12).

56. We find a similar account of intension in the discussion of reflective judgment in Hegel, *Science of Logic*, 646–47, and in Bradley, *Logic*, vol. 1, 113. We find this also in Peirce, in his accounting of "collection," in *Reasoning and the Logic of Things*, esp. 157–58.

57. I find that characterizing generic propositions as concerning extensional reach and universals as concerning intensional depth goes a long way to alleviating the concerns of Ernest Nagel and others who see slippage in Dewey's characterization of propositions, especially those of the All-Some variety.

58. Dewey invokes Peirce's notion of "leading principles" as analogous to his functioning of universals in operations. In a footnote on page 108, Dewey notes Peirce's aversion to nominalism and his sympathy with scholastic realism; forming universals is a natural operation for Peirce, and through their use, existential material becomes more amenable (Dewey uses the term "reasonable") to practical consequences (LW 11, 108). See also the discussion of "leading Principles" in

Thayer, *The Logic of Pragmatism*, footnote, 218. Dewey does not indicate either his approval or disapproval of Peirce's antipathy toward nominalism.

59. In a paragraph, Dewey lays aside the objection that possibility is thwarted in this distinction between logical forms. For possibility is also a logical form; in a universal conception (All men are mortal), there are a potentially infinite number of possibilities of application of the concepts humanity and mortality. This, of course, concerns merely logical possibility; it does not concern actual or existential possibility. This is a separate (though not completely unrelated) issue and is dealt with by Sleeper, *The Necessity of Pragmatism*, 138.

60. H. S. Thayer seems to get hung up on this point. Thayer, *The Logic of Pragmatism*, 94–95. But Dewey is clear that the relationship of universals to generic propositions *is* one of (hierarchical) ordering, even as the forms are signs of operations, and not fixed and final.

61. Dewey discusses the nominalism/realism debate at some length toward the end of the essay, and finds features in nominalism to his liking. This has led some to downplay the significance of Peirce's role in helping Dewey to see through the issues involved in building an account of universals. But Dewey's praise for nominalism only applies to the importance it attaches to symbols—an importance that cannot be denied in the case of Peirce. Other features of nominalism, especially its lack of an operational basis for those symbols, come under attack. See James Feibleman, *An Introduction to Peirce's Philosophy Interpreted as a System*, 474–75; Sleeper, *The Necessity of Pragmatism*, 138. Note that for Sleeper, Dewey's insistence that there are no "unactualized possibles" for sensation rules out Firsts in Peirce's sense, and is a point separating the two. Sleeper might claim there are no Firsts for Dewey; for every quality had in an experience is already a feature of that experience—a Second. And this rules out Firsts, or so it seems; or (to put the point differently), Peirce's Seconds are Dewey's Firsts. Of course, this begs the question of what is First in the Second (for Peirce), and we arrive back where we began.

62. The text cited in the article for especial consideration is Stebbing, *A Modern Introduction to Logic*.

63. Of course, Peirce "solved" this problem by referring to these objects as degenerate Thirds, or Thirds of second-degree degeneration, involving false attribution (relation) of perceptual material to a mythical concept. Dewey solves the problem through drawing the distinction between generic or general uses of propositions and uses of universals and claiming that the problem is an invalid one for universals. See C. S. Peirce, "A Guess at the Riddle," in *The Essential Peirce*, vol. 1, ed. N. Hauser and C. Kloesel (Bloomington: Indiana University Press, 1992), 255.

64. Dewey recognizes the work Russell, Stebbing, and other modern logicians have done on distinguishing singulars of a kind from members of an extensive kind. Though Russell is not directly cited for claiming this distinction

in the 1938 *Logic*, Dewey doubtless has him in mind. See Russell, *Our Knowledge of the External World as a Field for Scientific Method in Philosophy*, especially the discussion of induction and role of extension therein (48). See also Stebbing, *A Modern Introduction to Logic*. Stebbing is among the first to question the historical understanding of intension and extension as playing an inverse dialectical role to one another; a role in which intension and extension run together with denotation and connotation, and intension gets drained as extension gets filled out. In this understanding, when connotation is drained, extension in increased, and when connation is filled in, intension is decreased. Stebbing, like Dewey, is critical of this move, common to empirical logicians such as Mill and W. Stanley Jevons (Stebbing has Jevons in mind in L. Susan Stebbing, *A Modern Elementary Logic*, 5th ed. (London: Methuen and Co., 1952), 106–7). For himself, Dewey gives the example of "ship" as regards "a ship" and "ship-ness" in chapter 18 of the 1938 *Logic*: Terms and Meanings. "Ship-ness" is thoroughly intensional; "The definition of ship, or being of the ship—character . . . has no extension" (LW 12, 358). Dewey's discussion of extension and intension in chapter 18 of the 1938 *Logic* owes to Russell, to Stebbing, to the earlier correspondence, and to this essay.

65. This is a reminder that not all experience is felt as settled; many individual experiences are indeterminate and cannot be called continuous or whole, as they do not satisfy the qualitative need for this. Instead, they are broken or lacking. In an experience, we grasp an event or situation as whole. But the event or situation may be qualitatively discordant, and the whole, on inspection, illusory. While it is true that a sense of completeness or unity pervades all experiencing, this is often not the case for individual experiences, wherein certain features or traits are in discord with others, and resolution or balance is unavailable. It is precisely this lack of completeness and its accompanying traits (continuity, wholeness, balance) that the human organism, through the use of inquiry, attempts to address. It is the function of inquiry to situate events in a serial-temporal order such that they become complete in a larger experience.

66. Thomas Burke, "What Is a Situation?," *History and Philosophy of Logic* 21 (2000): 95–113. As should doubtless be obvious, "situations" here refer not merely to indeterminate or problematic situations, as at LW 12, 108, but rather to all situations or events that constitute having an experience, together with the qualitative features and traits of that experience. Matthew Brown chides Burke for considering only indeterminate or problematic situations as situations; in this and the preceding chapter, I have expanded on Burke's characterization. See Matthew Brown, "John Dewey's Logic of Science," *HOPOS* 2, no. 2 (2012): 258–306, 277.

67. Thomas Goudge, "The Views of Charles Peirce on the Given in Experience," *Journal of Philosophy* 32 (1935): 533–44. At this time, volume 1 of *The Collected Papers of Charles Saunders Peirce* had recently been published by Paul

Weiss and Charles Hartshorne, receiving long-overdue attention. Both Goudge and Dewey were reading these volumes. The selections Goudge and Dewey quote refer to volume 1 of the *Papers*. On Dewey and Goudge, see Sleeper, *The Necessity of Pragmatism*, esp. 165–67.

68. "We see that the idea of a quality is the idea of a phenomenon or partial phenomenon considered as a monad, without reference to its parts or components and *without reference to anything else*. We must not consider whether it exists or it is only imaginary, because *existence* depends upon its subject having its place in the general scheme of the universe. An element separate from everything else and in no world but itself, may be said, *when we come to reflect upon it*, to be merely potential. But we must not even attend to any determinate absence of other things; we are to consider the total as a unit" (italics Dewey's). Further, Dewey quotes Peirce at CP 1, 425 (italics Dewey's): "When we say that qualities are general, are partical [sic] determinations, etc., all that is true of qualities *reflected upon*; but these things do *not belong* to the quality-element of experience."

69. Dewey will consider "controlled reveries" as "logical non-existential modes" of mathematical propositions—that is, as abstract propositions, in a draft for chapter 23 of the 1938 *Logic*. Dewey Papers, *Logic*, II, 102, Box 53, File 11, 35.

70. We may recall Dewey's description of the "denotative method" at LW 1, 372 as "pointing-to."

71. Dewey makes it clear that the dynamic object (as actual object, or actualization) is the linchpin on which possibility (First) and generality (Third) turn. For "Peirce's most characteristic philosophical contribution, namely, his original theory of the relation between the existential and the logical, is wholly meaningless if it is not seen that he is speaking of possibility and generality as ways or modes *that with respect to actualization are potential and general*, being actualized only under individualized conditions of interaction with other things (i.e., other triads) (LW 11, 89, italics mine).

72. This augurs against Sleeper's reading of Dewey on Peirce, wherein a wholesale denial of Firsts seems to be argued for. See Sleeper, *The Necessity of Pragmatism*, 138–39.

73. Peirce, Letter to Lady Welby, December 23, 1908, CP 8, 342–76.

74. Obviously, this is but an outline, and a great deal of textual support would be needed to support the claim. Nor do I suppose complete congruence could be demonstrated between the two accounts. My point is rather that there are similarities in the overall pattern of each account that make them causal and, most importantly, that Dewey used Peirce's understanding of causality to buttress his own.

75. I suppose Peirce could be read similarly, as endorsing a Second (action/reaction) that invokes no further account of matter (as Third). But that would be for functional purposes only.

76. John Dewey, *Charles Saunders Peirce: Collected Papers of Charles Sanders Peirce*, New Republic 81 (1935): 338–39; John Dewey, *Charles Saunders Peirce: Collected Papers of Charles Sanders Peirce*, New Republic 89 (1937): 415–16. Again, I reject Ralph Sleeper's characterization of Peirce's theory of continuity (Synechism) as a "guarantee of eventual objectivity" (Sleeper, *The Necessity of Pragmatism*, 167). And I reject Sleeper's implication that Dewey himself saw it that way. I think Sidney Ratner is correct in his conclusion that Dewey, like Peirce, did not think that the "ideal limit" of inquiry was an antecedent idea that actually regulated inquiry, but rather a consequence of the consensus of scientific inquirers upon a rigorously conducted problem. Sidney Ratner, introduction to *John Dewey and Arthur F. Bentley*, 18.

77. In this last remark, Dewey is not quite correct regarding Peirce's account of sensations. For Peirce, as sensations in the larger activity of perceiving, they are Seconds of Thirds; the element of Secondness in habit or rule or perceiving, which is itself an activity of judging.

78. Consider Peirce's understanding of truth in 1905. In his first of a series on papers published on Pragmatism for the *Monist*, he says, "I hold that truth's independence of individual opinions is due (so far as there is any 'truth') to its being the predestined result to which sufficient inquiry would ultimately lead." C. S. Peirce, "Pragmatism," in *The Essential Peirce*, vol. 2, ed. The Peirce Edition Project (Bloomington, IN: Indiana University Press, 1998), 419.

79. Note Dewey will apply the same probabilistic force to inductive descriptive generalizations in chapter 22 of the 1938 *Logic*; relations are gauged in terms of their probability interpreted in the guise of frequency distributions (LW 12, 465–66). See also Peirce, CP 5, 179.

80. See my discussion of "the complete act of thought" in Johnston, *John Dewey's Earlier Theory of Inquiry*, 150–52.

81. E.g., H. S. Thayer and V. T. Thayer, Introduction (MW 6, xiii).

82. Cheryl Misak provides a judicious estimation of the way verification was used descriptively by the classical (and later) pragmatists. See Misak, *The American Pragmatists*, 166–67. A volume could be written on the understanding of verification from the classical pragmatists through to the linguistic idealists and the ways in which the latter take up (and in many cases misrepresent) the understandings of the former. Robert Brandom is emblematic of this misrepresentation; one that colors his estimation of the contribution of classical pragmatism to contemporary linguistic idealism. Brandom distinguishes legitimate doxastic commitments, which are based in inferences provided by the language game ("circumstances") with the practical bearings of classical pragmatism ("consequences"), dependent on observation (and, for Brandom, the myth of the given) rather than inference. See Robert Brandom, *Articulating Reasons: An Introduction to Inferentialism* (Cambridge: Harvard University Press, 2000), 174.

I do not defend Dewey's understanding of verification here; I only insist it has to do first and foremost with experimental corroboration.

83. Dewey adds a potential sixth trait—the trait of "forecast" or "prognosis" (LW 8, 208). This is said to tie the present situation (of inquiry) to the past and the future. This forecast is prediction; the probability or likelihood of the current conclusion being successful in a future state of affairs. Together with past and present, the forecast ties together the entire (temporal) spectrum of inquiry's phases. Past is immediately relevant to us because of our present evaluation; the future is at hand because of our forecast with respect to our (now conclusive) hypothesis.

84. Thus, in characterizing a situation as replete with physical and social conditions, the editors of *Dewey's Logical Theory* mislead us (though not intentionally) in claiming that the ordinary objects of the environment are somehow present-to-hand for us as a result of their existential features. It is rather the case that this environment is already a conceptual field as a result of habits produced through already enacted inquiries, and that the qualitative features we experience when we experience such an environment are largely predictable because of the habits formed as a result of these traits and the logical work done in reflecting upon them. While it is true that we can experience anew when we encounter such environments, we very often find little in the way of novel traits of existence in ordinary situations and this owing to the previous work of reflection on similar situations. It is in this way we can talk of immediate meanings and relations without begging the question of novel traits of existence. F. Thomas Burke, D. Micah Hester, and Robert B. Talisse, introduction to *Dewey's Logical Theory: New Studies and Interpretations* (Nashville, TN: Vanderbilt University Press, 2002), xv.

85. Some might say Dewey finally broke through in his accounting of "transaction" in *Knowing and the Known* (with Arthur Bentley). This was certainly a concern of some long-standing, as evidenced in the Dewey-Bentley correspondence. (See in particular, Dewey to Bentley, November 9, 1943, where Dewey discusses the proper understanding of "events" and the question of their "determination," and specifically claims that a case of knowing is a case of an event [Dewey to Bentley, November 9, 1943, in *John Dewey and Arthur F. Bentley*, 186–88].) Ratner seems to adopt this conclusion in his introduction to the Dewey-Bentley correspondence. Notice, though, this does not solve the problem of how *existential* traits line up in an inquiry; for if inquiry is an event unto itself, and inquiry has its own traits (including the trait of completeness), we are still left with the question of conjoining the traits of existence and the traits of inquiry. See Sidney Ratner, introduction to *John Dewey and Arthur F. Bentley*, 40.

86. Dewey refers the reader to the account of situations first developed in the 1938 *Logic*, chapter 4: "Common Sense and Scientific Inquiry," 72–73. Notice, *pace* Thomas Burke (Burke, "What Is a Situation?," 110) that this account

does not consider situations as *merely* indeterminate or problematic, in contrast to Dewey's understanding of situation at LW 12, 108. For more on "situation," see also Richard Gale, "Russell's Drill Sergeant and Bricklayer and Dewey's Logic," *Journal of Philosophy* 56, no. 9 (1959): 401–6.

87. The helix/spiral/corkscrew metaphor of Thomas Burke is especially apt in this regard. See Tom Burke, *Dewey's New Logic*, 158–60. In this metaphor, there is a doubling back of inquiry from whole (situation)-to-part (experimentally treated phenomena) and part-to-whole. The whole returned to is no longer the whole of the original situation, nor is the part first examined in inquiry. (Dewey has maintained a similar view as early as *How We Think*, 1st ed. [MW 6, 242].) By contrast, less-than-careful readers forget or overlook the double nature of experience. For example, H. S. Thayer, in his otherwise cogent analysis of situations, claims, "[I]f Dewey defines inquiry in such a way that the definition necessarily involves or entails the notion of inquiry effecting an 'existential transformation,' I should say the definition is inadequate. For there seem to be cases where investigations occur, having all of the features described by Dewey's making up the pattern of inquiries, except one. That one feature is that the investigations do not effect an 'existential transformation,' or reshaping of the antecedent material which sets the problem of investigation" (Thayer, *The Logic of Pragmatism*, 173–74). This problem is dissolved once it is remembered that "existential transformation" involves the ordering of traits of existence, and not (merely) changes in observable phenomena. The spectrum of what counts as an "existential transformation" is much broader than changes in observable phenomena. A more egregious example comes in Lowell Nissen's misunderstanding of the role of the inquirer in "obscure" and "indeterminate" situations. For Nissen, that "the initial situation of inquiry is indeterminate [is] either false or a commonplace" (Nissen, *John Dewey's Theory of Inquiry and Truth*, 26–27). It is false if it is meant to be understood that all find a "discordant situation" to be such; uninteresting or uncontroversial if a single inquirer finds a "discordant situation" perplexing (Nissen, *John Dewey's Theory of Inquiry and Truth*, 26–27). If we adopt Nissen's characterization of the relationship of subject to situation, we must conclude that "the situation is indeterminate with the respect to the inquirer" (Nissen, *John Dewey's Theory of Inquiry and Truth*, 27). Nissen distinguishes the situation from the inquirer in these passages; a distinction Dewey himself does not maintain, except for functional purposes. For Dewey, the situation is already one with the inquirer; whereas for Nissen, the situation is separate and apart from the inquirer. Nissen pulls apart the organic connection between inquirer and event, only to put them back together again in his triumphant conclusion that Dewey left them separate.

References

Alexander, Thomas. *John Dewey's Theory of Art, Experience, and Nature: The Horizons of Feeling.* Albany, NY: State University of New York Press, 1987.
———. "The Aesthetics of Reality: The Development of Dewey's Ecological Theory of Experience." In *Dewey's Logical Theory: New Studies and Interpretations.* Edited by F. Thomas Burke, D. Micah Hester, and R. B. Talisse. Nashville, TN: Vanderbilt University Press, 2002.
———. "Dewey's Denotative-Empirical Method: A Thread Through the Labyrinth." *Journal of Speculative Philosophy* 18, no. 3 (2004): 248–56.
Barry, Frederick. *The Scientific Habit of Thought: An Informal Discussion of the Source and Character of Dependable Knowledge.* New York: Columbia University Press, 1927.
Bentley, Arthur. *Linguistic Analysis of Mathematics.* Bloomington, IN: Principia Press, 1932.
Boas, Franz. *The Mind of Primitive Man.* New York: Macmillan & Co., 1911.
———. "The Methods of Ethnology" [1920]. In *Race, Language, and Culture,* by Franz Boaz, 281–89. Chicago: University of Chicago Press, 1940.
Boisvert, Raymond. *Dewey's Metaphysics.* New York: Fordham Press, 1988.
———. "Dewey's Metaphysics: Ground-map of the Prototypically Real." In *Reading Dewey: Interpretations of a Postmodern Generations,* edited by L. Hickman, 149–65. Bloomington: Indiana University Press, 1995.
Brandom, Robert. *Articulating Reasons: An Introduction to Inferentialism.* Cambridge, MA: Harvard University Press, 2000.
———. *Perspectives on Pragmatism: Classic, Recent, and Contemporary.* Cambridge, MA: Harvard University Press, 2011.
Bridgman, Percy William. *The Logic of Modern Physics.* New York: MacMillan and Co., 1927.
Brown, Matthew. "John Dewey's Logic of Science." *HOPOS* 2, no. 2 (2012): 258–306.
Burke, F. Thomas. *Dewey's New Logic: A Reply to Russell.* Chicago: University of Chicago Press, 1994.

———. "What Is a Situation?" *History and Philosophy of Logic* 21 (2000): 95–113.
———. "Prospects for Mathematizing Dewey's Logical Theory." In *Dewey's Logical Theory: New Studies and Interpretations*, edited by F. T. Burke, D. M. Hester, and R. B. Talisse, 121–60. Nashville: Vanderbilt University Press, 2002.
———. "Qualities, Universals, Kinds, and the New Riddle of Induction." In *Dewey's Logical Theory: New Studies and Interpretations*, edited by F. Thomas Burke, D. Micah Hester, and Robert B. Talisse, 225–36. Nashville: Vanderbilt University Press, 2002.
Burke, F. Thomas, D. Micah Hester, and Robert B. Talisse. Introduction to *Dewey's Logical Theory: New Studies and Interpretations*, by F. Thomas Burke, D. Micah Hester, and Robert B. Talisse, xi–xxiv. Nashville, TN: Vanderbilt University Press, 2002.
Chemlin, Paul. "John Dewey's Theoretical Framework from 1903–1916: Prefigurations of a Naturalistic Metaphysics." *The Pluralist* 12, no. 2 (2017): 57–77.
Colapietro, Vincent. "Experimental Logic: Normative Theory or Natural History." In *Dewey's Logical Theory: New Studies and Interpretations*, edited by F. T. Burke, D. M. Hester, and R. B. Talisse, 43–71. Nashville: Vanderbilt University Press, 2002.
Cornforth, Maurice. In *Defense of Philosophy: Against Positivism and Pragmatism*. New York: Lawrence and Wishart, 1950.
Crosser, Paul. *The Nihilism of John Dewey*. New York: The Philosophical Library, 1955.
Cunningham, Craig. "Dewey's Metaphysics and the Self." *Studies in Philosophy and Education* 13 (1994): 343–60.
Dalton, Thomas. *Becoming John Dewey: Dilemmas of a Philosopher and Naturalist*. Bloomington: Indiana University Press, 2002.
Dewey, John. Dewey Papers, Boxes 52–53, Special Collections Research Center, Morris Library, Southern Illinois University.
———. "Is Logic a Dualistic Science?" *Open Court* III (January 1890): 2040–43.
———. "The Reflex-Arc Concept in Psychology." *Psychological Review* III (July 1896): 357–70.
———. "Tychism." In *Dictionary of Philosophy and Psychology*. Vol. 2, edited by James Mark Baldwin. New York: Macmillan Co., 1902.
———. *Studies in Logical Theory*. Chicago: University of Chicago Press, 1903.
———. "The Postulate of Immediate Empiricism." *The Journal of Philosophy, Psychology, and Scientific Methods* 2, no. 15 (1905): 158–67.
———. *How We Think*. New York: Henry, Holt & Co., 1910.
———. "The Short-Cut to Realism Examined." *Journal of Philosophy, Psychology, and Scientific Methods* 7, no. 15 (1910): 553–57.
———. "Rejoinder to Dr. Spaulding." *Journal of Philosophy, Psychology and Scientific Methods* 8 (1911): 77–79.

———. "The Existence of the World as a Logical Problem." *Philosophical Review* 24 (1915): 357–70.

———. "The Subject-Matter of Metaphysical Inquiry." *The Journal of Philosophy, Psychology and Scientific Methods* 12, no. 13 (1915): 337–45.

———. "The Logic of Judgments of Practice." *Journal of Philosophy, Psychology, and Scientific Methods* 12, no. 19 (1915): 505–23.

———. *Essays in Experimental Logic.* Chicago: University of Chicago Press, 1916.

———. "The Pragmatism of Peirce." *Journal of Philosophy, Psychology, and Scientific Methods* 13 (1916): 709–15.

———. "The Concept of the Neutral in Recent Epistemology." *Journal of Philosophy, Psychology, and Scientific Methods* 14 (1917): 161–63.

———. *Reconstruction in Philosophy.* New York: Henry, Holt & Co., 1920.

———. *Human Nature and Conduct: An Introduction to Social Psychology.* New York: Henry, Holt & Co., 1922.

———. "Realism without Monism or Dualism." *Journal of Philosophy* 19 (1922): 309–17.

———. "An Analysis of Reflective Thought." *Journal of Philosophy, Psychology, and Scientific Methods* XV (1922): 673–81.

———. "China and the West." *Dial* 74 (1923): 193–96.

———. "Science, Belief and the Public." *New Republic* 38 (1924): 143–45.

———. "Logical Method and the Law." *Cornell Review* 10 (December 1924).

———. "The Development of American Pragmatism." In *Studies in the History of Ideas* 2, edited by the Department of Philosophy, Columbia University, 353–77. New York: Columbia University Press, 1925.

———. *Experience and Nature.* New York: Henry, Holt & Co., 1925.

———. *The Public and Its Problems: An Essay in Political Inquiry.* New York: Henry, Holt & Co., 1927.

———. "Half-hearted Naturalism." *The Journal of Philosophy* 24, no. 3 (1927): 57–64.

———. "Meaning and Existence." *Journal of Philosophy* 25 (1928): 345–53.

———. *Experience and Nature.* 2nd ed. New York: Henry, Holt & Co., 1929.

———. *The Quest for Certainty: A Study of the Relation of Knowledge and Action.* New York: Minton, Balch & Co., 1929.

———. "From Absolutism to Experimentalism." In *Contemporary American philosophy.* Vol. II, edited by G. P. Adams and W. P. Montague, 12–27. New York: The Macmillan Co., 1930.

———. "Conduct and Experience." In *Psychologies of 1930*, edited by Carl Murchison, 409–22. Worcester, MA: Clark University Press, 1930.

———. "Qualitative Thought." *Symposium* 1 (1930): 5–32.

———. *Philosophy and Civilization.* New York: Minton, Balch, and Co., 1931.

———. *How We Think: A Restatement of the Relation of Reflective Thinking to the Educative Process.* Boston: D.C. Heath and Co., 1933.

———. *Art as Experience*. New York: Minton, Balch, and Co., 1934.
———. "The Founder of Pragmatism." *Collected Papers of Charles Saunders Peirce*. Vol. 5: *Pragmatism and Pragmaticism*. Edited by Charles Hartshorne and Paul Weiss. Cambridge, MA: Harvard University Press, 1934. *New Republic* 81, no. 30 (January 1935): 338–39.
———. "Peirce's Theory of Quality." *Journal of Philosophy* 32 (1935): 701–8.
———. "Characteristics and Characters: Kinds and Classes." *Journal of Philosophy* 33 (1936): 253–61.
———. "What Are Universals?" *Journal of Philosophy* 33 (1936): 281–88.
———. "Religion, Science, and Philosophy: Review of Bertrand Russell's *Religion and Science*." *Southern Review* 2 (Summer 1936): 53–62.
———. "Authority and Social Change." *School and Society* 44, no. 10 (October 1936): 457–66.
———. "General Propositions, Kinds, and Classes." *Journal of Philosophy* 33 (1936): 673–80.
———. *Collected Papers of Charles Saunders Peirce*. 6 vols. Edited by Charles Hartshorne and Paul Weiss. Cambridge, MA: Harvard University Press, 1931–1934. *New Republic* 89, no. 3 (February 1937): 415–16.
———. *Logic: The Theory of Inquiry*. New York: Henry, Holt & Co., 1938.
———. "Outlines of a Critical Theory on Ethics." In *The Early Works of John Dewey*. Vol. 3 1892–1894, edited by Jo Ann Boydston. Carbondale: Southern Illinois University Press, 1967.
———. "Experience, Nature, and Value: A Rejoinder." In *The Philosophy of John Dewey*, edited by P. A. Schilpp and L. E. Hahn, 515–608. La Salle, IL: Open Court, 1989.
———. *Lectures on Ethics, 1900–1901*. Edited by D. Koch. Carbondale: Southern Illinois University Press, 1991.
———. *The Collected Works of John Dewey 1882–1953*. Edited by Jo Ann Boydston. Carbondale: Southern Illinois University Press 1969–1991. Early Works (EW) 1882–1898. Middle Works (MW) 1899–1924. Later Works (LW) 1925–1953.
———. *The Correspondence of John Dewey*. Vol. 1 1881–1918. Edited by Larry Hickman. Carbondale: Southern Illinois University Press, 2002.
———. *The Correspondence of John Dewey*. Vol. 2 1919–1939. Edited by Larry Hickman. Carbondale: Southern Illinois University Press, 2003.
———. "Types of Logical Theory 1915 and 1916." In *The Lectures of John Dewey*. Vol. 1, edited by Donald Koch. Carbondale: Southern Illinois University Press, 2012.
———. "Types of Logical Theory 1927–1928." In *The Lectures of John Dewey*. Vol. 2, edited by Donald Koch. Carbondale: Southern Illinois University Press, 2012.

———. *Unmodern and Modern Philosophy*. Edited by Phillip Dean. Carbondale: Southern Illinois University Press, 2012.

Dewey, John, and Arthur Bentley. "Transactions as Known and Named." *Journal of Philosophy* XLIII (1946): 533–51. Republished in John Dewey and Arthur Bentley. *Knowing and the Known*. Boston: Beacon Press, 1949.

Dewey, Robert. *The Philosophy of John Dewey: A Critical Exposition of his Method, Metaphysics, and Theory of Knowledge*. Dordrecht: Springer, 1977.

Drake, Durant. "What Kind of Realism?" *Philosophy, Psychology, and Scientific Methods* 9 (1912): 149–54.

Duran, Jane. "Russell on Pragmatism." *Russell: The Journal of the Bertrand Russell Archives* 14 (Summer 1994): 31–37.

Dykhuizen, George. *The Life and Mind of John Dewey*. Carbondale: Southern Illinois University Press, 1973.

Eddington, Arthur Stanley. *The Nature of the Physical World*. New York: Macmillan and Co., 1928.

Einstein, Albert. *Relativity: The Special and General Theory*. Translated by R. W. Lawson. New York: Henry Holt and Co., 1920.

Feibleman, James. "The Influence of Peirce on Dewey's Logic." *Education* 66, no. 1 (1945): 18–24.

———. *An Introduction to Peirce's Philosophy Interpreted as a System*. Boston: MIT Press, 1970.

Feynman, Richard, Robert Leighton, and Matthew Sands. *The Feynman Lectures on Physics*. Vol. 1. New York: Basic Books, 2006.

———. *The Feynman Lectures on Physics*. Vol. 3. New York: Basic Books, 2006.

Gale, Richard. "Russell's Drill Sergeant and Bricklayer and Dewey's Logic." *Journal of Philosophy* 56, no. 9 (1959): 401–6.

Garrett, Roland. "Dewey's Struggle with the Ineffable." *Transactions of the Charles S. Peirce Society* 9, no. 2 (1973): 95–109.

Garrison, James. "The 'Permanent Deposit' of Hegel in John Dewey's Philosophy." *Educational Theory* 56, no. 1 (2006): 1–37.

Goldenweiser, Alexander. *Early Civilization*. New York: F.S. Crofts and Co, 1922.

Goldman, Alvin. "A Causal Theory of Knowing." *The Journal of Philosophy* 64, no. 12 (1967): 357–72.

Good, James, and James Garrison. "Dewey, Hegel and Causation." *Journal of Speculative Philosophy* 24, no. 2 (2010): 101–20.

Goudge, Thomas. "The Views of Charles Peirce on the Given in Experience." *Journal of Philosophy* 32 (1935): 533–44.

Gouinlock, James. Introduction to *The Later Works of John Dewey*. Vol. 2: 1925–1927. Edited by Jo Ann Boydston, ix–xxxvi. Carbondale: Southern Illinois University Press, 1984.

Haldane, J. B. S. *Possible Worlds*. Edinburgh: Edinburgh University Press, 1927.

Hall, Everett W. "Some Meanings of Meaning in Dewey's Experience and Nature." *Journal of Philosophy* 25 (1928): 169–81.
Hegel, G. W. F. *Science of Logic*. Translated by A. V. Miller. New York: Humanities Press, 1969.
Heisenberg, Werner. *Physics and Philosophy*. London: Penguin Books, 2000.
Hickman, Larry. *John Dewey's Pragmatic Technology*. Bloomington: Indiana University Press, 1990.
———. "Dewey's Theory of Inquiry." In *Reading Dewey: Interpretations for a Postmodern Generation*, edited by L. Hickman, 166–86. Bloomington, IN: Indiana University Press, 1995.
Hildebrand, David. "The Importance of Experience and Situations in Democracy and Education." *Educational Theory* 66, nos. 1–2 (2016): 73–88.
Hobhouse, Leonard. *The Theory of Knowledge: A Contribution to Some Problems of Logic and Metaphysics*. New York: Macmillan & Co., 1895.
Holt, E. B. *The New Realism*. New York: MacMillan, 1912.
Holt, E. B. et al. "The Program and First Platform of Six Realists." *Journal of Philosophy, Psychology and Scientific Methods* 7 (1910): 393–401.
Huxley, Julian. *Scientific Research and Social Needs*. London: Watts and Co., 1934.
Jackson, Phillip. *John Dewey and the Lessons of Art*. New Haven: Yale University Press, 1998.
———. *John Dewey and the Philosopher's Task*. New York: Teachers College Press, 2001.
James, William. *Principles of Psychology*. Vol. 2. New York: Dover Press, 1918.
Jevons, William Stanley. *The Principles of Science: A Treatise of Logic and Scientific Method*. London: Macmillan & Co., 1887.
Johnson, William Ernest. *Logic: Parts 1–3*. Cambridge: Cambridge University Press, 1921–1924.
Johnston, James Scott. *John Dewey's Earlier Logical Theory*. Albany, NY: State University of New York Press, 2014.
Kadlec, Alison. *Dewey's Critical Pragmatism*. Lexington, KY: Lexington Books, 2007.
Kant, Immanuel. "The Critique of Pure Reason." In *The Cambridge Edition of the Works of Immanuel Kant*, edited by Paul Guyer and Allen Wood. Cambridge: Cambridge University Press, 1998.
Kennedy, Gail. "Dewey's Logic and Theory of Knowledge." In *Guide to the Works of John Dewey*, edited by J. Boydston, 61–97. Carbondale: Southern Illinois University Press, 1972.
Koch, Donald. Introduction to *The Lectures of John Dewey*. Vol. 1., edited by Donald Koch. Carbondale: Southern Illinois University Press, 2012.
Klyce, Scudder. *The Universe*. Winchester, MA, 1921.
———. *Dewey's Suppressed Psychology*. Winchester, MA, 1927.
Lakatos, Imre. "Falsification and the Methodology of Scientific Research Programmes." In *Criticism and the Growth of Knowledge*, edited by I. Lakatos and A. Musgrave, 91–196. Cambridge: Cambridge University Press, 1970.

Laplace, Pierre-Simon. *A Philosophical Essay on Probabilities*. Translated by F. W. Truscott and F. L. Emory. New York: John Wiley and Sons, 1902.
Lecky, William Edward Hartpole. *History of the Rise and Influence of the Spirit of Rationalism in Europe*. 2 vols. London: Longman, Roberts and Green, 1865.
Levine, Daniel. "Randolph Bourne, John Dewey, and the Legacy of Liberalism." *The Antioch Review* 29, no. 2 (Summer 1969): 534–44.
Lippmann, Walter. *The Method of Freedom*. New York: Macmillan Co, 1934.
———. *Public Opinion*. New York: Harcourt, Brace and Co., 2004.
Lovejoy, Arthur. "Pragmatism vs. the Pragmatist." In *Essays in Critical Realism*, edited by Durant Drake, 35–81. London: Macmillan and Co., 1920.
Madison, Charles A. "Oral History Interview. 8 November 1967. 5. Kathleen Paolos, Textual Commentary." In *John Dewey. Logic: The Theory of Inquiry. The Later Works of John Dewey*. Vol. 13: 1938–1939, edited by Jo Ann Boydston. Carbondale: Southern Illinois University Press, 1986.
Malinowski, Bronislaw. "The Problem of Meaning in Primitive Languages." In *The Meaning of Meaning*, by C. K. Ogden and I. A. Richards. New York: Harcourt, Brace, and Co, 1923.
———. "Culture." In *Encyclopedia of the Social Sciences*. Vol. 4, edited by E. R. Seligman and A. Johnson. New York: Macmillan Co, 1931.
Maxwell, J. C. "The Scientific Papers of James Clerk Maxwell." Vol. 2, edited by W. D. Niven. Cambridge: Cambridge University Press, 1890.
McDougall, William. *An Introduction to Social Psychology*. London: Methuen & Co. 1908.
Mead, G. H. "Social Consciousness and the Consciousness of Meaning." *Psychological Bulletin* 7 (1910): 397–405.
Mendell, Mark. "Dewey and the Logic of Legal Reasoning." *Transactions of the Charles S. Peirce Society* 30, no. 3 (1994): 575–635.
Merz, John Theodore. *History of European Thought in the 19th Century*. 4th ed. Edinburgh: William Blackwood and Sons, 1932.
Meyer, Max. *Psychology of the Other-one*. 2nd ed. New York: Columbia University Press, 1922.
Mill, J. S. *Studies in Logic, Rationcinative and Inductive: Being a Connected View of the Principles of Evidence and the Methods of Scientific Investigations*. People's Edition. London: Longmans, Green, and Co., 1889.
Mozur, Gerald. "Dewey on Time and Individuality." *Transactions of the Charles S. Peirce Society* 27, no. 3 (1991): 321–40.
Nagel, Ernest. *Sovereign Reason and Other Studies in the Philosophy of Science*. Glencoe, IL: The Free Press, 1954.
———. Introduction to "Logic: The Theory of Inquiry." *The Later Works of John Dewey*. Vol. 12: 1938, edited by Jo Ann Boydston, vii–xxiii. Carbondale: Southern Illinois University Press, 1986.
Nissen, Lowell. *John Dewey's Theory of Inquiry and Truth*. The Hague: Mouton and Co., 1966.

Noble, Edmund. *Purposive Evolution: The Link Between Science and Religion*. New York: Henry Holt and Co., 1926.

Newton, Isaac. *Optiks, or, A Treatise of the Reflections, Refractions, Inflections and Colours of Light*. 3rd ed. London: William and John Innys, 1721.

———. *The Mathematical Principles of Natural Philosophy*. Vol. 2. Translated by A. Motte. London: Benjamin Mosse, 1729.

Peirce, Charles S. *The Collected Papers of Charles S. Pierce*. Vols. 1–6. Edited by Charles Hartshorne and Paul Weiss. Cambridge, MA: Harvard University Press, 1931–1934.

———. *The Collected Papers of Charles S. Peirce*. Vols. 7–8. Edited by A.W. Burks. Cambridge, MA: Harvard University Press, 1958.

———. "Logic." In *Dictionary of Philosophy and Psychology*, edited by James Mark Baldwin, 647–703. New York: Macmillan and Co., 1905.

———. "Pragmatism." *The Monist* 15 (April 1905): 161–81.

———. *Reasoning and the Logic of Things*. Edited by Douglas Ketner and Hilary Putnam. Cambridge, MA: Harvard University Press, 1992.

———. "The Fixation of Belief." In *The Essential Peirce*. Vol. 1, edited by C. Kloessel and N. Hauser, 109–23. Bloomington, IN: Indiana University Press, 1992.

———. "A Guess at the Riddle." In *The Essential Peirce*. Vol. 1, edited by N. Hauser and C. Kloesel, 245–79. Bloomington, IN: Indiana University Press, 1992.

———. "What Pragmatism Is." In *The Essential Peirce*. Vol. 2, edited by The Peirce Edition Project, 331–45. Bloomington, IN: Indiana University Press, 1998.

———. "Pragmatism." In *The Essential Peirce*. Vol. 2, edited by The Peirce Edition Project, 398–433. Bloomington, IN: Indiana University Press, 1998.

Perry, R. B. "The Ego-Centric Predicament." *Journal of Philosophy* 7 (1910): 514.

Ratner, Sidney. Introduction to *John Dewey and Arthur F. Bentley: A Philosophical Correspondence 1932–1951*, edited by Sidney Ratner and Jules Altman, with James E. Wheeler, 347. New Brunswick, NJ: Rutgers University Press, 1964.

Reichenbach, Hans. "Dewey's Theory of Science." In *The Philosophy of John Dewey*, edited by P. A. Schilpp and L. E. Hahn, 157–92. La Salle, IL: Open Court, 1989.

Reiser, Oliver. *Philosophy and the Concepts of Modern Science*. New York: Macmillan and Co., 1935.

Rosenthal, Sandra, "John Dewey: Scientific Method and Lived Immediacy." *Transactions of the Charles S. Peirce Society* 17, no. 4 (1981): 358–68.

Russell, Bertrand. *Our Knowledge of the External World as a Field for Scientific Method in Philosophy*. Chicago and London: Open Court Publishing, Inc., 1914.

———. *Logical Atomism*. New York: Macmillan & Co., 1918/1924.

———. *The Analysis of Matter*. New York: Harcourt, Brace & Co., 1927.
———. *Religion and Science*. New York: Henry Holt and Co., 1935.
———. "Professor Dewey's Essays in Experimental Logic." In *Dewey and His Critics: Essays from the Journal of Philosophy*, edited by Sidney Morgenbesser. New York: Journal of Philosophy, Inc., 1977.
———. *History of Western Philosophy*. London: George Allen & Unwin, 1979.
———. "Dewey's New Logic." In *The Philosophy of John Dewey*, edited by P. A. Schilpp and L. E. Hahn, 135–56. La Salle: Open Court, 1989.
Robinson, Daniel Sommer. "An Alleged New Discovery in Logic." *Journal of Philosophy, Psychology, and Scientific Methods* 14 (1917): 225–37.
Rogers, Melvin. *The Undiscovered Dewey: Religion, Morality, and the Ethos of Democracy*. New York: Columbia University Press, 2009.
Ryan, Alan. *John Dewey and the High Tide of American Liberalism*. New York: Norton, 1995.
Santayana, George. "Dewey's Naturalistic Metaphysics." *The Journal of Philosophy* 22, no. 25 (1925): 673–88.
Siegfried, Hans. "Dewey's Logical Forms." In *Dewey's Logical Theory: New Studies and Interpretations*, edited by F. Thomas Burke, D. Micah Hester, and R. B. Talisse, 180–201. Nashville: Vanderbilt University Press, 2002.
Shook, John. *Dewey's Empirical Theory of Knowledge and Reality*. Nashville, TN: Vanderbilt University Press, 2000.
———. "Dewey and Quine on the Logic of What There Is." In *Dewey's Logical Theory: New Studies and Interpretations*, edited by F. Thomas Burke, G. Micah Hester, and Robert B. Talisse, 93–120. Nashville, TN: Vanderbilt University Press, 2002.
Sleeper, Ralph. *The Necessity of Pragmatism: John Dewey's Conception of Philosophy*. Urbana: University of Illinois Press, 1986.
Spaulding, E. B. "Realism: A Reply to Professor Dewey and an Exposition." *Journal of Philosophy, Psychology and Scientific Methods* 8 (1911): 63–77.
Stebbing, L. Susan. *A Modern Introduction to Logic*. New York: Thomas Y. Crowell Co., 1930.
———. *A Modern Elementary Logic*. 5th ed. London: Methuen and Co., 1952.
Stuhr, John. "Dewey's Notion of a Qualitative Experience." *Transactions of the Charles S. Peirce Society* 15, no. 1 (1979): 68–82.
———. "Dewey's Reconstruction of Metaphysics." *Transactions of the Charles S. Peirce Society* 28, no. 2 (1992): 161–76.
Suppes, Patrick. "Nagel's Lectures on Dewey's Logic." In *Philosophy, Science, and Method, Essays in Honor of Ernest Nagel*, by S. Morgenbesser, P. Suppes, and M. White, 2–25. New York: St. Martin's Press, 1969.
Thayer, H. S. *The Logic of Pragmatism*. New York: Humanities Press, 1952.
Thayer, H. S., and V. T. Thayer. Introduction to *The Middle Works of John Dewey 1899–1924*. Vol. 6: "How We Think" and Selected Essays 1910–1911, by

John Dewey, edited by Jo Ann Boydston, xi–xviii. Carbondale: Southern Illinois University Press, 1978.

Toulmin, Stephen. Introduction to *The Later Works of John Dewey 1925–1952*. Vol. 4: *The Quest for Certainty*, 1929, by John Dewey, edited by Jo Ann Boydston, ix–xvii. Carbondale: Southern Illinois University Press, 1984.

Tylor, Edward. *Primitive Culture*. 3rd ed., vol. 1. London: John Murray, 1891.

Venn, John. *The Principles of Empirical or Inductive Logic*. London and New York: Macmillan & Co., 1889.

Wells, Harry. *Pragmatism: Philosophy of Imperialism*. New York: International Publishers, 1954.

Whewell, William. *The Philosophy of the Inductive Sciences, Founded upon Their History*. 2 vols. London: J.W. Parker, 1840.

Westbrook, Robert. *John Dewey and American Democracy*. Ithaca: Cornell University Press, 1991.

White, Andrew Dickson. *A History of Warfare of Science with Theology in Christendom*. 2 vols. New York: D. Appleton and Co., 1896.

White, Morton. *The Origins of John Dewey's Instrumentalism*. New York: Columbia University Press, 1943.

Index

Actuals, actuality, 162–163, 165, 171, 173, 206
Adams, G. P.
  and *Contemporary American Philosophy: Personal Statements* vol. II (1930), 179
Adamson, Robert
  and Aristotle, 182
  and Development of Greek Philosophy, 182
Alexander, Thomas, 209
  and *John Dewey's Theory of Art, Experience and Nature* (1987), 201, 208, 209
  and "The Aesthetics of Reality: The Development of Dewey's Ecological Theory of Experience" (2002), 208
  and "Dewey's Denotative-Empirical Method: A Thread Through the Labyrinth" (2004), 198
Altman, Jules
  and *John Dewey and Arthur Bentley: A Philosophical Correspondence* (1964), 183
Analysis, 2–5, 29, 98, 103, 116, 149, 153, 165, 200, 222
  See also Russell, *The Analysis of Matter*

Anthropology, 10, 92, 103
Aristotle, 2, 9, 10, 16–17, 21–22, 38, 59–61, 112–113, 115, 118, 181–182, 184, 193–195, 205
  and *Organon*, 21, 182
  and Logic, 182
Art, 94–96, 126, 129, 137, 142, 195, 201
  See also Dewey, *Art as Experience*
  See also Jackson, *John Dewey as the Lessons of Art*

Baldwin, James Mark
  and *Dictionary of Philosophy and Psychology* (1902, 1905), 190, 211
Barnes, Albert, 21, 27, 32, 188, 213
Barnett, Samuel, 102, 203
Barry, Frederick, 108, 203, 207
  and *The Scientific Habit of Thought: An Informal Discussion of the Source and Character of Dependable Knowledge* (1927), 184, 203
Benedict, Ruth, 186
Benn, R. B.
  and *Greek Philosophers*, vol. I, 182

Bentley, Arthur, 11, 30, 31, 32, 131, 183, 186
  and *Linguistic Analysis of Mathematics* (1932), 31, 186
  and *Behavior, Knowledge and Fact*, 186
  and "Transactions as Known and Named" (1946), 207
  and *Knowing and the Known* (1949), 208, 221
Boas, Franz, 2, 10, 26–27
  and *The Mind of Primitive Man* (1911), 185, 201
  and "The Methods of Ethnology" (1920), 185
Bohn, Henry George, 182
Bohr, Neils, 2, 10, 21, 24, 28, 102, 104, 184, 185, 202, 203
Boisvert, Raymond
  and *Dewey's Metaphysics* (1988), 179, 181, 182, 188, 193
  and "Dewey's Metaphysics: Ground-map of the Prototypically Real" (1995), 198, 199, 209
Bonsaquet, Bernard, 202
Bourne, Randolph, 181
Boydston, Jo Ann, 184
  and *Guide to the Works of John Dewey* (1972), 202
Bradley, F. H., 39, 65, 116, 202, 206
  and *Principles of Logic*, 205, 206, 216
Brandom, Robert, 220
  and *Articulating Reasons: An Introduction to Inferentialism* (2000), 210, 220
  and *Perspectives on Pragmatism: Classic, Recent, and Contemporary* (2011), 210

Bridgman, Percy, 2, 108, 203, 204, 207
  and *The Logic of Modern Physics* (1927), 184
Broad, C. D., 202
Brown, Matthew
  and "John Dewey's Logic of Science" (2012), 218
Burke, Thomas, 195, 206, 212, 213, 221
  and *Dewey's New Logic: A Reply to Russell* (1994), 183, 212, 213, 215, 222
  and "What is a situation?" (2000), 218, 221
  and *Dewey's Logical Theory: New Studies and Interpretations* (2002), 185, 196, 208, 213, 215, 221
  and "Prospects for Mathematizing Dewey's Logical Theory" (2002), 196, 206
  and "Qualities, Universals, Kinds, and the New Riddle of Induction" (2002), 215
  and *History and Philosophy of Logic*, 218

Causality, 7, 10, 14, 31, 43, 49, 75, 84, 97, 104–105, 108, 114, 120–121, 132, 134, 139, 144, 146–147, 161–162, 164–165, 169–173, 188, 190–191, 195, 205, 209–210, 219, 227
  See also Goldman, "A Causal Theory of Knowing"
  See also Good and Garrison, "Dewey, Hegel and Causation"
Causation
  See Causality

Chemlin, Paul
  and "John Dewey's Theoretical Framework from 1903–1916: Prefigurations of a Naturalistic Metaphysics" (2017), 180, 188
Colapietro, Vincent
  and "Experimental Logic: Normative Theory or Natural History" (2002), 212
Common sense, 148, 175–177, 214
  and scientific inquiry, 72, 126, 132, 145, 221
Continuity, 4, 6–11, 14, 20, 23, 27–28, 31–33, 37–49, 51–53, 55, 58, 66, 70–89, 92–94, 104–105, 112, 125–126, 129, 131–140, 161, 165–166, 169–173, 187–191, 197–199, 204, 208–214, 218, 220
  Double continuity, 4–7, 10, 14, 20, 28, 31–32, 44, 77, 132, 161, 169, 173, 209
Control, in logical theory, 14, 60–61, 72, 98, 105, 108, 110, 117–118, 145, 148, 151–152, 169, 176, 194, 204, 207, 219
Cornforth, Maurice
  and *In Defense of Philosophy: Against Positivism and Pragmatism* (1950), 187
Crosser, Paul
  and *The Nihilism of John Dewey* (1955), 187
Cunningham, Craig
  and "Dewey's Metaphysics and the Self" (1994), 198, 201, 208

Dalton, Thomas, 209, 210
  and *Becoming John Dewey: Dilemmas of a Philosopher and Naturalist* (2002), 181, 183, 188, 209, 212
Darwin, Charles, 2, 86
Davis, Alice, 30
Dean, Phillip
  and *Unmodern and Modern Philosophy* (2012), 182
Deduction, 2, 4, 12, 15–18, 22, 29, 33, 52, 59–62, 65, 69–76, 89, 98, 101–102, 108, 115–119, 126, 128, 148–149, 170, 176, 195, 200, 206
Descartes, René, 64
Dewey, John
  and "Is Logic a Dualistic Science" (1890), 1, 179
  and "The Present Position of Logical Theory" (1891), 116, 206
  and "The Reflex-Arc Concept in Psychology" (1896), 93, 201
  and *School and Society* (1899), 15
  and "Some Stages of Logical Thought" (1900), 103
  and "Logical Conditions of a Scientific Treatment of Morality" (1903), 103
  and *Studies in Logical Theory* (1903), 9, 11, 13, 15–17, 33, 35, 43, 45–46, 53, 58, 66, 101–103, 113, 118, 128, 179, 181–183, 196, 205
  and "The Postulate of Immediate Empiricism" (1905), 105, 171, 185
  and *How We Think* (1910, 1933), 1, 4, 29, 33, 35, 41–42, 45–46, 52–53, 79, 98, 101, 116–117, 119, 132–133, 135–136, 139–141, 147, 149, 166–170, 172–173, 179, 186, 192, 196,

236 / Index

Dewey, John *(continued)*
205–206, 209–210, 214, 222
and "The Short-Cut to Realism Examined" (1910), 180
and "Rejoinder to Dr. Spaulding" (1911), 180
and "The Existence of the World as Logical Problem" (1915), 12, 180
and "The Subject-Matter of Metaphysical Inquiry" (1915), 193
and "The Logic of Judgments of Practice" (1915), 4, 11, 18, 33, 35–36, 41–42, 62, 101, 127, 186
and *Democracy and Education* (1916), 14–15, 37–38, 42, 44, 45–47, 49–50, 53–55, 58, 70–71, 73, 79, 94, 98, 109, 140, 182, 189, 207
and *Essays in Experimental Logic* (1916), 1, 3–4, 9, 11, 13–15, 20, 33, 35–41, 44, 46, 53, 58–59, 65–66, 70, 72, 75–76, 78–80, 88, 101, 103, 144, 149, 168, 179, 188–189, 193, 195–196, 202–203, 205, 208
and "Logical Objects" (1916), 36, 64–65, 72
and "The Pragmatism of Peirce" (1916), 10, 19, 23, 36, 46, 48–49, 53, 71, 73, 94, 146, 179, 183
and "The Concept of the Neutral in Recent Epistemology" (1917), 188
and "Concerning Novelties in Logic: a Reply to Mr. Robinson" (1917), 36
and *Reconstruction in Philosophy* (1920), 20, 24, 26, 37–38, 44–45, 56–57, 66–68, 70–73, 78–79, 94, 103, 118, 120–121, 125, 183, 189, 196
and *Human Nature and Conduct* (1922), 14, 20, 26, 37, 46, 49–52, 70–71, 73, 77, 80, 91, 94, 136, 139, 140, 183, 197
and "Realism without Monism or Dualism" (1922), 189
and "An Analysis of Reflective Thought" (1922), 196
and "China and the West," (1923) 183
and "Science, Belief and the Public" (1924), 53, 58–59, 192
and "Logical Method and the Law" (1924), 36, 68–70, 72, 196–197
and "The Development of American Pragmatism" (1925), 23, 76–77, 86–87, 184
and *Experience and Nature* (1925, 1929), 4–6, 10, 14, 20–21, 23, 26–27, 33, 39, 40, 44–45, 51, 55, 71, 73, 75–88, 90–96, 100–101, 105–106, 120–122, 125, 129, 131–133, 135–139, 141, 146, 161–162, 172, 180–181, 185, 188–189, 191, 197–198, 200–202, 207–209, 211, 214
and *Studies in the History of Ideas* (1925), 77, 86
and *The Public and Its Problems* (1927), 28, 57, 76, 94, 96–101, 126, 129, 142, 144, 181, 185, 202
and "Half-hearted Naturalism" (1927), 199
and "Meaning and Existence" (1928), 76–77, 87–88, 200
and "The Applicability of Logic to Existence" (1929), 76

and *Characters and Events* (1929), 192
and *The Quest for Certainty* (1929), 5, 25–26, 28, 73, 76, 86, 88–89, 91, 94, 100, 102, 104, 108, 120, 132, 139, 149, 170, 184, 186, 192, 194, 204, 207
and "From Absolutism to Experimentalism" (1930), 179
and "Conduct and Experience" (1930), 76, 92–94, 201
and "Qualitative Thought" (1930), 10, 20, 28, 44, 76–77, 83, 88–91, 129, 132, 135, 172, 189, 200, 208
and *Philosophy and Civilization* (1931), 101, 202
and "Science and Society" (1931), 94, 100–101
and *Art as Experience* (1934), 6, 14, 44, 55, 126, 132, 135–139, 142–143, 148, 161–162, 169, 172–173, 180, 198, 202, 210–211, 214
and "The Founder of Pragmatism" (1935), 186
and "Peirce's Theory of Meaning" (1935), 146, 162–165, 171, 173
and "Peirce's Theory of Quality" (1935), 133, 147, 186, 201, 210
and "Authority and Social Change" (1936), 132, 142–144, 210–211
and "Characteristics and Characters: Kinds and Classes" (1936), 5, 29, 32, 131, 145–147, 152–160, 171, 173, 186, 213, 215
and "General Propositions, Kinds, and Classes" (1936), 5, 29, 32, 131, 145–147, 152–160, 171, 173, 186, 213, 215
and "Religion, Science, and Philosophy: Review of Bertrand Russell's *Religion and Science*" (1936), 142, 144–145, 210–211
and "What Are Universals?" (1936), 5, 29, 32, 131, 145–147, 152–160, 171, 173, 186, 213, 215
and *Collected Papers of Charles Saunders Peirce* (1935, 1937), 30, 76, 133, 146–147, 162, 165–166, 171, 186, 218, 220
and *Logic: The Theory of Inquiry* (1938), 4–6, 11, 14, 18–19, 21, 28–29, 31–32, 43, 53, 55, 59–60, 80, 83, 85, 87, 90–93, 117, 120, 124–126, 128, 131–132, 139–141, 143–149, 151–156, 164–173, 175–177, 184, 191–192, 205–206, 209, 211–217, 219–221
and *Theory of Valuation* (1939), 35, 187
and *"Transactions and Known and Named"* (1946), *207*
and *Knowing and the Known* (1949), 208, 221
and *Outlines of a Critical Theory on Ethics* (1967), 17, 182
and "Experience, Knowledge, and Value: A Rejoinder," 212
and "Experience, Nature, and Value: A Rejoinder" (1989), 214
and *Lectures on Ethics* (1991), 17, 129, 182, 184, 191
and *Unmodern and Modern Philosophy* (2012), 182
and Types of Logical Theory, 18, 22–23, 25–26, 28–29, 32, 38–39, 59–62, 70, 72–73, 75–76, 98–99, 102, 106–119, 126, 131, 146, 149–150, 156,

Dewey, John *(continued)*
    170, 181, 184, 186, 188,
    193–196, 198, 202, 205–206,
    211, 215
  and 1915–16, 119
  and *Liberalism and Social Action*,
    210
  and "Freedom," 210
Dewey, Robert
  and *The Philosophy of John Dewey:
    A Critical Exposition of his
    Method, Metaphysics, and Theory
    of Knowledge* (1977), 185, 207
Drake, Durant, 196
  and "What kind of realism?"
    (1912), 196
Duran, Jane
  and "Russell on Pragmatism"
    (1994), 183, 192
Dwight, Marion E., 98, 107, 184,
    206
Dykhuizen, George
  and *The Life and Mind of John
    Dewey* (1973), 181, 212

Eddington, Arthur Stanley, 2, 10, 21,
    24, 86, 108, 120, 207
  and *The Nature of the Physical
    World* (1928), 184
Einstein, Albert, 2, 10, 21, 25–26,
    86, 120–122, 127, 184–185,
    202, 207
  and *Relativity: The Special and
    General Theory* (1920), 184,
    207
Emory, F. L.
  and *A Philosophical Essay on
    Probabilities* (1902), 184
Epistemology, 5, 24, 31, 57, 58, 88,
    103, 149, 177, 188, 194
Ethics, inquiry and
Euclid, 206

Experience
  Immediate, 3, 20, 28, 32, 37, 40,
    79, 83, 88–89, 91, 93–94, 105,
    132–139, 161–165, 172, 188,
    191, 198, 205, 209–210,
    221
  Gross and macroscopic, 14, 33,
    45, 85, 91, 95, 125, 129, 132,
    134, 169, 172
  As refined, 27, 30–32, 79, 85–86,
    125, 132, 134, 136–139,
    161–162, 164–165, 169, 172,
    199
  As metaphysics, 139

Feibleman, James, 191
  and "The Influence of Peirce on
    Dewey's Logic" (1945), 190
  and *An Introduction to Peirce's
    Philosophy Interpreted as a System*
    (1970), 190, 217
Feynman, Richard
  and *The Feynman Lectures on
    Physics* (2006), 185
Firstness, 162, 163
Freedom, in inquiry, 87, 96, 124,
    139–144, 160, 173, 211

Gale, Richard
  and "Russell's Drill Sergeant and
    Bricklayer and Dewey's Logic"
    (1956), 222
Garrett, Roland
  and "Dewey's Struggle with the
    Ineffable" (1973), 198
Garrison, James, 198, 214
  and "The 'Permanent Deposit'
    of Hegel in John Dewey's
    Philosophy" (2006), 179, 188,
    192, 195
  and "Dewey, Hegel, and
    Causation" (2010), 195

Gauss, Carl Friedrich, 206
Goldenweiser, Alexander, 201
   and *Early Civilization* (1922), 201
Goldman, Alvin
   and "A Causal Theory of Knowing" (1967), 190
Gomperz, Samuel
   and *Greek Thinkers*, vol. 4, 182
Good, James
   and "Dewey, Hegel, and Causation" (2010), 195
Goudge, Thomas, 162, 219
   and "The Views of Charles Peirce on the Given in Experience" (1935), 218
Gouinlock, James
   and "Introduction" to *The Later Works of John Dewey* (1984), 200
Gruen, William, 204

Habits, 6, 13–14, 20, 24, 33, 37, 41–55, 70–75, 81, 87, 91–94, 98, 113, 124, 133, 136, 139–145, 162–164, 168, 187–191, 199, 212, 220–221
Hahn, L. E.
   and *The Philosophy of John Dewey* (1989), 183, 212, 214
Haldane, J. B. S.
   and *Possible Worlds* (1927), 204
   and "Some Enemies of Science," 204
Hall, Everett W.
   and "Some Meanings of Meaning in Dewey's Experience and Nature" (1928), 87, 200
Hall, C. Everett, 90, 199
Hartshorne, Charles, 219
   and *Collected Papers of Charles Saunders Peirce* (1931–1934), 186, 218

Hauser, N.
   and *The Essential Peirce* (1992), 192, 217
Hegel, G. W. F., 2, 7, 19, 116, 179, 181, 195, 201, 205
   and *The Science of Logic* (1969), 195, 204–206, 215–216
   and *Encyclopedia of the Philosophical Sciences in Outline*, 202
Heisenberg, Werner, 2, 10, 21, 24–26, 28, 102, 104–106, 120–121–122, 127, 184, 202–204
   and *Physics and Philosophy* (2000), 185
Hester, D. Micah
   and *Dewey's Logical Theory: New Studies and Interpretations* (2002), 185, 196, 208, 213, 215, 221
Hickman, Larry
   and *John Dewey's Pragmatic Technology* (1990), 182, 193, 202, 211
   and *Reading Dewey: Interpretations of Postmodern Generations* (1995), 198, 215
   and "Dewey's Theory of Inquiry" (1995), 215
Hildebrand, David, 189
   and "The Importance of Experience and Situations in *Democracy and Education* (2016), 189
Hobhouse, Leonard, 202
   and *The Theory of Knowledge: A Contribution to Some Problems of Logic and Metaphysics* (1895), 182–184
Holmes, Oliver Wendell, 197
Holt, E. B., 180
   and "The Program and First Platform of Six Realists" (1910), 180, 192
   and *The New Realism* (1912), 180

Holt, Henry, 30
Hook, Sidney, 11, 21, 25–28, 30–32, 102–107, 131, 146, 148–149, 153–154, 171, 175–177, 184, 186, 203, 207, 212, 216
Hume, David, 194
Huxley, Julian
  and *Scientific Research and Social Needs* (1934), 211

Idealism, 3, 11–13, 16, 19, 27, 35, 37, 40, 58–60, 67–68, 70, 107, 149, 177, 180, 188, 191, 195–196, 210, 214, 220
  Absolute Idealism, 13, 37, 39
Immediacy, 3–4, 17, 20, 40, 45, 51–52, 80–83, 90, 150, 172, 201, 208
  Immediate knowledge, 82–83, 132, 188
  See also experience, immediate
  See also meanings, immediate
Indeterminacy, 6, 14, 24, 26, 28, 33, 36, 37, 41, 73, 76, 90, 104–105, 122, 127, 129, 133, 173, 204, 218
Induction, 2, 4, 15–17, 22, 29–33, 52, 59, 61–65, 72–76, 82, 98, 101–102, 108–119, 126, 128, 148–149, 157–158, 168, 170, 176, 194–195, 200, 204, 206, 218, 220
Inference, 2, 3, 6, 14, 21, 22–23, 32–33, 41, 43–44, 58–65, 73, 76–77, 84–85, 89, 93, 98, 109–119, 122, 126–129, 132, 141, 151–152, 155–156, 160, 172–173, 176, 189, 193, 195, 206, 215–216, 220

Jackson, Phillip
  and *John Dewey and the Lessons of Art* (1998), 209
  and *John Dewey and the Philosopher's Task* (2001), 201
James, William, 1, 2, 11, 17, 38–39, 55, 59, 87, 179, 188, 200
  and *Principles of Psychology* (1918), vol. 2, 182
Jevons, Walter, 12
Jevons, William Stanley, 218
  and *The Principles of Science: A treatise of Logic and Scientific Method* (1887), 182, 184
Johnson, A.
  and *Encyclopedia of the Social Sciences* (1931), 201
Johnson, William Ernest
  and *Logic: Parts 1–3* (1921–24), 182, 184
Johnston, James Scott
  and *John Dewey's Earlier Logical Theory* (2014), 32, 179–181, 183, 187–188, 196, 209, 220
Judgments 4, 9–11, 15, 18, 21–23, 28–29, 33, 35–38, 41–46, 58–68, 72, 98–103, 106–116, 120, 124–135, 145, 148, 151, 155–156, 158, 160, 166, 169–171, 176, 186, 193–196, 203–205, 208, 210, 215–216

Kadlec, Alison
  and *Dewey's Critical Pragmatism* (2007), 185, 207
Kant, 1, 12, 106–107, 194, 204
  and *The Critique of Pure Reason* (1998), 204
Kennedy, Gail
  and "Dewey's Logic and Theory of Knowledge" (1972), 202
Kloessel, C.
  and *The Essential Peirce* (1992), 192, 217

Klyce, Scudder, 10, 16, 19–20, 27, 38–39, 62–63, 72, 102–104, 106–107, 183–184, 187–188, 193, 197, 202, 204
and *The Universe* (1921), 20, 187, 188
and *Dewey's Suppressed Psychology* (1927), 20, 203
Koch, Donald
and *The Lectures of John Dewey* (2012), 181, 184, 188, 191

Lakatos, Imre
and "Falsification and the Methodology of Scientific Research Programmes" (1970), 185, 203
and *Criticism and the Growth of Knowledge* (1970), 185
Language, 6, 14, 20, 27, 45–46, 50, 55, 66, 81–82, 87, 91–92, 100, 115, 124–125, 127, 139, 140–141, 144, 168, 170, 176, 185, 192, 199, 201, 207, 210, 220
Laplace, Pierre-Simon
and *A Philosophical Essay on Probabilities* (1902), 184
Lawson, R. W.
and *Relativity, The Special and General Theory* (1920), 184
Lecky, William Edward Hartpole
and *History of the Rise and Influence of the Spirit of Rationalism in Europe* (1865), 211
Leighton, Robert
and *The Feynman Lectures on Physics* (2006), 185
Levine, Daniel
and "Randolph Bourne, John Dewey, and the Legacy of Liberalism" (1969), 181

Lippman, Walter
and *The Method of Freedom* (1934), 211
and *Public Opinion* (2004), 192
Locke, John, 12, 17–18, 59, 68, 82, 182, 194, 196
Logic
Formal, 1, 10, 22, 29, 31, 62–63, 113, 124, 193
Symbolic, 15
Empirical, 184, 202, 218
Lorentz, H. A., 25, 207
Lotze, Rudolph Hermann, 1, 202
Lotze, R. M., 12
Lovejoy, Arthur, 12, 180, 189
and "Pragmatism vs. the Pragmatist" (1920), 189

Madison, Charles A., 186
Malinowski, Bronislaw
and "The Problem of Meaning in Primitive Languages" (1923), 201
"Culture" (1931), 201
Martin, W. T., 180
Mathematics, 2, 15, 18, 21–26, 33, 58, 61–64, 96–99, 108, 114–116, 122–128, 148–150, 176, 183–185, 193, 206–207, 219
Maxwell, James Clerk, 25, 207
and *The Scientific Papers of James Clerk Maxwell* (1890), 184
McDougall, William, 189
and *An Introduction to Social Psychology* (1890), *190*
McGilvary, E. B., 12, 180
Mead, G. H., 2, 82, 92, 141, 199
and "Social Consciousness and the Consciousness of Meaning" (1910), 199, 201, 210
Meanings, 6, 13–14, 19, 23–25, 27, 32–33, 36–52, 60, 63, 73,

Meanings *(continued)*
   76–96, 106–107, 114–119, 125–126, 129, 132–136, 140–141, 146, 152, 160–163, 168, 171–173, 183, 190–191, 196, 199–201, 204, 208, 210, 212, 218–221
   Immediate, 24, 51, 77, 80–83, 87–88, 94–95, 125, 129, 199, 215, 221
Mendell, Mark
   and "Dewey and the Logic of Legal Reasoning" (1994), 197
Merz, John Theodore
   and *History of European Thought in the 19th Century* (1932), 205
Meyer, Max, 92
   and *Psychology of the Other-one* (1922), 201
Michelson, Albert, 25, 120–121
Mill, J. S., 2, 9–10, 12, 15–18, 21–22, 61–62, 75, 118, 150–151, 153, 157–158, 160, 182, 184, 195, 202, 205–206, 218
   and *Studies in Logic, Ratiocinative and Inductive: Being a Connected View of the Principles of Evidence and the Methods of Scientific Investigations* (1889), 182
Miller, A. V.
   and *The Science of Logic* (1969), 195
Misak, Cheryl
   and *The American Pragmatists*, 220
Montague, W. P., 180
   and *Contemporary American Philosophy: Personal Statements vol. II* (1930), 179
Moore, G. E., 194

Morgenbesser, Sidney
   and *Philosophy, Science, and Method, Essays in Honor of Ernest Nagel* (1969), 208
   and *Dewey and His Critics: Essays from the Journal of Philosophy* (1977), 181
Morley, Edward, 25, 120–121
Motte, A.
   and *The Mathematical Principles of Natural Philosophy* (1729), 185
Mozur, Gerald
   and "Dewey on Time and Individuality" (1991), 199, 201, 203
Murchison, Carl, 93, 201
Musgrave, A.
   and *Criticism and the Growth of Knowledge* (1970), 185

Nagel, Ernest, 147, 184, 186, 208, 213–214, 216
   and *Sovereign Reason and Other Studies in the Philosophy of Science* (1954), 213
   and Introduction to "Logic: The Theory of Inquiry" (1986), 213, 216
Nature, 4, 15, 27–29, 35–36, 53, 56, 68, 71, 84–85, 88, 91, 96, 99, 101, 113, 118–119, 121, 124, 127–128, 133–134, 139, 142–145, 159–160, 166, 169, 170, 172–173, 185, 194–195, 202–210, 222
Newton, Isaac, 2, 25, 103–105, 120–121, 207
   and *The Mathematical Principles of Natural Philosophy* (1729), 185, 206

and *Optiks, or, A Treatise of the Reflections, Refractions, Inflections and Colours of Light* (1721), 185
Nissen, Lowell, 213
and *John Dewey's Theory of Inquiry and Truth* (1966), 213, 222
Niven, W. D.
and *The Scientific Papers of James Clerk Maxwell* (1890), 184
Noble, Edmund
and *Purposive Evolution: The Link Between Science and Religion* (1926), 185

Objects, 3, 14, 18, 25, 30–32, 35–36, 38, 41–42, 46, 48, 50, 64–65, 72, 78–80, 85–95, 100, 103–105, 108–112, 115, 121–122, 134, 137–138, 141–142, 149–151, 156, 160–165, 171–173, 187–191, 190–191, 194–196, 198–200, 203, 208, 210, 211–214, 219, 221
Ogden, C. K.
and *The Meaning of Meaning* (1923), 201
Order, in logical theory, 3, 10, 14, 26, 28, 33, 44, 49, 53, 56, 63, 73, 83–86, 105, 108, 123, 125, 126, 131–134, 139, 146, 153, 157–161, 164, 167, 169–172, 175, 189, 199, 204–205, 209, 212, 215, 217–218, 222
Otto, M. C., 199

Paolos, Kathleen, 186, 213–215
Pattern of inquiry 3–4, 10, 21, 29, 43, 126, 133, 139, 147–150, 166–69, 172–173, 176, 209, 214, 222

Peirce, C. S., 1, 2, 7, 10, 16, 19, 21, 23–24, 30–31, 36, 46, 48–49, 53, 55, 67–68, 70–73, 75, 82, 86–87, 94, 133, 146–147, 162–166, 171–173, 179, 183–187, 190–192, 197–201, 206, 209–212, 217–220
and "How to Make Our Ideas Clear" (1878), 86–87, 196, 199
and "Pragmatism" (1905), 220
and "Logic" (1905), 211
and *Collected Papers of Charles Saunders Peirce* (1931–34), 30, 76, 133, 146–147, 162, 165–166, 171, 186, 218, 220
and *The Essential Peirce* (1992–98), 192, 217
and "The Fixation of Belief (1992), 192, 199
and "A Guess at the Riddle" (1992), 217
and *Reasoning and the Logic of Things* (1992), 216
and "Pragmatism" (1998), 220
and "What Pragmatism Is" (1998), 86–87, 192, 200
and "Chance, Love, and Logic," 202
and "Induction, Deduction, Hypothesis," 206
and "The Categories Defended," 212
Perry, R. B., 180, 194
and "The Ego-Centric Predicament" (1910), 191
Pitkin, Walter, 180
Planck, Max, 2, 10, 21, 24–26, 102, 104, 106, 185, 203–204
Plato, 54
Potentials, potentiality, 63, 82, 88–89, 149, 152, 159, 162–163, 166, 195, 217, 219

244 / Index

Pragmatism, 7, 11–12, 19, 23, 35–39, 46, 48, 53, 55, 59, 67, 70–73, 76–77, 86–87, 92, 94, 113, 146, 167, 179–193, 197, 200, 202, 205, 207, 210–222
Propositions
  Existential, 15–16, 28, 32, 60–63, 72, 90–91, 99, 102, 109–111, 116, 126–129, 146, 150, 157–158, 171, 173, 193–195, 210, 212, 215–216
  Singular, 153, 215
  Particular, 152
  Generic, 4–5, 28–29, 31, 107, 111, 128, 131, 146–147, 152–160, 167, 171–173, 213, 216, 217
  Universal, 11, 15, 23, 29, 59, 63, 70, 76, 102, 128, 152–153, 155–156, 171, 194
Psychology, 1, 5, 11–13, 17–24, 28, 32, 36, 42, 50, 65, 70, 75, 92–93, 98, 102–104, 115, 120, 127, 144–145, 158, 180–183, 185, 187–190, 194–196, 199, 201, 203, 205, 207, 211, 216

Quine, Willard Van Orman, 213

Ratner, Joseph, 11, 21, 25–27, 30–32, 131, 147, 148, 149, 150, 151, 152, 153, 154, 156, 158, 170, 171, 184, 192, 199, 214
Ratner, Sidney, 131, 149, 220
  and *John Dewey and Arthur Bentley: A Philosophical Correspondence* (1964), 183, 220, 221
Realism, 3, 14–16, 19–20, 24, 26, 33, 48, 59–60, 64, 72, 149, 171, 177, 181, 189, 191, 195–196, 202, 203, 216–217
  Critical, 11, 12, 13, 35–37, 58, 61, 180, 194
  New, 12, 35–37, 58, 180, 194
  Analytic (Neo), 11, 13, 35–37, 61, 75
  Six Realists, 11–13, 180, 192
Reality, 17–19, 27, 30, 40, 48, 49, 53, 55, 72–73, 87, 105, 147, 162–166, 172–173, 190, 194, 204, 207, 208, 212
Recursion, 46–47, 69, 114, 133, 205–207, 209
  and inquiry, 29, 41, 166, 172–173
Reflection 4, 11, 13–14, 38–41, 44–47, 60, 71, 75–81, 84–86, 91, 129, 132, 140, 149, 161, 167–170, 173, 185–190, 196–197, 200, 209, 216, 221
Reichenbach, Hans, 211, 214
  and "Dewey's Theory of Science" (1989), 214
Reiser, Oliver, 31
  and *Philosophy and the Concepts of Modern Science* (1935), 186, 211, 214
Richards, I. A.
  and *The Meaning of Meaning* (1923), 201
Riemann, Bernhard, 206
Robinson, Daniel Sommer, 36, 65–66, 72
  and "An Alleged New Discovery in Logic" (1917), 65, 187, 196
Rogers, Melvin
  and *The Undiscovered Dewey: Religion, Morality, and the Ethos of Democracy* (2009), 212
Rorty, Richard, 81, 192
Rosenthal, Sandra B.
  and "John Dewey: Scientific

Method and Lived Immediacy"
(1981), 200, 208
Royce, Josiah, 39
Russell, Bertrand, 9–13, 15–16,
18–19, 22–23, 35, 46, 58–60,
62–65, 70, 72, 75, 82, 115,
132, 142, 144–145, 180–181,
183, 192, 194, 198, 202,
205–206, 211, 217, 222
and *Our Knowledge of the External
World as a Field for Scientific
Method in Philosophy (1914)*, 62,
195, 218
and *Logical Atomism* (1924), 184,
193
and *The Analysis of Matter* (1927),
184
and *Religion and Science* (1935),
132, 142, 144–145, 182, 184,
210–211
and *Library of Living Philosophers*
(1939), 18
and "Professor Dewey's Essays in
Experimental Logic" (1977),
181, 190–192, 205
and *A History of Western Philosophy*
(1979), 18, 183, 187
and *The Problem of the External
World as a Field for Scientific
Method in Philosophy*, 18
and *Introduction to Mathematical
Philosophy*, 205
Rutherford, William, 21
Ryan, Alan
and *John Dewey and the High Tide
of American Liberalism* (1995),
181, 185, 212

Sands, Matthew
and *The Feynman Lectures on
Physics* (2006), 185
Santayana, George, 199

and "Dewey's Naturalistic
Metaphysics" (1925), 199
Schiller, F. C. S., 202
Schilpp, Paul Arthur
and *The Philosophy of John Dewey*
(1989), 183, 212, 214
Schrödinger, Erwin, 25
Secondness, 162–163, 165, 200, 210,
220
Seligman, E. R.
and *Encyclopedia of the Social
Sciences* (1931), 201
Shook, John
and *Dewey's Empirical Theory of
Knowledge and Reality* (2000),
190, 213
Siegfried, Hans
and "Dewey's Logical Forms"
(2002), 185, 207, 215
Signs, 6, 14, 26, 33, 43, 82, 88, 91,
93, 104, 121, 141, 146, 152,
202, 206, 210, 212
Sigwart, Christoph, 202
Situations, 3, 13, 24, 26, 28, 33, 38–44,
46–47, 50–52, 60, 66, 68–71, 76,
94, 97–100, 104–105, 111–112,
123, 125–127, 132–133, 136,
146, 150, 161, 164, 167–168,
170, 172, 189, 198, 201, 205,
209, 218, 221, 222
Indeterminate situation, 13, 41–42,
64, 66, 70, 79, 95, 98, 133–
134, 147, 168, 170, 222
Sleeper, Ralph, 212, 213
and *The Necessity of Pragmatism: John
Dewey's Conception of Philosophy*
(1986), 181, 183, 193, 205,
212, 215, 217, 219–220
Spaulding, E. B., 12, 180–181, 194
and "Realism: A Reply to Professor
Dewey and an Exposition"
(1911), 181

St. Hilaire, Barthélemy
  and Translation of Aristotle's *Logic*, 182
Stebbing, L. Susan, 32, 217
  and *A Modern Introduction to Logic* (1930), 186, 217–218
  and *A Modern Elementary Logic* (1952), 218
Stuhr, John
  and "Dewey's Notion of a Qualitative Experience" (1979), 200
  and "Dewey's Reconstruction of Metaphysics" (1992), 209
Suppes, Patrick
  and "Nagel's Lectures on Dewey's Logic" (1969), 208, 213
  and *Philosophy, Science, and Method, Essays in Honor of Ernest Nagel* (1969), 208
Symbols, 33, 123, 140–141, 150, 173, 206
Synthesis, 2–4, 29, 98–99, 116, 165, 201, 213

Talisse, R. B.
  and *Dewey's Logical Theory: New Studies and Interpretations* (2002), 185, 196, 208, 213, 215, 221
Temporality, 10–11, 13–14, 20–21, 24–28, 31–33, 37, 39–40, 43–44, 46, 49–50, 58, 60, 71, 73, 77–78, 83–85, 88–89, 93, 95, 100, 102–105, 108–109, 112, 118, 120, 121, 125–126, 128–129, 131–132, 134, 137–139, 148, 161, 169, 173, 176, 189, 198–199, 201, 204, 207, 209, 210, 218, 221
Thayer, H. S., 213, 220, 222
  and *The Logic of Pragmatism* (1952), 213, 217, 222
Thayer, V. T., 220
Thinking, thought, 5, 11, 29, 37–47, 50–53, 55, 57, 60–61, 63, 67–71, 73, 75, 78, 82, 88, 90–91, 95–96, 98, 100, 104, 108, 113–115, 118, 124, 127–129, 133, 135, 137, 139–140, 145, 149, 166–170, 179–180, 186, 189–190, 199, 202–203, 205, 209, 211–212, 220
Thirdness, and Peirce, 162, 164–165, 200
Toulmin, Stephen
  and "Introduction" to *The Later Works of John Dewey* (1984), 200
Traits of existence, 3–4, 6–7, 41, 44, 51, 58, 73, 75–84, 90, 94, 104, 129, 132–133, 163, 168–170, 172, 198–199, 201, 204, 209, 221–222
Trotsky, Leon, 30
Truscott, F. W.
  and *A Philosophical Essay on Probabilities* (1902), 184
Truth, 19, 27, 35, 49, 53–54, 59, 61, 65, 67–68, 106–107, 113, 127, 139, 147, 164, 166, 183, 190, 192–193, 195–197, 200, 204, 206, 208, 215, 218–221
Tylor, Edward
  and *Primitive Culture* (1891), 201

Veazie, Walter B., 181
Venn, John, 184, 202
  and *The Principles of Empirical or Inductive Logic* (1889), 183–184

Wallace, William
  and *Outlines of the Philosophy of Aristotle*, 182
Weiss, Paul, 218
  and *Collected Papers of Charles Saunders Peirce* (1931–34), 186, 218
Welby, Lady, 219
Wells, Harry
  and *Pragmatism: Philosophy of Imperialism* (1954), 187
Westbrook, Robert
  and *John Dewey and American Democracy* (1991), 180–181, 212
Wheeler, J. E.
  and *John Dewey and Arthur Bentley: A Philosophical Correspondence* (1964), 183
Whewell, William
  and *The Philosophy of the Inductive Sciences, Founded upon Their History* (1840), 182
White, Andrew Dickson
  and *A History of Warfare of Science with Theology in Christendom* (1896), 211
White, Morton, 213
  and *The Origins of John Dewey's Instrumentalism* (1943), 213
  and *Philosophy, Science, and Method, Essays in Honor of Ernest Nagel* (1969), 208
Windelband, Wilhelm
  and *Aristotle's Logic*, 182
Woodbridge, F. H., 2, 16, 181

www.ingramcontent.com/pod-product-compliance
Lightning Source LLC
Chambersburg PA
CBHW020646230426
43665CB00008B/334